# Using Computers in
# Qualitative Research

# Using Computers in Qualitative Research

*edited by*
Nigel G. Fielding and
Raymond M. Lee

SAGE Publications

London · Newbury Park · New Delhi

First published 1991    Reprinted 1991

SAGE Publications Ltd
6 Bonhill Street
London EC2A 4PU

SAGE Publications India Pvt Ltd
32, M-Block Market
Greater Kailash - I
New Delhi 110 048

SAGE Publications Inc
2455 Teller Road
Newbury Park, California 91320

**British Library Cataloguing in Publication data**

Using computers in qualitative research.
   1. Research. Use of computers
   I. Fielding, Nigel   II. Lee, Raymond M.
   001.40285

ISBN 0–8039–8424–3
ISBN 0–8039–8425–1 pbk

**Library of Congress catalog card number 90–53679**

Typeset by Photoprint, Torquay
Printed in Great Britain by Billing and Sons Ltd, Worcester

# Contents

# The Contributors

Professor Michael Agar, Department of Anthropology, University of Maryland

Anne V. Akeroyd, Department of Sociology, University of York

Pat Allatt, Teesside Business School, Teesside Polytechnic

Lynn D. Benson, Teesside Business School, Teesside Polytechnic

Elizabeth (Betsy) S. Cordingley, British Telecom Research Laboratory, Ipswich

John Davies, Department of Computer Science, University of Liverpool

Nigel G. Fielding, Department of Sociology, University of Surrey

Anthony Finkelstein, Department of Computing, Imperial College, University of London

Michael D. Fischer, Centre for Social Anthropology and Computing, University of Kent

Professor David R. Heise, Department of Sociology, University of Indiana

Raymond M. Lee, Department of Social Policy and Social Science, Royal Holloway and Bedford New College, University of London

Lyn Richards, Sociology Department, La Trobe University

Tom Richards, Department of Computer Science and Computer Engineering, La Trobe University

Professor John Seidel, Qualis Research Associates, Corvallis, Oregon

Renata Tesch, Qualitative Research Management, Desert Hot Springs, California

# 1

# Computing for Qualitative Research: Options, Problems and Potential

*Raymond M. Lee and Nigel G. Fielding*

Until recently, those who analysed qualitative data in the form of interview transcripts, verbal protocols, ethnographic fieldnotes and the like had to rely on little more than scissors, a copier and piles of paper. In the past few years, however, there has been considerable progress in the analysis of qualitative data using a variety of specially written computer programs. In July 1989, as the latest in an annual series of meetings which are published in the 'Surrey Series in Theory and Method' (past volumes available variously from Sage or Gower Publications), we organized an international symposium at the University of Surrey to assess these developments. The sessions consisted of profiles of techniques in use or which were emerging, practical demonstrations, evaluative papers and seminar discussions. The three principal themes of the symposium, described below, are reflected in our selection of chapters for this book. In making our selection, we aimed to produce a book which was both a state-of-the-art review and a primer that would offer those with little computing experience sufficient background to select programs with which to try their hand at the computer analysis of qualitative data. To these ends a 'Resources' section is included, and there is a comprehensive index and bibliography, and a commentary between the sections of the book.

Our first principal theme was an exploration of the sorts of research problems the programs can and cannot handle, at present or in the near future. Qualitative computing in the social sciences emerged in a serious way only in the 1980s. There are at present around a dozen programs on the market or under development, each with different characteristics and facilities. We wanted, therefore, to compare the principal programs, identifying their strengths and limitations. At the very least we hope to spare colleagues the wasted effort of reinventing the wheel. We are gratified to report that, in putting together, for example, the designer of the ETHNOGRAPH, John Seidel, and those of NUDIST, Lyn and Tom Richards, we have encouraged a fruitful interchange of ideas on matters both technical and conceptual (see, for example, Seidel, 1990).

Our second theme related to the teaching of computer-based techniques in qualitative research. We are now poised to train the first generation of qualitative researchers on whom issues relating to computerization may weigh as heavily as topics such as fieldwork ethics and analytic reflexivity. We intended, therefore, to collate existing practice among those who have begun to incorporate qualitative analysis programs into their research methods teaching.

The third and broadest theme was the implications of the development of computer-based techniques for the craft of qualitative research. We would not be true to our roots in qualitative research if we did not acknowledge the substantial reservations many in the specialism feel about facilitating analysis using computer programs. We wanted to give those reservations an airing, but more particularly we wanted our contributors to assess the impact of these procedures on the formalization and systematization of qualitative analysis. Contributions by Agar, Seidel, the Richards, Heise and others in this volume address this issue and we further discuss the matter below.

We should note here that the programs now available have grown out of qualitative research itself; developments have been driven by the needs of the research community rather than being the products of a competitive market-driven situation. The range of projects where these programs have been applied seems to confirm our view that the programs are with us to stay. Whatever our view of their role, qualitative researchers can no longer safely afford to ignore these developments. Drawing simply on the experience of those who attended the symposium there have been applications in studies of gerontology, educational evaluation, medical sociology, welfare benefits, the ethnography of urban Pakistan, the organization of software design teams, the nature of political scandals, organization discourse, police recruit training, steelworkers in Brazil, and social networks in suburbia. In short, the programs are starting to register right across the substantive domains of social science, and in the disciplines of sociology, psychology, anthropology, computer science, politics, criminology, history and geography.

It was scholars in the humanities, especially those such as biblical scholars who had to deal with very large bodies of textual material (see, for example, Busa, 1980; Choueka, 1980; Morton, 1980), who were attracted relatively early on to the use of computers with non-numeric data. Later, anthropologists began to show an interest in using computers both in the field and for the analysis of ethnographic data (Weinberg, 1974; Kirk, 1981). More recently, sociologists and applied social researchers interested in field research have begun to make use of the computer. Indeed, Kenneth Hinze (1987), in a review of current trends in sociology computing based on in-depth interviews with leading figures in the field, has suggested that 'computer use in qualitative sociology is advancing faster than in quantitative sociology'.

Computers offer advantages to the field researcher which arise both from the nature of the fieldwork task and from the characteristic form taken by field data themselves. Field research depends on immersion in the fieldwork, on non-direction, and on some attempt to remain true to the understandings of those studied and their modes of expression. The data thereby produced are usually textual in character, voluminous and difficult to handle (Sproull and Sproull, 1982; Podolefsky and McCarty, 1983). Moreover, the material produced is analytically demanding. It requires the analyst to 'cut' the data in a number of different ways across a range of cases (Agar, 1983); activities which are time-consuming, inconvenient and fatiguing.

Gerson (1984) has characterized the computer as a tireless, endlessly efficient clerk who never forgets, while Brent (1984) comments that a computer will do anything which is possible on paper but more easily and more efficiently. Faced with a large and relatively unsystematized body of field material, computers provide a speedy means of recording data in a written form and permit it to be retrieved very rapidly. Flexibility is possible (Becker et al., 1984) because, for example, ideas which occur to an analyst some time after the data collection process can be inserted at the appropriate place, say in previously entered fieldnotes. New codes can be added at will or material coded in several different ways at once. At the same time, the raw data remain close at hand and are ready for inspection.

It has been suggested that the quality of data analysis will be enhanced by the use of computers (Conrad and Reinharz, 1984). The computer, for example, makes it easier to find deviant cases or to extract small but significant pieces of information buried within a larger mass of material. Furthermore, simply by reducing the amount of paper and the extent to which it needs to be shuffled, analytic processes become less unwieldly, more pleasant and less tedious for the analyst. As a result the mechanics of field research should become less likely to get in the way of analytic processes.

Tesch (1989) argues that the use of computers in qualitative research will produce real savings in terms of the amount of time

4 *Using computers in qualitative research*

needed to carry out a qualitative study. She also argues that using a computer makes qualitative analysis less tiring. Although she acknowledges that some people would regard this as a trivial point she argues that facilitating the analytic process allows the direction of mental energy towards analytic rather than mechanical tasks. The ability to handle large quantities of data with relative ease means that researchers are no longer tempted to disregard new data because its incorporation would necessitate a lengthy and time-consuming process of recoding. Finally, she argues that the computer encourages researchers to 'play' with the data, a process which fosters analytic insight.

A further advantage is that, potentially, computers offer the possibility of new ways of working. Team research – in theory – becomes easier because data, fieldnotes and so on may be shared simply by transmitting them electronically down telephone lines to colleagues at distant sites. The computer makes easier, too, the replication of analytic procedures, potentially increasing the validity of research and permitting the possibility of secondary analysis (Conrad and Reinharz, 1984).

**Software for qualitative data analysis**

As Renata Tesch points out in this volume a range of different kinds of program are available for the analysis of textual data, not all suitable for qualitative research. These include: text management databases, concordance programs, 'chunking and coding' programs, 'qualitative modelling' programs and expert systems. Text management databases are commercially available programs which allow the user to search very quickly through a large number of files in order to locate a pre-specified text. Concordance programs, like OCP (the Oxford Concordance Program) or BYU Concordance, are widely used in the humanities to carry out syntactical analysis, indexing, concordancing, authorship studies and so on. The particular forte of such programs is their ability to generate for large bodies of text breakdowns, say, of the frequency with which particular words or combinations of words are used, to produce 'key word in context' lists, indexes and concordances. One difficulty with using these programs for ethnographic research is what Grant Blank (1989: 10) has referred to as the 'Goldilocks problem'; 'there can't be too much structure in the database, yet there can't be too little structure. The amount of structure has to be just right.' In the kinds of literary applications for which concordance programs are most useful, it is quite appropriate to specify a fixed amount of context, and to take the letter, the word or the line as a basic unit of analysis.

In many social science applications, however, one would not want to be constrained in this way. The context for an utterance can be a word, a few lines or several paragraphs. One wants to be able to work with user-defined 'chunks' of text.

*Chunking and coding programs*
From the user's point of view 'chunking and coding' programs tend to work in similar ways. Text to be analysed – fieldnotes, transcripts and the like – is typed into the computer. It is then inspected and codes are assigned to those segments which are of interest to the analyst. The computer can then be asked to recover codes or combinations of codes and to display them together with the text with which they are associated.

The authors of programs of this kind have usually been at pains to stress that what is being computerized is the mechanical aspect of qualitative data analysis and that the essentially interpretive work of generating codes is a task left to the analyst. As the developers of the ETHNOGRAPH, Seidel and Clark, put it:

> We would like again to emphasize the distinction between the mechanical and the thinking aspects of ethnographic research. The mechanical part is usually some type of cut-and-paste operation where large masses of data are disassembled and then reassembled in terms of some analytic/conceptual scheme developed by the researcher . . . It [the ETHNOGRAPH] relies on the researcher to make sense of the data. The programs facilitate this process by enhancing the efficiency of the mechanical parts of the work. (1984: 123)

*Qualitative 'modelling' programs*
The term 'modelling' may be a strange one to use in the context of qualitative research, and we use it with some caution. What we have in mind here are programs such as ETHNO which attempt to take qualitative data and to lay bare their underlying structure. David Heise's chapter conveys both the procedures and the larger purposes of such programs. The work is important in the formal modelling of human action and to the concerns of mathematical sociology, for example, in securing a more adequate empirical base for prediction and explanation than is offered by simple rational choice theory.

*Expert systems*
As some writers have pointed out (see, for example, Lyman, 1984), the computer can be regarded as having within it a relatively 'primitive' theory of knowledge masquerading as technological sophistication. Ironically, however, the developments in new

technology which are likely to be of most interest to qualitative social scientists are precisely those in which the brute power of the computer to 'crunch words' is replaced by 'knowledge-based systems' (Brent, 1984). The attempt here is to harness developments in artificial intelligence in order to effect what Gerson (1984) has characterized metaphorically as the transition from computer-as-clerk to computer-as-research-assistant.

## Teaching

One important but relatively unremarked aspect of computer technology in qualitative research is its potential use in teaching. Traditionally, little attention seems to have been paid to the teaching of qualitative analysis. One reason for this is that analytic strategies have not commonly been codified. To the extent that they may become so under the influence of the computer, it may mean that pedagogical strategies need to be rethought. Lyn and Tom Richards (this volume) argue that pedagogy may also have implications for the design of programs. In particular, they suggest that teaching is facilitated where programs allow multi-user access, something relatively uncommon among existing programs. In the even longer term, information technology and the new media may have even more far-reaching pedagogic consequences. Implicit in much teaching about field research methods is what might be called an 'initiation pedagogy'. We assume that research, and particularly the first research experience, is a rite of passage. The pedagogical assumption here is that the only way to learn about research is to do it, even if this is at some psychic cost to the neophyte. In the future the advent of CD-ROM, multimedia, intelligent simulation and 'virtual reality' may mean that students can be initiated through simulated social worlds.

## Problematic aspects

It is likely that computers will bring real benefits to qualitative researchers, making their work easier, more productive and potentially more thorough. An underlying worry must remain, however: to what extent will the advent of computers change the craft of social research in unanticipated ways? Is the computer, as some writers have suggested, a genie in the bottle which, once released, will transform the activity of field research in unnoticed and unwelcome ways?

Undoubtedly, some of the enthusiasm seen in the United States for computer-assisted field research arises out of a concern to destigmatize qualitative research in an environment which is not entirely sympathetic towards it, by finding ways to make qualitative research look more 'scientific'. More fundamentally, as a tool in our culture the computer is overlain by a variety of symbolic meanings that stress its technical character, and which in other contexts have encouraged the exclusion of women. This is a point made by Peter Lyman, who evaluated an experiment in which humanities faculty at Stanford University were given microcomputers and word processing software for use in their work. Lyman argues that the computer is embedded in a technical culture. As he put it:

> While the cybernetic model [implicit in computing] may be a useful paradigm for knowledge, it is markedly different from that of qualitative research which emphasizes diagnosis, not control, and interpretation, not explanation. In learning to use the computer the fieldworker is consuming a culture of control, not just a tool. (1984: 86–7)

Some of those studied by Lyman clearly felt that the use of computers was a vehicle through which university power holders could impose and enforce values of productivity at variance with their own humanistic convictions. For others the computer itself was embedded as a cultural artefact within what Lyman describes as 'an everyday male culture of aggressive images of control which constitute a cultural barrier to some users'.

At the more mundane level the computer may well alter the work styles of qualitative researchers. There are a number of possible scenarios. Ragin and Becker (1989) argue that as both quantitative and qualitative researchers are no longer dependent on mainframe computers the traditional gulf between 'variable-oriented' (quantitative) and 'case-oriented' (qualitative) researchers will tend to narrow. For both groups the microcomputer encourages closeness to the data and an intensive, interactive analytic style. This in turn may encourage a certain degree of methodological convergence as quantitative researchers find the detailed analysis of subpopulations easier and qualitative researchers are able to examine comparative contrasts within their case materials more fully.

An alternative view is that qualitative researchers may need to be cautious about the use of computer technology lest – as with some kinds of quantitative research – method comes to define substance (Freidheim, 1984). One straightforward illustration of the impact of computer technology in sociology can be obtained simply by comparing the manual for the original version of spss with the User's Guide for its lineal descendant, spss-x. While the former ran to 343 pages and detailed only 12 statistical procedures, the latter describes 22 procedures, many of a complex multivariate kind, in a total of 806 pages. Yet even writers like Lieberson (1985), who are committed to quantitative methods, have argued that statistical sophistication has not necessarily been accompanied by greater theoretical acumen.

There is the possibility that the use of computers may tempt qualitative researchers into 'quick and dirty' research with its attendant danger of premature theoretical closure. A number of more subtle consequences can also be envisaged. These include the loss of what the Richards (1989) call the 'untypable': the fleeting notes, doodles and marginalia within which insight is often captured. The ability to do complex analysis can also lead to a situation where more and more complicated indexing structures become inevitable to deal with a proliferation of codes. There is the continual difficulty for some (for example, Drass, 1989) that many of the existing programs, because they operate on the coded segments principle, do not permit the analysis of temporal sequences in data, while some researchers in the sociolinguistics tradition have also found available software limiting in certain respects (see, for example, ten Have, 1990).

Of course, the ultimate fear here is of Frankenstein's monster. It is susceptible to the same caveats, too. Like the monster, the programs are misunderstood. The programs are innocent of guile. It is their misapplication which poses the threat. It was exposure to human depravity which made a threat of Frankenstein's creation. Equally, the untutored use of analysis programs can certainly produce banal, unedifying and off-target analyses. But the fault would lie with the user. This is why teaching the use of the programs to novice researchers has to be embedded in a pedagogy which has a sense of the exemplars of qualitative analysis, rather than as skills and techniques to be mechanically applied.

The nightmare is rehearsed in this book in the contributions by Agar and Seidel. In essence, the anxiety comes from the fear that the machine will 'take over' the analysis. Researchers, and their audiences, will be seduced by the convenience and credibility of the program's rendering of sense. As we celebrate the program's output, and especially its form, we will no longer have an awareness of the process by which this product was brought about. Qualitative research, especially ethnography, will be commodified, without the knowledge of process that formerly made the final analysis a product we could believe in.

It would be foolish to think others have not faced this trial. It is familiar to those committed to the secondary analysis of statistical data. The operations to be learned are of such complexity that they easily divert attention from the logic and research design issues that actually govern the adequacy of an analysis. The ETHNOGRAPH, the most widespread program, itself emerged out of a graduate methods seminar (not a software house or a multinational). In other words, the program users remain largely located in academic settings (including applied research institutes and consultancies). Of course, these locations are no guarantee against philistinism. But these are the social institutions most directly expected to maintain intellectual standards. A good example of what can happen where such institutions are not involved is the case of 'creative nonfiction', whose integrity is continually subject to the blurring of fact and fiction (Agar, 1990).

This reference to guardianship of intellectual standards is more than a pious convention. It can be put at a very direct instrumental level. The increasing competitiveness of academic life in recent years, which all have noticed and many lament, has reinforced the salience of conventional mechanisms for according vocational status at an individual level. Pre-eminent among the mechanisms is publication, including conference presentations. It is the means by which our work is known outside our daily round. Without a track record available for assessment by the wider intellectual community, we get no tenure, no citations, no invitations to international conferences, no headhunting.

This is, of course, cynical. Many of us publish because we have science to do, results to report, allegiances to defend. But the point is that we publish. Publication is controlled by peer review. We sometimes suspect it may be weaker in some avenues, say book publication, than others, say journal articles, but it features in both, and with a vengeance when we pursue funds to support our work. So a great deal of the running is being made, and being braked, by colleagues in the role of referees. Referees are important at all times but critical at times of technical innovation. By definition they are established scholars, who can be expected to have clear views and preferences. We do not expect evenhandedness, though some are evenhanded. Generally, however, editors use referees in the plural, in the knowledge that out of the clash of differently committed minds will come the sensible verdict. As technical innovations begin to register through submissions for publication, they will encounter a majority of referees who are unfamiliar with the innovations but who are wholly familiar with the conventions of the field and with its lineage. They will, in short, apply prevailing standards of adequacy to the new material. Their mental set is likely to be sceptical. They have certain competencies and are sure of them. Innovations have a tough test to pass here, and we also should not neglect the low motives that can be attributed to status competition, which can affect processes of review and accreditation. Qualitative writing, qualitative research, will still be submitted to qualitative publication outlets. The journals associated with qualitative work will naturally maintain refereeing groups particularly knowledgeable about and committed to qualitative paradigms of explanation. In our experience these are especially jealous, and rightly so, in their defence of these canons and their epistemological base. So program-based analysis is likely to attract particularly stringent refereeing. This argument applies most strongly to work published in the academic sphere. It is true that it applies less strongly to applied research. But our spirit of collegiality should not blind us to status considerations here too. Many applied researchers are committed to their work, in evaluation research and especially in educational research. Many are not; theirs is a temporary berth while they pursue an academic position. But even the former group want their work to be endorsed as credible and respected by the research community, if for no other reason than to continue to get funding or to advance in the hierarchy of their government departments, institutes and consultancies. In our own specialisms we soon learn who has a reputation for 'quick and dirty' research. The orientation to peer review of workers in applied settings may be less direct than that of the full-time academics, but it is only a matter of degree.

We mean to depict the peer review system not as perfect, but simply as the most immediately available solace from the nightmare. It seems to us there are other sources of reassurance in the face of new technology. One of them is to consider the nature of scholarly and research working arrangements. The assumption that researchers will be drawn to the technical fix on its advantages of speed and apparent credibility is an absolutist vision that does not stop to ponder what we would be doing with the time thus freed. Scholarship and research are reflective, time-intensive activities, and the people who do this work are usually drawn to it by these very qualities. Is it realistic that we would all be mounting twice as many studies assuming these programs halve our work? If so, who is going to pay for all the new research? And if the answer is that we will be able to spend twice as long in the field, and collect incrementally more data, won't that bring us back to square one in analysis time? It seems to us that the dream of more time to devote to more fulfilling analysis and more sophisticated reporting is at least as plausible as the nightmare of the ethnographer as cultural dope who presses a button and gets a PhD.

**Innovation, diffusion and development**

When asking developers to provide information about programs for the 'Resources' section of this book, we collected information about the nature and timing of the development process for dedicated qualitative analysis programs. Broadly speaking, there seem to have been three phases of development. Around the beginning of the 1980s, early, rudimentary programs for simple textual analysis usually based on mainframe computers began to be adapted for use on microcomputers. Examples are the LISPQUAL program by Kriss Drass which became TAP in its microcomputer version, and the ETHNOGRAPH developed by Seidel and Clark. These programs were intended for use on MS-DOS machines, that is, IBM PCS and compatibles. In the late 1980s, programs for Macintosh computers began to be available, as the advent of a program known as HyperCard made the development of complex applications available to non-experts. A third phase which has been developing has been the use of expert systems and knowledge-based applications, though this work remains relatively underused among qualitative researchers. The late 1980s also began to see the development of a *community* of developers and users.

While there has clearly been no lack of innovation, Tesch (1989) has argued that there has still been a lack of diffusion of qualitative analysis programs. She argues that there is a lack of awareness by many researchers of the kind of dedicated software now available. Commercial programs are more widely known even if they are not well adapted to the specific needs of qualitative researchers. Some researchers, she argues, have been hostile to computerization because of its association in their mind with positivistic forms of research.

Our view is that the issue may be less whether the software has or has not diffused, but rather how this has taken place. We have at least some information on the user base of the most widely used program, the ETHNOGRAPH. Since March 1988 and up to January 1990, a total of 1600 copies of the ETHNOGRAPH had been shipped. Of the 115 users who had signed up to be listed for networking, the largest group (33) were in education, followed by nursing research (27), sociologists (17), anthropologists (13), other health disciplines, e.g. occupational therapy (11), psychologists (9), and individuals from other fields including criminology and political science. What these figures suggest is that the technology has been diffusing to those in applied areas. Our experience of acting as resources for individuals interested in the computer-assisted analysis of textual data is that many are postgraduate students. In other words, we suspect the adoption of the innovation represented by the use of computers in qualitative research has been highly instrumental. Having said this, it is also important to note how even proponents of the use of computers in qualitative research have not pushed their use as far as might have been the case. Kling and Iacono (1988) speak of 'computerization movements', loose groupings of activists who attempt to foster increasing computerization. These activists try to mobilize resources and build commitments to the use of computers by reference to an ideology which stresses the benefits which flow from the increasing penetration of computer technology into wider realms of society. Interestingly, such a movement appears not to be a present feature of the diffusion of computers into qualitative research. There are a number of reasons for this. One is the reticence of developers themselves to make claims which might encourage the view that computers will produce alienation from the traditional labour process in qualitative research. Indeed, among those who have been most concerned to maintain a cautious posture towards computers are precisely people like John Seidel, Lyn Richards and Michael Agar whose involvement has been long-standing, and who have been at the forefront of developments. The established route to qualitative analysis skills has been such that even (especially?) the designers of the programs are not naive advocates of the technical fix.

**Future developments**

What of the future? Starting with the programs themselves, Tesch (1989) points to the need for yet another major technological innovation in qualitative research – the computer transcription of speech. Clearly this would eliminate a tedious chore, but one from which the researcher-as-transcriber gains deep familiarity with the data. One current program (HyperResearch) allows one to code directly off audio tape. It is not clear whether this method is too cumbersome for large bodies of material.

Devault (1990) has noted that transcription is often regarded simply as a mechanical task often left to subordinates. It is possible that hardware for speech transcription will encourage this trend. Paradoxically, however, the likely inability of equipment to operate in anything other than a relatively coarse-grained way may encourage analysts to attend closely to the 'rough-cut' text. This is an important issue for feminist researchers because, as Devault points out, the women she interviewed often resorted to 'a halting, hesitant, tentative talk' which in her view 'signals the realm of not-quite articulated experience, where standard vocabulary is inadequate, and where a respondent tries to speak from experience and finds language wanting' (1990: 103).

In his celebrated essay 'On Intellectual Craftsmanship' (1959), C. Wright Mills pointed to a range of procedures, such as perspective by incongruity or the random remixing of existing file categories, for stimulating the sociological imagination. Ironically, many of those procedures graced with the name of 'creativity techniques' form a staple of management training. One challenge for software developers may be to utilize 'idea processing' or graphical software to help stimulate creativity and imagination. This may form an important part of programs which are designed to guide researchers rather in the manner of 'expert systems'. The prospect is there for the development of programs which will allow the display of analytic patterns using the kinds of graphical forms advocated, for example, by Miles and Huberman (1984).

Turning from program developments to the program-designing and program-using community, and applying the pragmatic view from our discussion of refereeing, it is remarkable that little academic credit is accorded for producing software. As Tesch (1989) observes, for many of the programs currently available software was developed in 'free time' or was only possible with the support of a university. The desirable and impressive humility of early developers may give way to commercial pressures unless sensible support is given within *academe*.

A final infrastructural issue concerns consumer advice and information. One of the things which is missing from the literature is independent evaluation of software. Although a number of writers (Drass, 1980; Agar, 1983) point to trials which suggest that computer-assisted analysis will replicate analyses previously carried out by hand while at the same time recovering additional patterns which remained unnoticed in the earlier analysis, little systematic evaluation is present. There is a pressing need for research based on field trials where different programs and different applications are compared.

We have no doubt that much of what we have written will soon be out of date, but, by the same token, for many the developments we describe will be new and exciting. Unlike substantive subdisciplines there is no existing institutional focus for these innovations. The networks of users and developers are scattered and not always well integrated. What we hope to do, therefore, is to lay a foundation to encourage colleagues to try these techniques and thus add to our grasp of what is, and is not, on offer to enhance qualitative knowledge.

# PART ONE

# USING COMPUTERS IN QUALITATIVE RESEARCH

The many uses to which dedicated programs may be put and the potential for confusion produced by commercially available software all suggest the need for a basic 'road map' of existing provision. Few people are better placed to survey the existing terrain than Renata Tesch. Tesch, who operates as a consultant and distributor for qualitative analysis software, as well as being an accomplished qualitative researcher in her own right, provides a comparison of analytic needs and program capabilities. Tesch proceeds from a taxonomy of qualitative research approaches. She suggests that there are three broad strands among qualitative researchers: those who are language oriented, those who are interpretively oriented and those concerned with the building of theory. Tesch carefully delineates the extent to which both commercially available and dedicated software packages will assist researchers, whatever their analytic predilections.

Many qualitative researchers by now use word processors and as a result have at least some basic familiarity with microcomputers. By and large, those in this position will have little difficulty in installing and running most of the dedicated programs for qualitative analysis that Tesch mentions. Complete novices will need to take advice from more experienced users or, in an academic environment, from their institution's computer centre. (They might also wish to consult an introductory text such as Davis, 1989.) Although mastery of a particular program will probably require a certain degree of perseverance, and can sometimes be a frustrating process, most users will require relatively little technical knowledge of computing.

The Richards, while cautious about the possible negative consequences of using computers in qualitative research, celebrate the ways in which using computers can encourage researchers to rethink the procedures they normally take for granted. They also encourage the rethinking of conventional terms and dichotomies, such as 'coding' and the qualitative–quantitative distinction. They relate their discussion to the development of the NUDIST program, providing in the process a sketch map of the program. NUDIST can facilitate the testing of alternative data coding/indexing choices. Its nodal structure allows running adjustments to indexed headers. In the Richards' view, this goes some way towards mitigating the rigidity imposed by programs based on assumptions and conventions which may not straightforwardly apply to the substantive problem in hand. Indeed, the time invested in using that flexibility means that program-aided analysis is unlikely to reduce overall analysis time. Systematicity, formalization and quality control through enhanced 'grounding' are benefits bought at considerable time costs. The Richards are explicit that this could inhibit inspiration and fruitful intuition. In team research it may be worth designating a team member who addresses the data conventionally, or for the team to work this way initially, to realize any such benefits.

NUDIST is a very powerful program which extends the range of analytic strategies conveniently available to qualitative researchers. Among the new tools available, which are readily facilitated by the computer, is the ability to produce the kind of matrix display strategies for qualitative data favoured by Miles and Huberman (1984: Chapter 6). The use of such strategies, however, raises an old question in an interesting new guise. Suppose in using complex search routines on qualitative data, which are then displayed in a matrix form, one encounters an empty cell in the matrix. The lack of coincidence of one category with another may be of considerable analytical significance. However, it may also come about simply because one has gathered data from a homogeneous sample with insufficient degrees of freedom in the data. As the use of computers in qualitative research develops, do qualitative researchers need to be reminded, as quantitative researchers have long been, of the 'gigo' principle – 'garbage in, garbage out'?

Both the Richards' chapter and that by John Davies reflect long periods of time spent in the development of particular programs. Both are also sensitive to the ways in which researchers actually interact with programs. Davies's chapter blends technical specification, cognitive psychology and ethnographic reflection to produce an insight into how programs come to be modified. One ironic feature of Davies's chapter is its implicit recognition that the relationship between computing and qualitative research need not always be in one direction. This is in terms of processes of elicitation. As Anthony Finkelstein pointed out at the Surrey Conference, the development of expert systems depends on developers eliciting knowledge from human experts. The techniques required to do this look suspiciously like those data collection skills developed and honed by qualitative researchers over the past 40 years.

# 2

# Software for Qualitative Researchers: Analysis Needs and Program Capabilities

*Renata Tesch*

'Qualitative analysis' has become the accepted term for the analysis of data that are not numeric. The concept, however, holds different meaning for different researchers, depending on the type of approach they use in their work. Qualitative research 'is not a unitary enterprise', as J. Gubrium observed (Gubrium, 1988: 23). Other scholars commented on the pluralism in qualitative sociology as early as 1977 (Bell and Newby, 1977: 10). Not only the nature of the data varies (responses to open-ended questions, narrative fieldnotes, interview transcripts, personal diaries, public documents, etc.), but, even if two researchers were to analyze the exact same text, their strategies and outcomes could be quite different, each justified and relevant in the light of their respective epistemological frameworks and research purposes. Therefore, when we consider computer software that can be used to assist the researcher in the analysis of qualitative data, we first need to take into account the variations in the processes that researchers employ when they try to make sense of their data.

## Types of qualitative research approaches

Before the term 'qualitative' was common, social science researchers who had no interest in setting up experimental conditions or conducting quantifiable surveys simply called their activities 'fieldwork' and their method of data collection 'participant observation'. Today, the methodological literature is replete with terms that describe the perspectives qualitative researchers adopt (for instance, 'naturalistic', 'interpretive', or 'phenomenological'), or the school of methodological thinking on which they base their stance (such as 'symbolic interactionism' or 'ethnomethodology'), or the research approach they use (ethnography, grounded theory, discourse analysis, etc.). These terms are quite fuzzy, that is, they may overlap with each other or they may not be of the same conceptual level. Consequently, it is difficult to distinguish clearly between terms that denote an epistemological stance and those that refer to method. Ethnomethodology or symbolic interactionism are 'general conceptions . . . of the nature of explanations of social activity' (Halfpenny, 1981: 565) at the same time as embodying directions for appropriate research strategies. Grounded theory is simultaneously a set of assumptions about the production of knowledge and a set of guidelines for empirical research work.

The investigative purpose and the overall design of a research project conducted within one of these conventions are obviously determined by such epistemological assumptions and methodological guidelines. Since the nature of the analysis process, in turn, depends on the purpose of the inquiry, I have assembled a list of approaches that sociologists describe in their methodological literature – without claiming completeness, and aware of the fact that some terms are epistemologically more inclusive than others – and then briefly stated their objectives. Focusing on purpose statements in this manner will enable us to compare some aspects of the differences in the analysis processes associated with each approach. The types included are: traditional content analysis, ethnographic content analysis, document 'case' study (including life history study), discourse analysis, event structure analysis, ethnoscience, holistic and structural ethnography, ethnography of communication, grounded theory, ethnomethodology, and symbolic interactionism.

Table 2.1 provides brief purpose descriptions for each of these approaches, in alphabetical order. Although at first glance each of these various approaches seems quite different from all the others, it is possible to detect commonalities among some of them and group them accordingly. For the purpose of this chapter I will concentrate mainly on those commonalities that pertain to the analysis process, since it is here that we must take into account the different purposes of software packages designed to assist the qualitative researcher.

## Types of qualitative analysis

The list of research approaches above can be divided roughly into three groups. I will call these groups 'language oriented', 'descriptive/ interpretive', and 'theory building'. The first of these has a number of subgroups. I found, however, that sorting research approaches into groups is a hazardous activity: not everything fits neatly in one and only one subgroup. Classifications of this kind do not 'mirror' reality; they are merely heuristic intellectual tools wherever there

Table 2.1  *Research types and purposes*

| Type of research | Purpose |
| --- | --- |
| Content analysis, classical | 'making replicable and valid inferences from data to their context' (Krippendorf, 1980: 21) 'objective, systematic, and quantitative description of the manifest content of communication' (Berelson, 1952: 489) 'making inferences by systematically and objectively identifying specified characteristics within text' (Stone et al., 1966: 5) |
| Content analysis, ethnographic | 'the reflexive analysis of documents' (Altheide, 1987: 65) 'used to document and understand the communication of meaning, as well as to verify theoretical relationships' (Altheide, 1987: 68) |
| Discourse analysis | 'the linguistic analysis of naturally occurring connected spoken or written discourse' (Stubbs, 1983: 1) providing 'insight into the forms and mechanisms of human communication and verbal interaction' (van Dijk, 1985: 4) |
| Document study, life history study, oral history | an 'unstructured and non-quantitative' approach using personal documents (Bailey, 1978: 273), often resulting in typologies, or 'through which to examine and analyse the subjective experience of individuals and their construction of the social world' (Jones, 1983: 147) |
| Ethnography ('classical', Werner and Schoepfle; 'holistic', Jacob; 'reflexive', Hammersley and Atkinson) | 'to describe and analyze all or part of a culture or community by describing the beliefs and practices of the group studied and showing how the various parts contribute to the culture as a unified, consistent whole' (Jacob, 1987: 10) |
| Ethnography ('structural', Gubrium) | 'classifies and highlights the social organization and distribution of subjective meanings as native and diverse field realities' (Gubrium, 1988: 26), being 'concerned with . . . cataloging their forms and relationships in time and space' (Gubrium, 1988: 26) where we 'think of culture as a cognitive map' (Spradley, 1979: 7), and where 'both tacit and explicit culture are revealed through speech' (Spradley, 1979: 7) |

Table 2.1   *Research types and purposes (continued)*

| Type of research | Purpose |
| --- | --- |
| Ethnography of communication ('microethnography') | focuses 'on the patterns of social interaction among members of a cultural group or among members of different cultural groups' in order to 'specify the processes of interaction and understand how these "micro" processes are related to larger "macro" issues of culture and social organization' (Jacob, 1987: 18) |
| Ethnomethodology ('articulative ethnography', Gubrium) | 'study how members of society, in the course of ongoing social interaction, make sense of "indexical" expressions. Indexicals are terms whose meaning is not universal, but is dependent upon the context' (Bailey, 1978: 249) 'how members of situations assemble reasonable understandings of the things and events of concern to them and, thereby, realize them as objects of everyday life' (Gubrium, 1988: 27) 'how people in society organize their activities in such a way that they make mutual sense, how people do things in such ways that others can recognize them for what they are' (Sharrock and Anderson, 1986: 56) |
| Ethnoscience (cognitive anthropology) | 'to understand participants' cultural categories and to identify the organizing principles that underlie these categories . . . through the study of semantic systems' (Jacob, 1987: 22) 'to define systematically the meaning of words, or labels – in short the names of things in the context of their use' (Werner and Schoepfle, 1987: 29) in order to 'construct lexical-semantic fields of linked propositions' (Werner and Schoepfle, 1987: 38) |
| Event structure analysis | to examine and represent series of events as logical structures, i.e., as elements and their connections (including the assumptions that govern these connections) that can serve as explanatory models for interpreting actual or folkloristic sequences of events (Heise and Lewis, 1988). |
| Grounded theory construction | to 'discover theory from data' through the 'general method of comparative analysis' (Glaser and Strauss, 1967: 1) |
| Symbolic interactionism | 'to see how the process of designation and |

Table 2.1   *Research types and purposes (continued)*

| Type of research | Purpose |
| --- | --- |
| | interpretation [participants are defining and interpreting each other's acts] is sustaining, undercutting, redirecting and transforming the ways in which the participants are fitting together their lines of action' (Blumer, 1969: 53) 'understanding how individuals are able to take one another's perspective and learn meanings and symbols in concrete instances of interaction' (Jacob, 1987: 29) |

are too many things to apprehend at once. The shortcomings of any kind of classification usually are that not all entities they organize have clear-cut boundaries. In many cases, the boundaries overlap or are fuzzy. It is important to keep that in mind when we are grouping research approaches.

*Language-oriented research approaches*
Researchers who employ language-oriented research approaches are interested in the usage of language and in the meaning of words. This type of analysis is predominant in classical content analysis, discourse analysis, ethnoscience, ethnography of communication, structural ethnography, symbolic interactionism, and ethnomethodology. In some of these approaches language is mostly considered a means of communication, in others it is seen as a manifestation of the culture in which it serves as the communication instrument. An example of the former is the study of political documents to see how the rhetoric of one political party differs from that of the other. An example of the latter is the identification of a system of terms that are shared among members of a subculture who attach to those terms certain meanings which remain obscure to outsiders.

Each of these main divisions has two subdivisions. When dealing with *language as communication*, one could be interested in the content of texts, as in the example above (content analysis). One could, however, also be interested in the process of communicating itself, that is, 'in the forms and mechanisms of human communication and verbal interaction' (van Dijk, 1985: 4) (discourse analysis, or conversation analysis).

There are again at least two ways in which *language as culture* can be studied. Some scholars study culture strictly in terms of 'lexical/

semantic relations and the lexical/semantic fields that the relations comprise' (Werner and Schoepfle, 1987, vol. 2: 15) (ethnoscience or cognitive anthropology). The results are often the development of diagrams that can be viewed as models of the cognitive structure of the culture as mirrored in its language. A simple example might be an inverted tree-type diagram of the general and subordinate terms used in a culture to distinguish between types of occupations or of foods, or any other sub-aspect of the culture.

The second type consists of research approaches that explore how human beings make sense of their interactions with each other. Symbolic interactionism concentrates on the symbolic environment, that is, things, actions and utterances as interpreted by others with whom one is in interaction. (Since symbolic interactionists consider the evolution of theory, or the development of conceptual schemes, a desirable outcome, this type of research will also be listed again in our last group, theory-building approaches.) The closely related ethnomethodology concentrates on how people make sense of 'indexical expressions' in communication. 'Indexicals are terms whose meaning is not universal, but is dependent upon the context' (Bailey, 1978: 249). In the preceding sentence the indexical term is 'whose'. Without context, we would not know that it stands for 'terms'.

Structural ethnography could be placed in both of the above mentioned subgroups. It uses classification of cultural terms and concepts as a research tool, as ethnoscience does, and at the same time it focuses on interpersonal meaning. The term structural ethnography is relatively new (Gubrium, 1988: 24) and is used to describe the 'traditional' way of conducting ethnography in sociology. Ethnography of communication (or microethnography) bridges the two main groups, communication and culture. Here researchers explicitly 'focus on the patterns of social interaction among members of a cultural group' (Jacob, 1987: 18). Ethnographers of communication do not work with words only, but include non-verbal communication, that is, behavior, in their study.

Ethnographic content analysis would fit partly into the language-as-communication group, and partly into the theory-building group, which will be described in the section on theory building. It actually is a fusion of quantitative and qualitative methods, which is advocated by David Altheide, who suggests viewing appropriate documents as ethnographic material. Such materials are appropriate in so far as they are 'products of social interaction' (Altheide, 1987: 66). The 'distinctive characteristic [of ethnographic content analysis] is the reflexive and highly interactive nature of the investigator, concepts, data collection and analysis' (Altheide, 1987: 68). In contrast to traditional content analysis, in ethnographic content analysis categories for sorting of data pieces are not established prior to the analysis, but partially emerge from the data, the context is taken into account, and 'data are often coded perceptually, so that one item may be relevant for several purposes' (Altheide, 1987: 69). Data are collected as the study is in progress, and the analysis sometimes leads to reconceptualizations which, in turn, require additional data. The inclusion of new data is, of course, possible only where data are contemporary, not historical. Ethnographic content analysis is, therefore, best suited to current affairs such as news media coverage and policy analysis.

*Descriptive/interpretive research approaches*
In reality, all types of qualitative research are descriptive to a certain extent, and all of them – being scientific work – contribute to theory (our next group). Although most researchers in this group maintain that theory generation is the ultimate goal of social science research, they are cautious about how much of this can be done in an individual study. Ethnographers, for instance, establish 'way-stations on the road to theory' such as 'concrete descriptions, typologies, or models', but 'there is no obligation on the part of an ethnographer to travel all the way [to theory] in any particular study' (Hammersley and Atkinson, 1983: 201). The findings of a study result in no more and no less than 'a coherent, valid, and analytically sound "account"' (Halfpenny, 1979: 817), that is, a narrative that either describes in an orderly and detailed manner the characteristics and the structure of the phenomenon, or provides an interpretation of what the phenomenon means to those who experience it. Therefore, the distinction I make is between the explicit intents of the analysis procedures. In descriptive/interpretive research the intent of the analysis is to gain insight into the human phenomenon or situation under study and to provide a systematic and illuminating description of the phenomenon, not explicitly to generate theory.

In sociology only two major research approaches fall into this group: classical/holistic ethnography, and life history studies, oral history, or document studies. (In other disciplines, such as education or psychology, this group would have the most entries, while language-oriented approaches hardly exist.) This does not mean, however, that the largest share of the qualitative research work in sociology is language oriented. It merely means that the variation among language-oriented approaches is greater; the volume of work done may actually be smaller.

Ethnography has its origin in anthropology, where it was used mainly to study exotic cultures. Social scientists then recognized that groups within cultures form their distinctive subcultures, and that these are sufficiently unique to warrant intensive examination and portrayal. 'Holistic ethnographers seek to describe and analyze all or part of a culture or community by describing the beliefs and practices of the group studied and showing how the various parts contribute to the culture as a unified, consistent whole' (Jacob, 1987: 10).

The methods of life history studies are, naturally, related to those historians employ, particularly to the practice of explication (which Barzun aptly describes as 'worming secrets out of manuscripts' (Barzun and Graff, 1977: 94)). A sociologist who does historical research, however, would go beyond explication toward interpretation, since s/he is concerned more with understanding the dynamics of human affairs than with historical documentation. In principle, two different sources of data are available: documents and oral narratives. Oral history is the practice of eliciting memories from elderly people in order to capture the culture of a bygone era. Document study allows the researcher to travel even further back when trying to gain 'insight into how those circumstances we experience as contemporary "reality" have been negotiated, constructed and reconstructed over time' (Goodson, 1985: 126).

*Theory-building research approaches*
In sociology, theory-building approaches are represented mostly in grounded theory construction and somewhat in symbolic interactionism. Event structure analysis also is theory oriented, but in quite a different way, as will be explained later.

The main difference between this group of research types and the previous group is that those researchers who seek 'connections' seek 'explanations'. They try to find out more than just *what is*; they also try to find out *why* it is. Seeking explanations is the same as 'theorizing'. It begins with attempting to establish linkages between/among the elements to the data that the researcher has identified and classified.

A single research project does not produce an entire social theory, but it can develop a set of theoretical propositions. Explanatory propositions are statements about relationships, such as 'X exists because . . .; given X, then Y will follow; X is necessary but not sufficient for Y to occur; X causes Y' (Miles and Huberman, 1984: 72). Consequently, the researcher's first analysis goal is to find the entities that s/he will call X or Y. In fact, the entire point of theory construction is 'to produce concepts that seem to fit the data' (Strauss, 1987: 28).

In grounded theory construction these entities are called 'categories'. Glaser and Strauss coined the term 'constant comparison' to describe the process of progressive category clarification and definition (Glaser and Strauss, 1967: 45). When the researcher then discerns that two or more of these categories are conceptually related in some way, rather than claiming that any 'theory' has been derived, all that has been achieved has been to 'construct hypotheses . . . and attempt to demonstrate support for those . . . hypotheses' (Bogdan and Taylor, 1975: 79). Although not strictly seeking generalizations, grounded theory is theory building in the sense that it aims at stripping away the particulars and arriving at some underlying principle that is likely to apply to similar situations.

As mentioned earlier, symbolic interactionism also searches for these kinds of underlying principles (and so does, to a degree, ethnomethodology). These two approaches are described in the section on language-oriented research approaches, above. The objective of symbolic interactionists is to discover 'how this process of designation and interpretation is sustaining, undercutting, redirecting, and transforming the ways in which the participants are fitting together their lines of action' (Blumer, 1969: 53). The 'how' is not only meant to apply to one individual, but is to be expressed as an 'underlying principle' that would be valid at least for the group of 'participants' studied.

Ethnographic content analysis (described in the section on language-oriented research approaches above) also is theory building, as well as language oriented. It 'is used to document and understand the communication of meaning, as well as to verify theoretical relationships' (Altheide, 1987: 68). The latter is done basically by applying grounded theory to documents, which means using constant comparison procedures. Ethnographic content analysis also uses many of the traditional content analysis procedures, but unlike content analysis (which employs fixed categories for coding of words and phrases) the researcher's own 'categories' and 'variables' initially merely guide the study, and others 'are allowed and expected to emerge throughout the study' (Altheide, 1987: 68).

Event structure analysis differs from other theory-building approaches; it does not seek any form of generalization. Instead, it seeks to discover underlying 'structures' of events. Events in real life or in stories happen in a chronological order. However, there is an underlying 'logical structure' according to which they happen. It would not make sense for some events to occur at certain points, because certain conditions have not been met. Furthermore, the story or actual event takes one particular turn every time a prior event is completed, although there are actually several possibilities of events that could occur instead. This is the kind of logical structure the event analyst is interested in. People cause certain events to happen by making choices in the actions they take. In the same way they prevent other events from occurring. But each situation offers only a limited number of choices, and certain events cannot occur before their prerequisites have taken place. Thus for any situation abstract logical structures of events can be generated and compared with actual event sequences. The results could provide clues about people's priorities or about norms in a culture. Event analysis can be applied not only to actual incidents, but to folk tales and other cultural narratives (Heise, 1988).

**Analysis needs**

The purposes of and the methodological steps in the analysis procedures are, of course, idiosyncratic for each qualitative research approach. However, there are some basic commonalities within each group. Before we turn our attention to these commonalities, however, let me point out a commonality that pertains to all groups.

In all qualitative analyses the process consists of two simultaneous activities. The *conceptual* operations involved can be carried out only in conjunction with or after the accomplishment of certain *mechanical* tasks in the management of the data. The researcher must engage in manipulative activities such as locating words or phrases in the text, comparing words with a 'dictionary' of terms representing analysis categories, making lists of words and alphabetizing them, adding reference information, counting occurrences of words or phrases, marking relevant text segments, attaching numeric or mnemonic codes, inserting key words or comments, extracting and assembling topically or thematically related segments, etc. This, of course, is where the computer becomes useful. It can with enormous speed perform technical tasks that previously had to be done painstakingly by hand. While the difference may appear trivial in terms of scholarship, the gain can be measured not only in savings of time, but in increased accuracy, and the potential for greater thoroughness can actually result in considerable investigative advantages (see Tesch, 1988).

The thinking, judging, deciding, interpreting, etc., are still done by the researcher. The computer does not make conceptual decisions, such as which words or themes are important to focus on, or which analytical step to take next. These intellectual tasks are still left entirely to the researcher. Even artificial intelligence cannot yet recognize the meaning of human language, especially as it changes according to context. Thus all the computer does is follow instructions regarding words, phrases or text segments previously designated by the researcher as analysis units.

Now let us look at some common analysis needs of qualitative research approaches. No matter which kind of qualitative analysis a researcher is using, many more than just two or three operations are involved. Some of these questions may be unique for the particular type of analysis, but many are shared among several approaches. Even if they are held in common, however, the importance of any operation varies greatly among the approaches. For some, a particular operation may be a central step, for others it may be just one of the many things to focus on. Space does not permit me to describe in detail the analysis operations of each of the kinds of research that have been mentioned so far (for details see Tesch, 1990). Instead, I will list the major manual operations required in qualitative research. The kinds of research approaches in which a particular operation is used (to a greater or lesser extent) will be mentioned. The operations list is not exhaustive. In order to focus on computer software, I will mention here only those for which corresponding functions exist in the programs whose capabilities I have studied. Each 'operation' here will later be referred to as a 'function' of some software. Since even within the same approach researchers carry out their analysis in idiosyncratic ways, and since it is impossible to remain up to date with the newest methodological twists, you might find yourself not mentioned under an 'operation' that you do, in fact, perform. The following is an overview, not a complete catalog.

*1. Locating individual words and phrases*   Many language-oriented researchers need to locate individual words and phrases as a first exploratory step (classical content analysis, ethnoscience, ethno-methodology, structural ethnography, ethnography of communi-cation, ethnographic content analysis). They might want to see whether a particular word or phrase is used in the text at hand (so it can be classified), whether two (or more) occur in the same piece of text, and whether they occur within a certain proximity of each other. In particular, content analysts and ethnoscientists might also want to discover whether synonyms of the word occur, not only the specific word itself.

*2. Creating alphabetic word lists, counting the frequency of the occurrence of words*   There is no kind of research in which the locating of individual words exhausts the analytic procedures. After (or without) such individual word searches, most researchers wish to enlarge the picture. For instance, they may need to know which words occur in the data text in order to get an overview of the vocabulary (content analysis, discourse, ethnography of communication). They might even do this first, pick out words of interest, then search for these to find their locations and see their context. In order to get a first idea about where the emphasis of a text lies, it is often useful to compare the frequencies of occurrence among the relevant words on the inventory list (content analysis, life history studies, document case studies).

*3. Creating indices (attaching source information to each occurrence) and 'key word in context' concordances*  Where it is important to compare the vocabulary of one piece of text with others, one could, of course, merely compare the frequency of occurrence of relevant words (content analysis). However, some researchers prefer to look at a list of the locations of each word or phrase. Such a list would look much like an index in the back of a book, but would provide information on several levels, such as document name, chapter number, page, and perhaps even paragraph number. This way, not only can the words be compared across texts, but their locations can be found and the context can be taken into consideration. Context is of special importance when the various usages of a word are of interest (content analysis, ethnoscience, ethnomethodology). The researcher creates what is commonly called a KWIC concordance (key word in context). In such a concordance, the word under consideration is listed, each occurrence surrounded by a specified range of content.

*4. Attaching key words to segments of text*  In speech or written text, an idea may be verbalized in many ways, without ever using the key word that precisely defines it (such as talking about one's various culinary experiences without ever using the term 'food' or the phrase 'culinary experience'). If the researcher wants to examine a text for topics, rather than for linguistic properties, s/he needs to break down the text into segments that represent topic-units or 'instances', and attach to each the appropriate key word (discourse analysis, ethnography of communication). Then all segments that deal with the same topic can be assembled by key word and interpreted.

*5. Attaching codes (categorization symbols) to segments of text*  The differences between key words and codes are: key words are one-word summaries of the content of a text segment, while codes are abbreviations of category names. Categories can be pictured as the conceptual equivalent of file folders, each labelled with the name of one aspect of the research project or one topic found in the data. They serve to organize data pieces. These categories may emerge during the analysis, or they may be developed beforehand, or partially either way. Key words are complete and normal English words, and there can be as many in a study as there are different topics contained in the text; codes are abbreviations or other made-up fragments. The number usually is kept to a manageable range, since each code represents an item or category in the researcher's system for organizing the data. This kind of organizing of data segment is common in ethnographic content analysis, classical ethnography, life history studies, oral history, document case studies, and grounded theory. It is a prerequisite for creating well-ordered narratives about the nature of the phenomenon investigated.

*6. Connecting codes (categories)*   Many researchers wish to go beyond mere classification and explore whether or not the phenomenon possesses a discernible structure, or whether or not linkages exist between/among particular categories. Most notably this is done in grounded theory, but to a lesser degree also in event structure analysis, ethnographic content analysis, discourse analysis and ethnography of communication, ethnoscience and structural ethnography, symbolic interactionism and ethnomethodology. The purpose is to develop propositional statements or to make assertions regarding the structure or the linkages, or to relate concepts in order to discover the underlying principles (by many researchers also referred to as the generation of hypotheses). In some cases, the researcher goes beyond mere generation and attempts, in a second step, to find support for her/his assertions or to verify them by negative case analysis, etc.

### Software capabilities

It would be convenient for researchers if an array of microcomputer programs were available, each facilitating the mechanical tasks of data management in the way best suited to exactly one of the approaches listed in the first section of this chapter. Unfortunately, this is not the case. The approaches are not sufficiently discrete to warrant such great diversity in computer programming, while, on the other hand, any given concrete study might well incorporate aspects from more than one research type. Furthermore, as indicated above, the specific research purpose and nature of the data can differ from study to study even within one approach, necessitating unique data management maneuvers. Programmers, therefore, attempt to gear their software toward operations that many types of analyses have in common. Not surprisingly, the programs fall into three main groups: packages for language-oriented research (which include literary analysis programs used in the humanities, which I did not include in this sociology-oriented context), qualitative analysis packages for descriptive/interpretive kinds of analysis, and qualitative analysis packages for theory-building research. Their functions, of course, overlap. Since there is not enough space here to introduce each program and then compare each with all the others, I will instead describe software capabilities by function, in the order of operations listed in the previous section.

Before I turn to that task, however, I wish to distinguish between two major kinds of software packages: those created by software companies for general use, and those created by academicians specifically for qualitative analysis. While the former are produced in the hope of finding a large range of applications, the latter are created on the basis of intimate knowledge of qualitative data management, seeking to support each step in its proper order. Therefore, when a researcher works with a 'general purpose' program, s/he must adapt it to her/his particular purpose, while 'academic' programs come ready for (and might even elicit) the researcher's first input.

One type of 'commercial' program included here is the database manager (DBM). So many different packages exist that if I listed only the names I currently know about, without trying to discover what else is available, it would be boring for the reader. Therefore, in the following I will refer to DBMs as a genre rather than provide individual names.

Database managers share the basic principle of efficiently storing and retrieving information, but beyond that the individual packages differ widely from each other by including enhancements of the basic functions or even incorporating entire additional concepts. This diversity, however, is moderate compared with the second type of commercial programs, which I will call text retrievers. These are the ones used extensively in language-oriented research approaches.

The reason I cautiously say 'I will call' is that in the computer literature some programs that retrieve words or chunks of text are also called text searching programs, search and retrieval software, knowledge access software, note takers, indexers, archivers, text database managers, concordance programs, content analysis programs, or they might be incorporated in desktop utilities or personal information managers. An individual review of each would require the space of a book, and even a list of names would be too lengthy to make sense for this chapter. I will, however, furnish individual program names occasionally where researchers have found a particular program especially convenient. Proliferation is not a problem with academic programs. Scholars are not full-time programmers, and even if they work with a programmer they usually cannot devote much time to software creation. Many of the packages started out as small assemblies of functions that doctoral students compiled for use in their own data analysis. Since these packages are more 'researcher friendly', having been developed explicitly for scholarly work, and since their number is still small, their names will be listed here, and referenced at the end of the chapter. ZyIndex and WordCruncher are two 'text retrievers' which were initially created in an academic environment, then made available to commercial software companies for distribution (WordCruncher was first named BYU Concordance by its Brigham Young University authors). QUALPRO, the ETHNOGRAPH, TAP, and HYPERQUAL are American programs marketed for the past several years. Textbase Alpha was developed in Denmark, and has been available in an English version for at least two years. Kwalitan is a Dutch package that is not yet translated into English. MAX comes from Berlin, and its developers are considering an English translation. All of these are basic qualitative analysis programs. The structure-depicting program ETHNO is American and has been used for many years. At the current edge of the development are the theory-building programs, most of which are likely to be ready for distribution in English versions by the time this chapter is published. The closest to the finish line are HyperResearch (name still tentative) from the US, and AQUAD from Germany. Next comes NUDIST from Australia, then ATLAS from Germany.

Another distinction we should not forget is the one between operating systems. The only two programs I know about that worked with Apple-DOS (CONTENT ANALYSIS and TEXT ANALYZER) are no longer obtainable. All other programs are for MS-DOS (IBM) or the Macintosh environment. (I am not including programs for mainframe computers here.) All programs named above work with MS-DOS, except the Macintosh programs HyperQual, HyperResearch, NUDIST, and ATLAS. NUDIST, which is currently working well as a mainframe program, is planned to be made available in MS-DOS and Macintosh versions as well.

*1. Locating individual words and phrases*   If a search for words and phrases is all a researcher wishes to do, there is no need to buy a specialized analysis program. All word processors search for words and phrases, with different degrees of sophistication. So do DBMS, usually with a higher number of search options than word processors. All text retrievers provide this function, of course, some explicitly being labelled 'search programs'. Of the qualitative analysis programs, Textbase Alpha and TAP also allow the user to search for words in the text. The ETHNOGRAPH will do so in its next version, scheduled to appear shortly. I am not familiar enough yet with the idiosyncratic details of the theory-building programs, but some of them will provide a simple search function as well.

Word processors produce a screen-full of text, in which the search string (word or phrase) is highlighted. In other words, they search only through the document currently active and on the screen (as do qualitative analysis programs). Some word processors have the facility to search through all files on a floppy disk or a subdirectory of a hard disk, then mark the files in which the search string was found. The user must then decide which marked file to display on the screen (usually, the search term is not highlighted in the file).

All DBMS search across all stored records. (A record is similar to a file; it contains data about one unit of text, such as everything pertaining to one person or the reference information for one book. Standard database managers let the user divide records into fields that contain a particular kind of information, such as the person's birth date, or the publisher of the book. All records are set up so that they have the same fields. Text-based managers don't require the structuring into fields.) In a standard structured DBM, the user would ask to search within one field across all records. As a result of the search, the program shows the records in which the specified field contains the search string. Text database managers highlight the search string in a certain amount of context. Each DBM, of course, varies in its actual display.

Text retrievers always search across all files or those marked by the user, and show the search result as a list of the file names in which the string was found. It is then up to the user to indicate which file to display; the search string will be highlighted. A few retrievers combine the two steps and show the beginnings of the text portions in which the string occurs (notably the Text Collector).

Since both text retrievers and DBMS are designed specifically for locating items in text imported from other sources or stored in their own databases, their programmers have invested a lot of effort in making searches useful. Searches can be either expanded or restricted. If, for instance, I do not find the term 'sociology' in a document, I could expand the search by using a 'wildcard'. The wildcard allows me to use a symbol (* or ?) in place of any character or group of characters. I could use a word's root ('sociolog*'), and in this way include in my search 'sociological', 'sociologist', etc.

Another expansion works through a 'fuzzy' search, in which a 'sound-alike' word is located, another one by using the operator 'OR' (a so-called Boolean operator) to include a synonym: 'research' OR 'investigation' OR 'inquiry'. Academic programs such as CONTENT ANALYSIS and WordCruncher will even allow one to set up an entire list of 'related terms' or a 'thesaurus' or 'dictionary' of synonyms. When too much is found, the user can delimit the search by specifying that the search string must occur near another term (proximity search), or in the same document with another term (Boolean operator 'AND'), or only if a specific other term is *not* in the document (NOT).

One of the most useful software facilities for the qualitative researcher is the 'cut-and-paste' feature. It allows the user to indicate context boundaries around the highlighted search string, then assemble the text segments in another document. Almost all text retrievers can do this, and some text-based DBMS as well (for instance, askSam).

*2. Creating alphabetic word lists, counting the frequency of the occurrence of words*   The program I use when I need to quickly get a list of the words in a document I am working on (for instance for creating a book index) is Word Match. It also counts the occurrence of each word, and that is all it does. This little program is simple, cheap and quite fast. WordCruncher provides the same services, and so do a number of text retrievers (the Text Collector, CONCORDANCE and ZyIndex), although not with the same ease as Word Match and WordCruncher. All of these programs make the results manageable by allowing the user to indicate that very common words, such as 'and', 'he', 'in' (noise words), should be ignored. They provide their own ignore-list, to which the user can add more such 'connecting words' or 'stop words'.

While all others produce an alphabetic list with frequency counts added, WordCruncher provides an additional small utility that sorts words by decreasing frequency. Furthermore, it will compare the word lists of several files, using all the words found in the first file.

*3. Creating indexes (attaching source information to each occurrence) and 'key word in context' concordances*   In the advertising literature about text retrievers much is said about the advantage of indexes. These indexes, however, are not meant for the user. They are internal devices that the programs create to speed up a search; a list of word locations is examined faster than the entire text. The location information is encoded according to an in-house scheme. Although some retrievers will print out their indexes, they are usually mere word lists, not useful indexes. The qualitative researcher needs an easily understandable system for making a record of word locations in texts. KWIC Text Indexer allows the user to subdivide a document into 'chunks', then adds to each word it lists the file name and chunk number. WordCruncher excels in the task of indexing; it furnishes reference information in the form of the (abbreviated) name of the 'book' (the entire document) in which the string occurs, and the number of the section and line in which it can be found. Words to be included in the index are selected by the user.

Constructing key word in context indexes is the sole reason for the existence of KWIC Text Index. Like Word Match, it is a simple and cheap program that makes a list of the words in a file or any 'chunk' of it, and sorts it alphabetically with reference information (see section 2 above). The output consists of individual lines, each line beginning with the 'key' word, followed by about 30 succeeding characters. In the middle of each line a '+' is inserted to mark the place where the 30 or so preceding characters are reproduced. At the end of the line, the program inserts the reference information. WordCruncher, a much more polished program, prints the 'citation' first (a location indicator), then 30 characters of text, the key word, and then another 30 characters.

*4. Attaching key words to segments of text*  Attaching key words to segments of text is similar to the cut-and-paste operation mentioned in section 1 above. Rather than retrieving words and phrases only, an entire segment of text is retrieved. The difference between the cut-and-paste method and the key word method is that cut-and-paste is done individually chunk by chunk, as the full text is on the screen (as one could also do a bit clumsily with a word processor by moving 'blocks' of text into another window or a second document). The key word method is much more elegant, because a single command retrieves all relevant segments and collates them. The computer 'knows' what the boundaries of the chunks are, since each is the content of a distinct 'field'. This kind of data manipulation is only possible, of course, if the data do not consist of continuous text, but are structured: chunks of information are placed into 'fields', the one or more key word(s) are attached that signify in some way the content of any particular field. A search is now done using a key word, and all fields that have the appropriate content are reproduced. This, of course, is the forte of standard structured database managers. All DBMS provide the facility, as do some advanced text retrievers, such as ZyIndex (attaching key words to entire files, however).

5. *Attaching codes (categorization symbols) to segments of text*    The difference between attaching key words and attaching codes to text segments is that codes (for an explanation of their nature see section 5 under 'analysis needs' above) are assigned not to predetermined chunks of text whose boundaries remain fixed. When 'coding', the researcher decides which sentences form a relevant meaning unit, then determines which code is appropriate and attaches it. Another code may be attached to the exact same segment, or smaller parts can be carved out from the segment and coded differently ('nesting' of segments). The next segment may begin within the current segment and end beyond it; in other words, segments may overlap. Unlike in a simple cut-and-paste operation, all these boundaries and attached codes remain stored and can be reused. They can also be changed partially (either segment boundaries or codes, or both) or the entire document can be resegmented and provided with additional codes, or totally recoded. Later, a search using one of the codes will result in a reproduction of all segments to which that code is attached, including reference information about the original location of the segment. All qualitative analysis programs offer these facilities.

QUALPRO is the most basic of the qualitative analysis programs. It invites the user to segment and code, then performs searches for the indicated segments and assembles them. These main functions are accomplished in a neat and straightforward manner, and the only additional function of QUALPRO is a count of the frequency of the occurrence of each code (a feature all qualitative analysis programs possess). All other programs (the ETHNOGRAPH, TAP, Textbase Alpha, HyperQual) contain a number of 'enhancements', some of which begin to facilitate theory building of a simple kind. For instance, if the data contain numerous segments that were coded with the same two codes (standing for concepts), there might be some connection between the two concepts. Therefore, the ETHNO-GRAPH, TAP and HyperQual permit the researcher to search for co-occurring codes and print out the segments which were coded with both (or more). The ETHNOGRAPH uses Boolean operators (see above under section 1), while TAP becomes even more sophisticated. It permits the researcher to specify the order in which the co-occurring codes were attached (first, then next, then next, etc.). TAP is the only program that will search for a sequence of codes, that is, for two (or more) codes, the first of which is attached to a segment which is followed immediately (or with interruption) by a segment that has the second code.

Another way of exploring relationships is to do 'selective' searches. In a selective search the program will not, as usual, search for a particular code or code combination through all data files, but will automatically select only those that satisfy a certain condition. The condition could be that all files must be interview transcriptions with female respondents. In this case, of course, the researcher must have indicated which transcriptions are from female interviewees. The ETHNOGRAPH and Textbase Alpha provide such a facility. They let the researcher 'code' entire files with certain characteristics, often socio-demographic variables such as age or home state, then specify which value the variable must have (for instance, *home state = Arizona*) for the file to be selected for the search. If the same search is done with another value (*home state = Idaho*), the researcher can use the two collections of data segments to explore whether differences seem to exist between the two groups.

Some qualitative analysis programs use the selection feature in combination with the code count to construct matrixes that may be inspected as they are, or even imported into common statistical packages for simple quantitative analyses. Textbase Alpha and MAX do so, and the ETHNOGRAPH will in its next version (4.0).

*6. Connecting codes (categories)*  The 'enhancement' features of qualitative analysis programs as described above do connect codes to a certain degree. The reason I have not listed the programs under this section's heading is that these features were meant mainly to sharpen the interpretation; they were not specifically designed for theory building. Programs that aim directly at relating conceptual categories begin with coding segments, and they also allow these segments to be assembled, but their main function is to discover and 'test' whether there are instances from which the researcher can discern that, for example, X is always present where Y occurs, or 'X exists because . . .; given X, then Y will follow; X is necessary but not sufficient for Y to occur; X causes Y', etc. (Miles and Huberman, 1984: 72). The programs invented for this purpose and being readied for distribution are HyperResearch, AQUAD, NUDIST and ATLAS.

The procedure that theory-building qualitative analysis programs employ is somewhat different from the ones described in the section above. Although a code is attached to a particular segment of text, the code now 'characterizes' the file in which it is present. Codes, therefore, are thought of more like 'values' of a variable. If the category or concept is 'relationship with parents', for instance, the corresponding codes could be 'nurturing', 'distant', 'mutually dependent', etc. Any given file will have one of these embedded, perhaps attached to several segments, all of which represent

evidence for (or instances of) the 'distance' in the family relationship, for instance. Let us assume that among the remaining
categories there is one that deals with the nature of social behavior.
The program might find that files 'characterized' by 'distant
relationship to parents' more often than not are also characterized
by 'uncommunicative behavior', while 'nurturing relationships' are
usually associated with some other kind of behavior. The researcher
then may instruct the program to see whether there is sufficient
disconfirming evidence (search for the opposite association, for
instance) to reject the developing hypothesis. If not, a tentative
proposition may be proclaimed.

Two of the programs under development, NUDIST and ATLAS,
provide facilities for the graphic representation of the relationships
between and among codes/categories. NUDIST uses hierarchical tree
structures only, while ATLAS works with boxes and arrows connecting
these clusters.

## Conclusion

This chapter has been no more than an introduction to the broad
range of software available to the qualitative researcher. Almost all
the programs mentioned here possess interesting features that I had
insufficient space to refer to, much less to describe. The information
provided is not adequate for deciding which program is the best for
a particular study. Although the actual operations a program
supports are the most significant criterion, attributes such as ease of
learning, compatibility with the programmers' work style, convenient extras and price will also enter into a judgement about the
suitability of a program. The aim of this chapter was to show how
diverse the assistance is that computers can offer qualitative
researchers, and to bring some order into the large, confusing
supply of software to enable the researcher to find her/his way
among the many options.

## Appendix 2.1: Software programs

Further details of programs marked with an asterisk may be found in the 'Resources'
section at the end of the book.

**askSam**™ (MS-DOS)
Seaside Software, PO Box 1428, Perry, FL, 32347. Tel.: (800) 327-5726. Price:
$295.00.

**Concordance**™ (MS-DOS)
Dataflight Software, 10573 West Pico Blvd, Los Angeles, CA 90064. Tel.: (213)
785-0623. Price: Version 4.0: $495.00; Version 3.0: $295.00.

\*ETHNO™ (MS-DOS)
National Collegiate Software Clearing House, Duke University Press, 6697 College
Station, Durham, NC 27708. Tel.: (919) 737-2468 or (919) 684-6837. Price: $35.00.
\*ETHNOGRAPH™ (MS-DOS)
Qualitative Research Management, 73425 Hilltop Road, Desert Hot Springs, CA
92240. Tel.: (619) 329-7026. Price: $150.00.
\*HyperQual™
Qualitative Research Management, 73425 Hilltop Road, Desert Hot Springs, CA
92240. Tel.: (619) 329-7026. Price: $125.00.
\*QUALPRO™ (MS-DOS)
Qualitative Research Management, 73425 Hilltop Road, Desert Hot Springs, CA
92240. Tel: (619) 329-7026. Price: $125.00.
\*TAP™
Qualitative Research Management, 73425 Hilltop Road, Desert Hot Springs, CA
92240. Tel.: (619) 329-7026. Price: $150.00.
\*Textbase Alpha™
Qualitative Research Management, 73425 Hilltop Road, Desert Hot Springs, CA
92240. Tel.: (619) 329-7026. Price: $150.00.
Text Collector™ (MS-DOS)
O'Neill Software, PO Box 26111, San Francisco, CA 94126. Tel.: (415) 398-2255.
Price: $69.00.
WordCruncher™ (MS-DOS)
Electronic Text Corporation, 5600 North University Ave., Provo, UT 84604. Tel.:
(801) 226-0616. Price: $299.00.
ZyIndex™ (MS-DOS)
ZyLab Corporation, 233 E. Erie St, Chicago, IL 60611. Tel.: (800) 544-6339 or (312)
642-2201. Price: $95.00 (Personal); $295.00 (Professional); $695.00 (Plus).

AQUAD™, \*ATLAS™, HyperResearch™, MAX™ and \*NUDIST™ will be distributed by
Qualitative Research Management when they are completed. For information call
(619) 329-7026.

# 3

# The Transformation of Qualitative Method: Computational Paradigms and Research Processes

## *Lyn Richards and Tom Richards*

In an area where there has been remarkably little cumulative methodological literature or discussion of data-handling processes, the introduction of computers has been possible with virtually no reflection on their significance. Few articles discuss computers in this context, and most concentrate on particular programs (for example, Drass, 1980; Podolefsky and McCarty, 1983; Seidel and Clark, 1984; Shelly and Sibert, 1986). Methods texts even recently published ignore the possibility of using computers (for example, Lofland and Lofland, 1984; Strauss, 1987). Exceptions are rare, and their discussions brief (for example, Burgess, 1984: Chapter 8). So far, only one comprehensive book attempts to explore the relationship between software and qualitative method (Tesch, 1990). There has been no wide-ranging discussion of the impacts of introducing computational methods and thinking, and no suggestion that they may profoundly change qualitative research.

Yet such changes have already taken place. In a previous paper, distinguishing four sorts of programs – those searching text, those offering database storage, the code-and-retrieve method and those performing concept-based analysis – we explored the impacts of each (Richards and Richards, 1989). This exercise produced a collection of impacts ranging from the advantages that speed and memory offer for clerical tasks to the abilities to locate occurrences of strings in text or perform rapid retrievals by keyword or Boolean searches using multiple codes – tasks impossible by manual means.

Every aspect of the handling of qualitative data is dramatically changed by computers. Text can be stored more efficiently and accessed in a far wider range of ways, more accurately – removing the uncertainty and tentativeness of conclusions. Text can be searched by codes attached to it or by strings occurring in it. Comparisons can be accurate, deviant cases can be pinpointed. Conclusions can be checked and verified. These changes follow very limited use of fairly simple software – yet they have remade the tasks of the qualitative researcher.

The present chapter argues that they have also transformed *thinking about* qualitative method. What we are seeing is more like a methodological revolution than, as so often implied, a mere improvement in conditions of clerical employment and a saving of pine forests. Like all revolutions, it has complex and not always desirable results. Three aspects of this transformation are considered here. First, computers, we argue, challenge the dichotomy of quantitative and qualitative method. Secondly, they encourage recognition of methodological diversity within qualitative research. And, thirdly, they alter the experience of research, reshaping the research process.

## Disposing of the dichotomy

'Qualitative' research has to contend with a negative definition – 'non-quantitative' handling of 'unstructured' data. The terms carry a tone of apology and often mean impressionistic analysis of messy data. The literature has until recently confirmed this dubious tone. Burdened with low status and reputation for untrustworthy results, qualitative methods writing has tended to stress defiantly the meaningfulness of unstructured data and the joys of getting them, rather than the challenges and techniques of handling the stuff. This imbalance has only very recently been remarked upon (Turner, 1981; Burgess, 1984; Strauss, 1987; Richards and Richards, 1987). There has been little attention in classic texts to techniques for sorting and analysing qualitative data. And only recently has there been a renewed insistence that they should be *rigorous* techniques.

The introduction of computers has coincided with, and is at most only partly responsible for, a growing concern for developing and justifying rigorous methods of data processing. That shift was happening anyway – driven by frustration at the continuing low status of qualitative research and its felt inability to counteract criticism. Recent texts criticize the tendency of ethnographers to justify statements merely by illustration with juicy quotes (for example, Agar, 1986). The increasing use of qualitative data in policy research is cited as part of 'a rehabilitation of data' (Cain and Finch, 1981; Finch, 1986). The cause of 'cautious positivism' in qualitative research (Silverman, 1985) has been strongly pursued in medical studies. Each of these influences pushes research emphases away from cheerful reliance on getting lots of the stuff or getting different sorts of stuff – indeed criticisms of the once-gospel rule of 'triangulation' recur in several recent works (Fielding and Fielding,

1986; Burgess, 1984). We are now urged to get 'better quality stuff' (Agar, 1980a).

One result is direct questioning of the dichotomy of qualitative and quantitative data analysis – either covertly, as data are smartened up, or overtly, as the bases for that dichotomy are questioned. The sets of loosely fitting dichotomies generally subsumed under qualitative/quantitative (soft/hard, holistic/ atomistic, inductive/deductive . . .) have long been open to question (Halfpenny, 1979; Burgess, 1984). Even without computer techniques, major growth areas of qualitative research in recent years have tended towards 'harder' analysis of 'soft' data. Educational evaluation studies stress various versions of quasi-variable analysis, embodied in matrix displays (Miles and Huberman, 1984), which, unlike juicy quotes, will impress policy-makers, though they may distort the data they compress.

Computer applications must be expected to reinforce any trend to 'dealing quite rigorously with soft data' (Norris, 1981: 348). Computerization removes barriers to scale and complexity of analyses. There are virtually no clerical limits to how *much* stuff you get now, and few to how complex it is. Thus, in the rethinking of qualitative methods, computer applications are highly likely to be lumped in with the push to quantification and respectable scale. Several programs, including our own, offer statistical summaries of the text retrievals they provide, so, whilst not confined to large-scale projects, they do remove the barriers to it. Our own program, in its mainframe version, supports multiple users with multiple indexing databases.

Whilst such developments are certainly not to be regretted, they must be monitored. Inevitably, if programs are seen only in terms of these abilities, they will be greeted with hostility by those committed to the traditional goals of field research and 'grounded theory'. Meanwhile, computer techniques are likely to be both funded and encouraged as part of a cleaning up operation on suspect social science. Since the early days of content analysis, computers have offered the opportunity to quantify a wide range of characteristics of text. They also extend the reach of 'qualitative' techniques to data collected by stereotypically 'positivist' means – write-ins on the most rigid of surveys can now be thoroughly analysed, rather than relegated to juicy illustrative quotes. So the computer offers a handy Trojan horse for infiltrating into qualitative research the narrowest goals of quantitative sociology. It reawakens a dream decades old of converting '"raw" phenomena into data which can be treated in essentially a scientific manner' (Cartwright,

1953: 435). That dream was of research conducted 'so as (1) to create reproducible or "objective" data, which (2) are susceptible to measurement and quantitative treatment, (3) have significance for some systematic theory, and (4) may be generalized beyond the specific set of material analyzed' (Cartwright, 1953: 435). To associate computational developments with such a return to the physics/chemistry virtues is pessimistic – but the warning should be made. We wish to resist that association. Contrary scholarly virtues celebrating (1) the non-experimental and person-related, (2) the non-numerically reducible, (3) the rich and suggestive, (4) idiosyncratic and specifically relevant results, are also capable of support by computer. These alternative scientific virtues can be pushed by computers through their presently existing barriers of complexity. It is our argument that recent developments in computer techniques celebrate and develop, rather than undermine, the methods traditionally associated with qualitative research. For example, our own program now supports the production of matrices from 'cross-tabulation' of categories: the cells contain not only statistical summaries of the results, but all the text they refer to. It also allows the results of searches for strings of characters in the text to be combined with indexing data, giving much more certainty that all occurrences of a category have been explored.

Programs should aim for goals strongly in the theoretical traditions of qualitative methods. It is possible now to offer computer support for full exploration of data patterns and pursuit of grounded theory (Richards and Richards, 1991). That computers also allow identification of deviant cases and enumeration of occurrences of patterns, verification of hypotheses, 'quasi-statistics' and grounding of claims in rigorous text searches will inevitably force reassessment of the relationship of qualitative and quantitative techniques – but the latter need not undermine the former. They offer then a rethinking of the entire dichotomy, a recognition that qualitative and quantitative methods are different modes of approach to information, not modes of information.

The transformation of methods promised by computers is not about numerical techniques. What present developments offer is a different bridging of the fictional gap between qualitative and quantitative analysis. The computer can allow detailed interrogation of complex data in the course of a process of explicit testing of theories. It can make thorough search and analysis procedures easily available. It can also promote a more rigorous pursuit of combinations of qualitative method and variable analysis. Much of the vocabulary of 'hard' quantitative research thus becomes appropriate to 'soft' data analysis. But these procedures can be carried out without sacrificing the detail and subtlety of the original data.

Given such priorities, computational developments can, we assert, serve to promote rigorous and convincing analysis without sacrificing the features of the qualitative tradition summarized in Agar's ode to ethnography: 'its openness, its willingness to approach complex behaviour in natural context, its lack of commitment to the common wisdom as encoded in social science theory, its methodological flexibility in adapting elicitation and observation to the situational and personal demands of the moment and its stress on the quality of the relationship within which the information exchange occurs. To lose this in an effort to approximate a different research tradition would be to kill it' (Agar, 1980a: 36).

### Celebrating diversity

Of course, qualitative research is not a single research tradition. The literature implies that it is – yet displays incompatible ways of doing it. The label 'qualitative analysis' has been normally applied, as though obviously appropriate, to practically anything that did not involve adding up, and to much that did. It is usual for book titles to imply that in discussing one method they cover all of qualitative methods. When techniques have been seriously described (for example, Lofland and Lofland, 1984; Strauss, 1987; Miles and Huberman, 1984) they are quite normally presented idiosyncratically, as *our* way, even the *only* way of doing it. Thus the field has acquired a series of manuals for particular makes of vehicle (often asserting that they are the only cars on the road), with little general literature on automotive engineering.

Looked at one way, the application of computers to qualitative research could worsen this situation. Necessarily, at least in the early design stages, software encapsulates a particular approach to handling data. Atomization is encouraged by specific software promotions aimed at particular methodological contexts, and by the tendency of developers, going commercial, to avoid academic reporting of their designs (Richards and Richards, 1991). If discussion of computer applications stays at the level of particular programs, it will confirm the spattered patterns of the methods literature. Instead of an uncoordinated set of manuals for different makes, we will have sales yards for software lining the highways to research funding – but still no cumulative literature on qualitative method.

Not only do computer techniques gloss over differences in

method: they also may flatten them out. Researchers will design their projects to fit known programs, and most programs are good at a limited set of tasks. Software, especially for IBMs, has achieved a plateau of competence in a very advanced version of the code-and-retrieve technique (Richards, forthcoming). However, qualitative analysis was never just about coding and retrieval. Most programs do more for large-scale, comparative and collaborative research (Gerson, 1984: 63) than fine examination of flows of thought or action and textual structures within texts. Most give no support to methods that rely on matrix displays of rich data and little to model building. And most are much better suited to theory testing than to grounded theory.

On the other hand, computer techniques could force critical comparative work on method. The fact that we all handle 'unstructured data' (a dubious term at best) is no longer sufficient basis for the assumption that we all play the same rules on the analytical games field. Linguistic analysis, for instance, needs a different approach from the techniques of 'grounded theory', a term widely adopted as an approving bumper sticker in qualitative studies, but less often given methodological discussion. The 'knowledge engineering' exercise required for the creation of software involves fine specification of the researcher's tools and tasks. To design programs to fit research approaches demands attention to variety – of sources and sorts of data, and relationships of data to theory. (To clarify your goals, try fitting your project to an inappropriate program!)

Different forms of qualitative analysis can and now must be sharply distinguished. No one existing computational method fits all qualitative research, any more than one statistical technique fits all quantitative projects. So computer applications arguably promote exploration of the variety of methods that are called qualitative, the different theoretical justifications, purposes and processes of data construction, the different shapes and challenges of the stuff qualitative researchers call data (Halfpenny, 1979). Sociology of science is only beginning to explore the different canons by which research quality can be judged, the antagonisms between them (Gerson, 1989). Our own current project includes a series of qualitative studies of qualitative researchers across the spectrum of techniques already affecting software development. (To give a simple example, discourse analysis required retrievals using information about chronological order of textual material and proximity to or enclosure in text coded in other categories; both could be included in our software, but had not been previously required.)

Even the vocabulary obscures major differences. Check the use of the verb 'to code' in any selection of recent texts! It describes entirely dissimilar processes, whose analytical goals are entirely different. In the argument below, those differences are important. Computer programs hitherto have supported only one sort of 'coding' of qualitative data.

'Coding' of data in the grounded theory approach refers to a process by which the researcher takes off from data documents – explores, examines, theorizes about emerging ideas (Glaser and Strauss, 1967). This is done via a series of steps stressing concept specification, constant comparison within the data and extrapolation beyond, and techniques for selecting and solidifying the strands of emerging theory. The resultant theory grows in memos, only loosely linked to the original data, and is justified by its ability to account for new instances. Recent adaptations of the method have specified clerical processes for ensuring concept definition and recording of specific instances and even accompanying text (see especially Turner, 1981; Martin and Turner, 1986). But the clerical emphasis remains on making new data documents – memos – rather than coding all original text for retrieval.

By contrast, in much research carrying the qualitative (and sometimes 'grounded theory') label, 'coding' refers to a process not unlike postcoding for quantitative analysis. The obvious thing to do with messy data is attach the same tag to all the stuff on one subject, and invent a way of finding all those tags. The goal is to collect extracts in a manageably few categories for efficient retrieval. Tesch (1990) has thoroughly explained the techniques involved. Miles and Huberman (1984), challenging the 'inductivist' claim that theory can only emerge from data, encapsulate prior theory in 'starter' codes. As further codes are generated, they are kept in orderly lists, and the search for unifying categories is done by 'pattern coding'. All codes are *systematically* applied to label segments for retrieval. That all text is thus coded is essential for the theory-testing goal; ultimately, any emerging pattern can and must be tested by retrieving *all* the instances that fit the theory.

The contrast between the two approaches to coding shows in the tone of accounts. In Strauss's writing, coding is an adventure, almost a game. Miles and Huberman warn, by contrast, that coding is 'hard, obsessive work'. But the two techniques are not incompatible. They can (and arguably should) be regarded as different loops of enquiry, theory production and testing, appropriate to different stages of research, types of data and, perhaps most importantly, different theoretical purposes. And software should support both.

**Remaking the research process**

In the current literature there are no accounts of how computer technology changes qualitative research. Indeed there seems to be a commitment to portraying computers as merely allowing us to do better and more easily what we were doing before. Yet, even when fairly simple programs are used, the task is altered. More complex ones reshape the research experience.

In what follows we draw on our own experience and that of other users of NUDIST (see 'Resources' section), so central aspects of its design are pertinent here (Richards and Richards, 1990). Clerical tasks of qualitative research – data recording, storage, and indexing – are handled in NUDIST by input into and exploration of separate text and index files. Data documents need not be online to be indexed. Indexing data can refer to finely defined extracts of text or to information about the text (thus to characteristics of people, or groups, who are the subjects of particular documents or parts of documents). Exploration and theory development are done in interplay of the original text with the conceptual structure used for and created by its exploration.

NUDIST invites (though it does not require) extremely fine-grained indexing (we avoid that ambiguous term 'coding'). It will store information in tree-structured indexes, which become the repository for references to documents and thinking about them. The index system is effectively unlimited not just in the number of categories but also in complexity of index structure. Categories (or nodes in a tree-structured index) have titles, carry comments and contain references to text. Researchers can input unlimited multiple indexing of text on finely distinguished subcategories of major conceptual 'trees'. (They can also do parsimonious indexing with simple flat index systems – but most accept the invitation to complexity.)

Searches can incorporate not only the knowledge of indexing of text units (which may be lines or paragraphs) but also the patterns of overlap or lack of overlap of units indexed at each category and the information about documents or sectors of documents. The results of any enquiry or of any text searching can be stored automatically as a new category in the index system, available then for further enquiries. A logically complete set of search and analysis operations is offered, exceeding the merely Boolean. And in the analysis process, getting back text is only one outcome. Researchers can browse the index or document system and move between them, with hypermedia techniques that allow constant interaction of indexing with the original text. The program enables rapid and safe interrogation and revision of the conceptual structure expressed in the index files and the indexing of text located there, as well as recording of comments at any node.

The program also encourages flexibility of the index system as prior theory is questioned, new categories emerge, and relationships between categories change. Indexing information can be added or altered at any time, with all entries automatically dated. The indexing system can be reshaped as required, sectors deleted or shifted, complete with all information stored there. It can also grow, accepting new nodes without limit – as the researcher adds new categories or creates them from combinations of old – and storing them in logical locations.

Each of these developments opens new aspects of qualitative procedures to computing. Here we concentrate on three areas. First, the coding process, and its place in the research timetable, are altered. Secondly, index systems take new priority, their construction and alteration changing the research process. And thirdly, the research process is remade by the ability to move between text and indexing data.

### 'Codes' and what to do with them

Most qualitative analysis software works with only one form of coding – the labelling of text in order to retrieve by category. Arguably, all qualitative analysis has to do some of this: all approaches involve 'a mechanical phase' through which 'data are structured and presented for interpretation' (Drass, 1980: 334). Computers are very good at this, celebrating it in database management.

Humans, however, are bad at two processes required if this way of handling text is not to restrict it. First, they need procedures for keeping track of and systematically using complex and rich collections of codes. This is especially important if the collection can (even must) keep growing after data processing is underway. Secondly, flexibility of systems is a problem. If the goal is theory construction, exploration of patterns in data, not merely retrieval of text, is required. Researchers need to wander through their data and their thinking about it, exploring and interrogating emerging patterns.

Keeping track of codes and using them systematically are less serious problems where there are fewer codes or the method synthesizes and collapses codes. In the grounded theory approach, the answer to codes that are generated like raindrops is to use memos to bring them together (in muddy puddles, then crystal-clear lakes?). Code-keeping is harder in the code-and-retrieve method, since it produces large and growing numbers of codes and requires that codes be systematically applied: all data already processed should be relabelled whenever a new label is invented.

So grounded theory produces, as theory emerges, an imploding collection of codes, and an expanding system of cumulative memos *about* the data. The code-and-retrieve approach produces a coding framework that grows as new categories are invented. In the development of qualitative analysis software, little attention has been paid to either cumulative memos or expanding code collections.

NUDIST aimed to support either or both approach in any project, and to open new possibilities for both. If a project is on any computer system, memos can of course be handled as just any other text, and indexed along with data documents. (If all lines of the memo are indexed at a node, it will all appear with retrievals from that node.) But memos are a motley lot, and some are mere comments on where thinking has got or on ideas still to be explored. In NUDIST these can be stored at that node, in a comment field that will be included in any further nodes constructed with this one (dated and labelled with the node where it originated). Memos can be added or deleted to any node at any time, so the thinking about node construction processes can be updated. The collapsing of codes central to grounded theorizing is supported by the ability to combine existing nodes into new nodes in the index system – and the program brings with those nodes not only all the data that have been indexed at them but also memos about them.

The expansion of categories, and challenge of using them, is a major problem for any technique. Manual methods mean dire consequences for those who keep revising code lists. Computer databases of course can always allow additions. But what to do with them is a new problem, as is what to do with text already processed each time a new category is introduced.

NUDIST invites expansion of indexes. New categories can be made in four ways. First, new nodes can be created simply by entering information about lines to be stored at that node. Secondly, the user can request a search of the text itself for strings of characters occurring there: the result of any such search becomes a new indexing node. Thirdly, new nodes can be formed out of old, through the exploration of relationships between categories. At any stage, a new index node can be created from the retrieval resulting from any enquiry about text coded in combinations of the current index nodes. And fourthly, any existing node can be relocated, complete with information stored there, and given a new name and pathname. Any new node can then be treated just like any other node in the index trees, explored, linked to other nodes and pursued in further enquiries.

## Index systems and their impact

Because the program will accept any number of index categories at any stage, it is essential that they be logically ordered. NUDIST locates all new categories within the tree-structured index system (always identifying a node by its pathname as well as its title) and supports pruning and shifting of any subtree so the index system can be kept efficient.

The categories must then be systematically used, however. In any system seeking to recall all data indexed at any node, the development of new nodes is problematic if the researcher is unwilling to re-process already indexed text whenever a new category 'emerges'. NUDIST helps in several ways.

Given the possibility of constant additions to or subtractions from the index system, of reshaping of it and revision, support for rethinking of data documents indexed earlier was essential. As emerging categories are incorporated and new made out of old, there are three methods for locating data in already processed documents that should belong there. Text search can be used to find occurrences of indicator words. A 'collect' operation can be used to gather together all the subcategories below any general node for recoding once new subcategories have appeared. Or fine indexing can be delayed, bulk categories used until finer categories are identified, then reindexing easily performed on that subset of data.

The computer will incorporate any number of such new categories, and redo any amount of indexing. So not some but *all* the stuff on the topic or combination of topics can be retrieved, *and* you can also keep asking questions about it . . . so long as your indexing categories are good enough, and your search and research procedures sufficiently thorough. There's the rub.

Two sets of problems emerged in the early experience with NUDIST. Both derive from the computer's ability to do well what researchers could not do before.

First, it can retrieve all material indexed at any node. Retrieving what? The aims of theory construction grounded in data require ability to move between the index system and the data it derives from and delineates. The ability to code and retrieve with computers highlights a problem always present in such techniques but never acute when they could not be performed perfectly. Coding for retrieval involves 'decontextualizing' data, taking it out of original context to 'recontextualize' in the new category (Seidel and Clark, 1984; Tesch, 1990). Qualitative method is about understanding data in their context. Offered a neat printout of all the stuff on one topic, researchers then often find it hard to recall the original context, the whole episode or conversation that made sense in the context of the segment now retained. Many say they find it harder – partly because they can have more documents on a computer system, partly because the neat retrieval process distances them from the messy original data.

In addition, they may well be tempted not to try to return to those documents, since the computer can of course give a total retrieval of everything indexed there, and most programs automatically produce information about the location. NUDIST provides, for any document text comes from, a paragraph of header information about the document itself and also allows subheaders inserted to identify speakers or give detail of context.

What about what wasn't indexed? Or what happened next? NUDIST makes movement back into the document rapid and easy, with hypermedia switching between databases, so contextual information can be browsed. Back in the document you can find out what other indexing was given those lines, and read different lines. Back in the index system you can browse memos about the node, or the context of that text. So retrieval becomes not so much a clerical as a theorizing task.

Secondly, the removal of barriers and presentation of such possibilities offer a sort of methodological anomie. Creating the index structure, given such freedom, can appear as a major challenge. In the prototype project for NUDIST (Richards, 1990), final (?) agreement on index structure took over a year, with further adaptations as it was tested. When the computer can do so much, the fear is that the human effort will provide inadequate conceptual fodder for the computer to munch. In NUDIST version 1.0, several projects hit serious failures of nerve at what was seen as a necessary early stage of proliferating index categories. Construction of categories loomed as a major stage on the research timetable. Indexing became a massive task, sometimes (since it had to be done well) an insuperable barrier to exploring the data. And the distance from what qualitative analysis was meant to be about was evident.

To strive for the perfect index is of course absurd. It also threatens endless projects! To keep reshaping index systems and reindexing already processed texts promises no publications. Re-thinking of this experience led to the provisions for improving and restructuring the index system as the project matures. Increasingly, we discovered, the research timetable is being altered.

*Reshaping the research experience*
Construction of the index system becomes important from the start
of the project and continues to the end, and is itself a theoretical
process. And growth of that indexing system becomes the indicator
of a project's development. Index system work, we have found,
demands clarification of categories. Concept definition 'forces the
theorist to formulate previously intuitive thoughts and wrestle with
the difficult task of expressing – explicitly and at length – the themes
inherent in incidents previously placed in a conceptual category on
the basis of global association' (Martin and Turner, 1986: 150).
Concepts can then be linked and links explored. Collect together all
nodes under a generic concept and they can be newly interrogated.

Experience in NUDIST served to expose the hidden model of a
sequential research process of data gathering and coding. An
identifying feature of qualitative research is that data collection and
analysis are integrated, 'inform or even "drive" each other' (Tesch,
1990: 95). But the code-first, think-next pattern learnt from survey
research leaks in, especially when the computer offers efficient
handling of very many codes. NUDIST version 2.0 tackled this model
directly, making movement between data, thinking about it and
indexing of it easy and quick, and supporting many ways of
incorporating rethinking about categories without imposing clerical
costs.

The result is to centre the research process around the index
system. Making, shaping and exploring it become theorizing tasks.
A startlingly high proportion of time can be spent 'in' the index
system – creating concepts, exploring relations between them and
with the data, making new concepts out of old and exploring those
in data. This is not a research procedure outlined in textbooks, and
it is foreign to either of the approaches to indexing described above.
It enables the construction and testing of theory in constant contact
with data.

All this means rethinking not only the importance of index
construction and indexing, but the way they are seen. Hitherto,
texts have urged efficiency, treating an index as a fixed object,
created, so to speak, before analysis starts. Indexing has to be
thought of instead as a *process*, and one that goes the length of the
project.

One result is that indexing processes are altered. Increasingly,
users have moved towards an indexing technique inverse to that
normal in quantitative analysis. There, researchers are urged to
make quantitative precoding categories as fine as possible – you can
always collapse them. But where the index database and the text
database are separately available, as in NUDIST, the researcher can

– and probably *should*, if there is any uncertainty about emerging categories – index deliberately in a more general category. All that text can be viewed and reindexed later, as grounded theory emerges. The hierarchical indexing structure supports this approach: a category can be split into a whole subtree of subcategories. Meanwhile, memos can be recorded and indexed, so emerging ideas stay with the data. Categories can be added or changed, and recoding done by gathering up all material indexed in the subtree below any category for reindexing. With such abilities, researchers may be advised to start with a very minimal index system. The final, but not the immediate goal, is a set of categories through which can be explored all emerging patterns. The index system will reflect at any time the thinking about the project – and at the start of the project this may be very limited.

By the end, indexing of any text can involve *as many* categories as justified by prior and emerging theory and necessary to explore them. This poses new problems of controlling and accessing systematically all nodes, avoiding using just the few easily remembered. It places new constraints on cooperative projects and the use of multiple coders and new emphases on verifying indexing. These problems required new processes. NUDIST provides efficient ways of accessing, browsing and exploring the entire index system; at any stage it will provide lists of all nodes and their location, or all indexing of any document(s) and all cross-indexing. The approach then encourages gradual development of index systems as complex as the project requires. In qualitative work (as in quantitative), pressure is normally for parsimony of categories in simple structures. Tree-structuring is normally done in a very bonsai fashion. But NUDIST encourages indexing as rich as the data deserve.

There are rewards, too, for a different *approach* to indexing. Basic research training normally teaches avoidance of multiple indexing – attaching many tags to the same segment – since 'decontextualizing' costs money and time. Thus researchers tend to conflate index categories, and try to build into categories the ideas emerging from text, rather than to index with multiple categories in such a way that those emerging ideas may be explored and tested, not merely retrieved. But the computer can support fine-grained indexing on any number of categories. Thus, researchers can reap the advantages of creating theoretically 'innocent' index categories that can be used to locate instances of an emerging pattern, rather than labels asserting that it has occurred here. Discovery of unexpected patterns is not pre-empted, and genuine testing of relationships is supported.

If the act of 'coding' and use of index systems are transformed –

so too are research routines. Analysis can begin with the first data collection and increasingly concentrates on exploring the conceptual index database. The ability to search *theoretically* encourages analysis that builds on and interrogates past searches. The ability to build new nodes from old offers serendipity – feeling through and freely exploring patterns. Asking further questions of an interesting result takes moments, so further questions get asked. These flights of theoretical fancy are grounded in data, since at any stage, text can be put to the conceptual structure being explored, and the routes of exploration retraced.

All this changes the relationship between theory and data in a first attempt to combine aspects of the 'grounded theory' approach with the detailed and rigorous retrieval of all text to test theory. But exploration is not merely an act of retrieval of all the stuff at one node – rather it is a fluid process. The possibility of removing the clerical barrier between researcher and data must now be taken seriously. Fluidity of text indexing and lightness in exploration of growing theory, and the facility to move between conceptual exploration and the words it is about, help free analysis from the tentacles of clerical tasks that have hitherto too often tied it down.

This has many implications. Earlier computer programs tended to drive qualitative analysis much more into the text – either to words and their frequency of occurrence, or to segments indexed for retrieval. For linguistic analysis this may be the required focus. But it can mean a surprisingly strong shift from what was the rhythm both of 'grounded theory' and of traditional ethnography – to get clear of the text (Glaser and Strauss, 1967). Even in pre-computer methods, in Strauss's words, 'People spend too damn much time being compulsive about their data. If you're going to go back to your data it's got to be theory directed' (1987: 7). NUDIST pushes analysis instead to exploration of index systems and their theoretical content – but without losing links with the text.

**Conclusions**

These developments directly feed in to the transformations we addressed in the first two sections of this chapter – new ways of thinking about the dichotomy of qualitative and quantitative and the varieties of methods that bear the qualitative badge.

The centrality of index systems and their manipulation opens new links to quantitative techniques. The combination of indexing on the subject matter of text with indexing of information about the text effectively provides a way of combining qualitative analysis with aspects of variable analysis. Quasi-statistics about the number of occurrences of words or themes are instantly computed, as are, in NUDIST, proportions of text in the file or files indexed at the specified category. The computer allows researchers to interrogate patterns, to keep asking questions and drawing together different levels, contexts, relationships to test their significance and to chase ideas about the ways they pattern data.

The literature glosses over possibilities of rigorously exploring and testing emerging theory; to achieve its emergence is usually enough. Qualitative analysis always aims for, but can rarely systematically achieve, abstraction and testing of theory deriving from the data. The potential of computer programs is that the goals of 'grounded theory' become accessible without the risk of jettisoning evidence for emerging themes, and with new abilities to interrogate them. That evidence can be examined in simultaneous analysis or subsequent reanalysis of data using different techniques. Comparative techniques can be applied to different databases in the same index structure. The mainframe version of NUDIST is designed explicitly for multi-user and multi-site projects, allowing differential access to index and data files by different levels of users. It is compatible with the Macintosh version, so users can take segments of data off the mainframes for detailed analysis on their micro-computers, or bring MACNUDIST files from the field to incorporate in the central databases. In a method which has always stressed comparison (meaning many things by that, too!), these possibilities may provide new transformations.

This chapter has focused on only three aspects of the ways computer techniques are transforming qualitative research. The story of transformation has of course hardly begun, and to note these areas in which research processes are remade is not to predict the outcome. In each area, indeed, we have identified positive results and problems. Computational techniques may drive quali-tative method away from its traditional base and towards the stereotypically quantitative. If this occurs, it will be very divisive. In many countries, qualitative studies are already an embattled minority, and hostility to computer approaches further divides researchers – into sceptics and enthusiasts. The enthusiasts all too often enthuse only about smart clerical tactics. A computer-induced concentration on relieving the burden of storing and sorting can easily produce a new sort of fetishism – with storage systems instead of with the joys of fieldwork. Serious debate can deal with such distortions. Given strong emphasis on theoretical goals and varieties of method, computing may push qualitative research towards far more subtle, varied, powerful and rigorous ways of doing what the method has always attempted to do.

# 4

# Automated Tools for Qualitative Research

## John Davies

In qualitative research, writing is the primary means of storing information and of analysing and interpreting its meaning. Manual methods in analysis have their drawbacks (Brent, 1984) and this has led to experimentation, and limited success, with programs such as: word processors, text databases, data indexing systems, and hypertext systems (Brent, 1984; Shapiro, 1984; Dey, 1988). The ETHNOGRAPH (Seidel and Clark, 1984) is one of the few commercially available programs designed specifically to assist researchers with the content analysis of their textual data. However, most systems to date suffer from poor interface design, lack of attention to system functionality, and inadequate (or non-existent) conceptual models of system operation presented to users.

This chapter describes a project carried out at the University of Edinburgh (Davies, 1988). There were two main aims: to develop an appropriate design methodology (which would overcome the weaknesses perceived in the design of current systems); and to design a set of automated, qualitative data analysis tools which would serve researchers without impeding the important conceptual processes forming the core of qualitative analysis. The notion of 'tools' was very important. The role of the computer technology was to enhance researchers' skills, not to automate them or to obstruct them with added complexity. There was a time limit of approximately six months.

Given the purpose of the proposed system, an innovative design approach was proposed: a collaborative process involving a group of researchers experienced in ethnography and a computer systems designer. Researchers were involved throughout, and continual communication to, and feedback from, them guided the design development.

The rest of this chapter is divided into four main sections: methods used in the project, a brief overview of the project stages, the final conceptual model and design, and a discussion of some of the issues raised by the project.

## Methods used in the project

Several hybrid methods were employed in developing the design. This section describes the main methods and discusses their use in the project.

*Iterative, collaborative design*

Many authors acknowledge an inability to predict with accuracy what will work well in practice, particularly when dealing with highly interactive systems (for example, Kelly, 1984; Shakel, 1986). An important part of the design approach therefore, was successive iteration towards a better design. This cyclical approach was used to develop models of analysis and prototype systems based on those models.

It was important that the design proceeded in incremental steps, with regular verification and evaluation by all those concerned to allow for any problems caused by differences in background, experience and area of expertise between the designer and researchers. This process would give the researchers time to better understand the alternatives available for the system, and the designer time to better understand the process of analysis.

*Design group meetings and data collection*

There were many meetings between researchers and the system designer during the course of the project. Apart from the data-gathering aspects of each meeting (discussed below), it was anticipated that meetings would be useful in several ways: to develop a rapport and feeling of cooperation, to demonstrate to researchers that they had some control over system design, and to help establish a common view of the project and common goals. A review of recent events (including new developments) was held at the beginning of each meeting; similarly, at the end, a short discussion was held concerning the progress of the meeting and confirming any future plans.

The main part of meetings varied as the project progressed. During the early phases of the project this was invariably an interview. As models were being developed, the main part consisted of discussions with researchers – to introduce a particular style of modelling and encourage researchers to criticize and correct initial modelling attempts. (Shorter interviews and discussions continued throughout the project.) When prototype systems were being developed, the main part of the meetings was taken up by tests of the systems by researchers, followed by short debriefing interviews.

At the start of the project, data collection covered broad areas with relatively little depth. As the project progressed, the data collection gradually became more in-depth and focused on relatively narrow issues. Several data-collection techniques were used during the project. One of the most important and widely used was the interview. The designer prepared the areas to be covered beforehand, noting questions to be asked. However, the wording and question order were not kept constant, and if a promising area was uncovered during the interview it was briefly examined. A debriefing interview followed each prototype test. The interview included questions raised by the test as well as those prepared beforehand. All interview data were collected in note form with an audio tape recorder as backup.

Direct observation was used to try and avoid the problem of distortion which can occur when recalling and commenting upon past events. Suchman (1983) discusses similar problems, arguing that the actual progression of events is only accessible through direct observation coupled with a precise recording procedure. Several factors were taken into account before the decision to use observation was made. The researchers were all highly skilled and used well-practised techniques. It was judged that these would not be significantly affected if time was allowed for the researcher to get used to the observer's presence. Also, a majority of the observations were to be carried out in surroundings familiar to the researcher. A point made by several researchers was that they had some experience of demonstrating and showing their analyses to others (for example, during supervisor–student sessions and meetings with other researchers), so being observed was often not a completely new experience.

Written material was collected by the designer throughout the project. Outlines of completed ethnographic projects were collected – overviews of the processes, methods and stages – together with card files, completed reports and examples of partial analysis from current projects. Sessions were conducted with researchers in which they carried out a preliminary analysis of data – manually, before any system prototypes were developed, and later using a prototype. The written material before the session was recorded for later comparison with the results of the session.

The final data-collection technique was that of thinking aloud (Ericsson and Simon, 1985). This was used periodically as a supplementary method to direct observation. Verbalizing was seen as a check on the retrospective reports, and as an effort to avoid the problem of subjects 'filling out' incomplete memories by interpreting or inferring. A typical session (recorded on audio tape) involved an observed researcher analysing data. The researcher had been asked to try to give a running commentary on what he/she was doing, but not to give detailed explanations or worry how the commentary sounded. Thinking aloud was also used during some of the prototype tests. As researchers were novices with the system, there was a danger that verbalizing would significantly affect their performance. So training sessions were held with a new system before it was tested.

Thinking aloud is a technique borrowed from cognitive psychology, and has been used in knowledge engineering and human–computer interaction. For example, Greenwell recommends it as a supplement to other techniques, 'to elicit detailed information concerning the task' (1988: 52). Mack et al. used it to investigate the learning of word processors, claiming that 'participants soon become accustomed to the thinking aloud task and to the routine of verbalising' (1983: 255). However, there is some controversy over the use of this technique. Diaper, for example, argues that a verbal report can contain distortions and omissions, and at best it is 'a simplified, general description of how the task should be performed' (1987: 288). None the less, I have found the collection of verbal reports to be worth while, if used with caution and as one of several techniques.

*Data analysis*
Data analysis was the process by which transcripts, notes, etc. were condensed and processed into intermediate representations. The process was iterative and qualitative, and there were several types of intermediate representations (each giving a different perspective on analysis), for example, graphical models, collections of themes and written descriptions.

The basic analysis procedure used by the designer is similar to the 'unitization' and 'categorization' described by Lincoln and Guba (1984). It consisted of first reading through the data, several times, and trying to identify meaningful sections of text. Initially these sections were taken directly from the data – the answers to questions, for example – and were written onto separate cards. These were then broken up into categories (which 'emerged' during analysis) and connections were sought between various categories. As more connections became apparent, a process of refining and sorting categories was started. This eventually led to an organization of the categories and the construction of one or more representations.

*Task analysis*
Task analysis has been used in psychology for a number of years. The technique divides tasks into pre-specified parts and relation-

ships, derived from theory. This task description provided another perspective on researchers' analysis and formed part of the cognitive model around which a first prototype was designed. The task description provided an initial functional outline (part of an overall system definition) of data used, methods utilized, etc., paralleling those in current use. By modelling the computer task environment on the current environment, researchers would be able to pursue the same goals, and the system would seem familiar and easier to use.

The GOMS model (Card et al., 1983) was used as a theoretical framework on which to base the task description. GOMS is a pure performance model, particularly suited to modelling experts. It divides tasks into Goals, Operators, Methods and Selection rules. The goals, methods, etc. were obtained from the data, where they were defined by researchers or inferred by the designer (the latter were checked with researchers before the model was constructed).

*Conceptual models*

A conceptual model is a representation of the basic principles and components around which a particular computer system is designed. The model takes account of the tasks, requirements and abilities of potential users, together with human information-processing considerations. The main purpose of the model is to enable the behaviour of the system to be anticipated and understood. If a system is to be seen as coherent and intelligible its construction must be based on an underlying conceptual model (Norman, 1987).

In system design, there are two main conceptual models: the designer's model, and the user's model (constructed from the model of system behaviour presented to him/her, the system image, previous use of computers, expectations, etc.). Significant problems can arise if the models are inconsistent. An attempt was made to minimize these problems by involving researchers in the design of the conceptual model, by developing the model iteratively, and by constructing a prototype system (incorporating the model) at each iteration. The objective was to develop a 'group conceptual model', shared by the designer and the researchers, as far as possible.

*Interface considerations*

The approach to interface design was guided by researchers' aims. An important aim was system transparency (attention can be focused on the task, not on operating the system). Researchers wanted the system's behaviour to be straightforward, easy to learn and to anticipate. They wanted to be able to perform tasks in a clear, intuitive and individual way, remaining in control of the system at all times.

One way of achieving some of these aims was to present the conceptual model in a consistent, clear and meaningful way. In addition, an action paradigm – a direct manipulation type approach (Schneiderman, 1983) – was used rather than the more traditional communication paradigm. Briefly, users carry out tasks by operating on visible system objects rather than having to learn and use complicated command language syntax. The operations are incremental, reversible, physical actions performed with a mouse or similar device. There is a continuous visual representation of the current system state giving the user constant feedback.

Psychological theory, particularly the metaphor of human information processing (Baecker and Buxton, 1987), was used to guide and constrain aspects of the interface design. The metaphor leads to useful concepts such as cognitive load – the cognitive resources required to perform a particular task. Keeping the load low (for example by ensuring system mechanisms are consistent) has a positive effect on factors such as learning time, user fatigue and ease of use.

*The prototype environment*
A prototype was an easily changed, working mock-up of a significant part of the proposed system. It was important for showing parts of the system to researchers, letting them see and try out several possibilities (interface styles, etc.), and for testing aspects of system performance. The prototypes also acted as focal points, adding an important dimension to the communication between researchers and designer. Working with a prototype is perhaps one of the most powerful ways of encouraging potential users to develop their ideas.

The Macintosh computer (*Inside Macintosh*, 1985) was chosen as the machine on which to implement the design prototypes. The philosophy behind the Macintosh parallels many of the guidelines given above: it provides a consistent graphical interface with metaphoric system representation. A high-level application development tool was also necessary to build prototypes quickly, as time was very limited. HyperCard (*HyperCard User's Guide*, 1987) was chosen because it provided the most powerful and adaptable development tool available; it is both a hypertext system and a programming language.

**Overview of project stages**

This section shows how the methods above were combined, and gives an indication of the developmental stages.

*Preliminary data collection and analysis*
This phase consisted of background reading for the designer, discussions between the designer and researchers, and interviews conducted by the designer. An analysis of transcripts from interviews and discussions led to an identification of themes from the analysis process and a detailed written description of each.

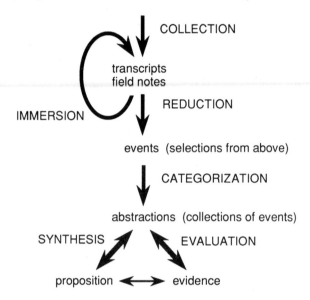

Figure 4.1   *One of the early graphical models of analysis*

A graphical model of analysis was also developed (Figure 4.1). It shows a sequence of activities (large arrows) and the results of each activity; the proposition–evidence link represents the mutual dependency of the two concepts. The sequential nature of the model represents the way in which the focus of analysis moves gradually from the top of the model to the bottom. It would be usual for more than one of the activities shown to be in progress at once.

*Data collection and task analysis*
Observational notes were made of researchers performing analysis on their own data, and researchers were asked to provide a running commentary. A copy of the data before the session was made to compare with the results of the session. Finally, a short interview was held to clarify and expand upon the observations.
    The data were analysed in the light of all the other data collected to date but more emphasis was placed on task-oriented factors. A

written form of the results was produced and they were also structured into a task model. A preliminary set of system requirements was also developed.

*Prototype systems*

A conceptual model was first developed to include: direct manipulation concepts, information from the various data and task analyses, and the set of system requirements. The design was then constructed to incorporate the conceptual model and the interface considerations described earlier. At this stage no attempt was made to implement a 'complete' system; the prototype represented a scene from a full working system. It dealt with the structuring of raw data, the facilities necessary for aiding the analysis of a single piece of data, and general navigation issues concerned with moving through the various system structures.

Each researcher completed a training exercise, then 'played' with the system until he/she was accustomed to it. The researcher was then asked to begin to analyse a single piece of data. Each test was observed and followed by a debriefing. Some tests involved thinking aloud.

The conceptual model was extended in the light of the test results, and a new design was constructed. From this a second prototype was implemented which simulated many more of the facilities offered by a full working system. It incorporated more data, and researchers were able to organize it within the system and to define the system structures as analysis progressed.

The second set of tests followed a similar format to that of the first set. Researchers were asked to use the system to organize pieces of data, and to assess other features by performing a short, preliminary analysis of some of the data (researchers were already familiar with the transcripts that made up the data). The results were used to refine the conceptual model, and from this a final design was produced. This is described in the next section.

**Final conceptual model and design**

The following description is a user-oriented view of the system, and combines parts of the conceptual model with examples (taken from the second prototype) of how those parts could be implemented and used.

All commands to the system are carried out by manipulating visual system objects, for example activating icons or labels, pushing 'buttons' on the screen, and selecting parts of text by 'dragging' the mouse. The metaphor of creating structures and moving through them is an important part of the system.

### Data input
A method of data input is proposed similar to that offered by the ETHNOGRAPH: researchers use their own word processors to create files which are then used by the system. Most researchers already have word processors and would prefer not to learn to use a new one. However, unlike the ETHNOGRAPH, this system does not require files to conform to any particular format.

### Organizing the data
The way in which data are organized dictates, to some extent, the way in which a researcher goes about his/her analysis. Researchers had used manual filing systems or the file-directory systems of various computers. All the systems were hierarchical, with the bottom of the hierarchy consisting of 'natural' pieces of data (for example, an interview transcript was often regarded as a single piece).

This system is used to organize the pieces of data into a hierarchical tree-like structure. The data pieces are leaves of the tree, and the layers in the tree represent the broader distinctions researchers made between collections of data pieces (for example, interviews with first-years and interviews with final-years). Each node of the tree contains information on the nodes below it.

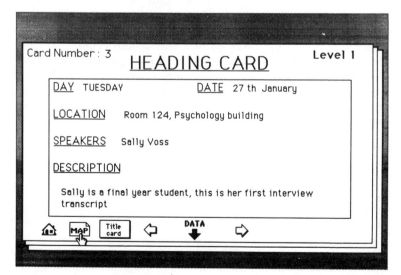

Figure 4.2   *A possible format for a heading card*

First, a 'heading card' is filled out for every piece of data. The heading card or 'face sheet' contains background details about its data (a standard, modifiable format for the heading card is provided). Figure 4.2 shows one example of a heading card. (The card also shows some of the icons used to access other screens.)

The system provides a visual representation of a researcher's data organization, called 'the map'. Figure 4.3 is a simple example constructed by one of the researchers (the heading card in Figure 4.2 is represented by the 'Sally Voss' node on the map). The map is set up at the beginning of analysis in a dialogue between the system and the researcher. It can be edited or restructured at any time using a similar dialogue. The map defines, and gives an overview of, a navigable structure. The user can move through the layers of the tree, and across the nodes at a given layer. The map screen provides a navigation aid, giving 'you are here' information, and can be used as a short-cut between any two locations in the system.

As more data are accumulated, the map will get unwieldy. The solution, similar to that used by MacCadd (Jones, 1986), requires the introduction of a new type of node – a submap node. When a map gets too big, a subtree is replaced by a single submap node. To view that part of the map, the user 'zooms in' on the appropriate node.

*Main analysis*
The basic methods used by researchers during analysis (use of

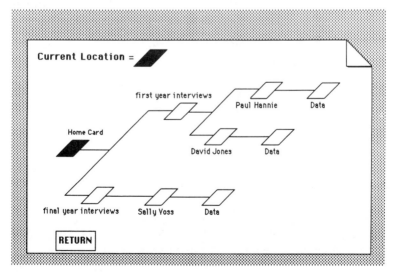

Figure 4.3 *An example of a map drawn by a researcher*

categories, etc.) were similar to those described elsewhere (for example, see Lincoln and Guba, 1984; and the 'data analysis' subsection of this chapter). Beyond these, however, two approaches were distinguished: 'vertical' and 'horizontal' analysis. Vertical analysis focused on one piece of data at a time, analysing to an intuitively specified depth. All the data had been read several times, so, though the focus was on one piece of data, the rest of the data were kept in mind. Horizontal analysis involved analysing across pieces of data, with more emphasis on the whole. Typically, analysis was carried out on a collection of data (for example, the first set of interviews for site one). When each piece of data had been analysed vertically to a similar depth, they were compared with each other. Horizontal analysis became more important as analysis progressed. Vertical and horizontal analysis were frequently combined in a highly individual and personal way by each researcher.

The system's underlying model of vertical analysis is represented by the 'lattice' (Figure 4.4). The number of levels is not fixed, but the model always follows this pattern. There are two basic loosely defined actions that can be performed on a piece of text: a 'summary' or an 'abstraction'. A summary is defined to be a quote from the text or a comment (an elaboration, explanation, note, etc.) on a particular piece of the text. An abstraction is defined to be a word or short phrase that attempts to capture something of the meaning of a piece of the text. Each action can be performed on any piece of text including an existing summary or abstraction.

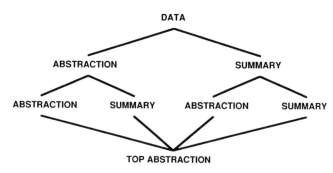

Figure 4.4    *The lattice model for vertical analysis*

When a summary action is performed, the summary is written on the next level of the lattice and an explicit link is formed between that summary and the piece of text it refers to. (A similar process occurs when an abstraction action is performed.) When analysis has progressed to a suitable depth, decided by the researcher, the spread of the lattice is reversed to a set of 'top abstractions'. There are no links between the levels of the lattice before analysis starts; they are created by the researcher as the data are analysed. The links can be traversed, so vertical analysis can be seen (from the system point of view) as constructing one or more paths between the data and the top abstraction level.

Horizontal analysis is catered for in two main ways. First, a view of a particular level of a given lattice can be compared with a chosen level of another lattice at any time. Secondly, the idea of bringing ideas together into a top abstraction level is taken one step further by bringing the top abstraction levels together into a 'group abstraction' (Figure 4.5).

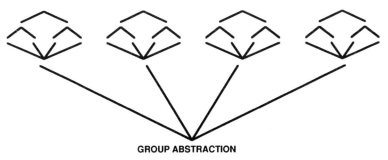

**GROUP ABSTRACTION**

Figure 4.5 *The vertical analysis model (Figure 4.4) extended to include horizontal analysis. The top abstractions for each piece of data are brought together into a group abstraction*

As with the map, the system provides a visual representation of the lattice. When the map is created, a default-sized lattice (the size of Figure 4.4) is supplied for each piece of data; the lattice depths are alterable. The lattices are shown as outlines at first, giving pictorial information of shape and depth. As analysis proceeds, the outlines are filled in automatically so that the progress of analysis can be charted. The filled-in parts of a lattice can be used for navigation in the same way as the rest of the map.

The main analysis starts from a data screen (for example, Figure 4.6). The data appear in a scrolling area covering most of the screen. The rectangles at the top of the screen are 'push buttons' activated with the mouse. When performing a summary, researchers wanted the system to take care of copying quotes automatically. So, instead of having a summary button, a summary action was divided into one of two possible actions: marking an 'event' (quote), or making a 'comment'. The basic underlying model is not changed, however; both actions are still summary actions and both store text in the same summary space at the next level of the lattice.

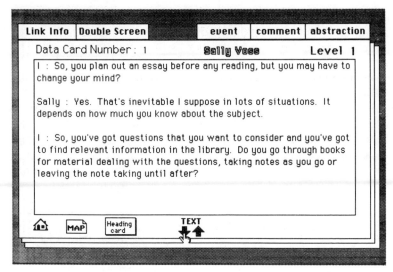

Figure 4.6 *A typical data screen*

To make a comment, the relevant piece of text is first selected, then the comment button is activated. A comment box appears at the bottom of the screen, and the comment is written inside (Figure 4.7). When the comment is complete, the 'end comment' button is activated and the system stores it in the summary space of the next

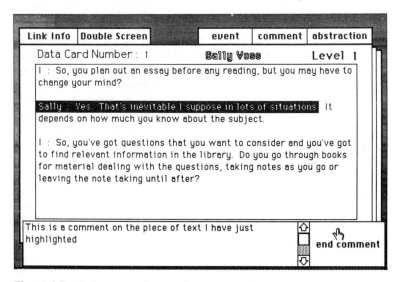

Figure 4.7 *A comment about to be completed (by activating the end comment button with the hand-shaped cursor)*

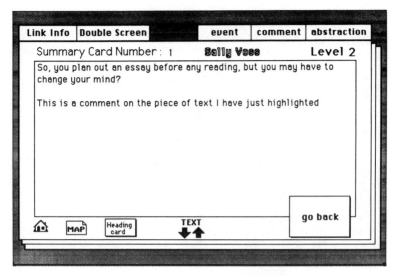

Figure 4.8 *A summary screen after a researcher has made two summaries (an event followed by a comment, from Figure 4.6)*

level of the lattice, and forms a link between that comment and the piece of text that was selected initially (Figure 4.8 shows the summary screen with an event followed by a comment, both from Figure 4.6). An event action is performed by merely selecting the text and activating the event button. An abstraction is performed in the same way as a comment, but using the abstraction button and the abstraction space of the next lattice level. Links are formed between the event and the original text, and between the abstraction and original text, as for a comment. The lattices are traversed using these bi-directional links.

Often researchers will need to compare two levels of a lattice. This can be done using the 'double screen' (Figure 4.9), which is called by activating the double screen button. Summaries or abstractions can be made from the left screen to the right, within the confines of the basic lattice structure, though any two levels can be compared and edited if necessary. The latter feature is useful when analysis-so-far needs to be compared across pieces of data (see horizontal analysis, above), as a screen from a given level of a particular lattice can be compared with any other lattice screen. The double screen is also useful when bringing ideas together into a top abstraction or group abstraction level.

As analysis develops, the relationships between abstractions increase in importance (they are often grouped, for example). A spatial metaphor is used to represent these relationships. For

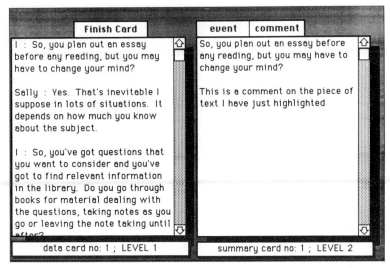

Figure 4.9   *The double screen showing two consecutive lattice levels: Figure 4.6 on the left, and Figure 4.8 on the right*

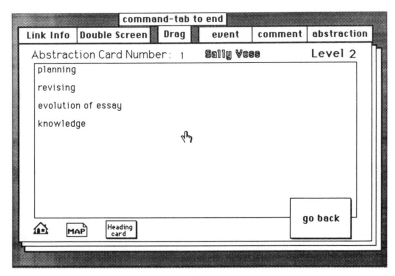

Figure 4.10   *An abstraction screen showing four abstractions about to be grouped (with the hand-shaped cursor)*

example, in Figure 4.10, if the three abstractions 'planning', 'revising' and 'evolution of essay' are more closely related to each other than to 'knowledge', they can be 'dragged' to positions on the screen to reflect this (Figure 4.11). This does not affect links to other lattice levels.

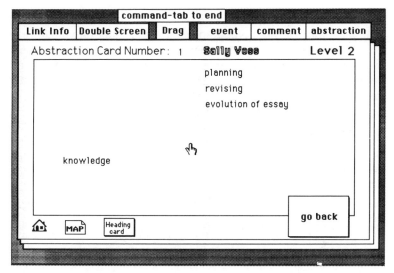

Figure 4.11 *The four abstractions after grouping (three of the abstractions are related to each other)*

It is often important to be able to pick out pieces of text from the original data referenced directly or indirectly (through more than one lattice level) by one or more abstractions. A search-and-extract facility is provided which will search for text referenced by: one or more particular abstractions, abstractions and NOT other(s), and heading card attributes in combination with abstractions. The search can be constrained to one or more pieces of data.

The system allows analysis to be 'undone' or 'unwound'. An 'experimental' analysis can be performed, where an idea or train of thought is followed to see if it leads anywhere. If it doesn't, the experimental summaries and/or abstractions can be undone. (See the final section for a discussion.)

*Output*
The system is able to send text from any screen (including text that could be brought onto the screen by scrolling) to a printer or a file. An important feature is the ability to print out the double screen, retaining the side-by-side relationship. The printout is important during analysis, to take away and study, and to discuss with other researchers (especially during team projects). Output to a file is important when constructing a document.

**Discussion**

This section briefly discusses some of the issues raised during the project.

*The design group*
The backbone of the methodology was the collaborative nature of the design. Initially, the designer's understanding of researchers' work was tenuous, while researchers' knowledge of computers and their potential was equally tenuous. This gap was successfully narrowed, if not bridged, by encouraging communication at all levels.

There was something of an initial 'culture clash'. All the researchers had suffered unpleasant experiences with poorly written programs and/or inconsiderate 'computer people, who kept trying to palm you off with statistics packages or word processors'. Some researchers doubted that the system designer – who was imagined to have a 'mechanistic approach to everything' – would ever be able to understand the 'very personal processes' of analysis. There was also a fear that the designer would try to automate analysis. The 'clash' was not one sided. The designer was apprehensive about working with a group of researchers, some of whom he imagined might be hostile to the idea of using computers in analysis.

However, the initial wariness subsided as the group got to know one another; indeed, something akin to 'team spirit' had developed by the end of the project. One helpful factor was that several researchers felt, given the advances in personal computers, that there must be a way of 'harnessing the beast' to aid analysis. Also, interest was aroused when it was discovered that a significant amount of the designer's data analysis was qualitative in nature. An important factor was the view, shared by all, that technology should be designed to integrate with human qualities such as experience and skill. One researcher commented:

> it [the second prototype] overcomes one of the irritations, which is that everybody is learning to respond to the machine. . . . You see it rather as a tool and that gives quite a different feel to it, you know, it feels much more like something that was designed for your benefit rather than something that was designed and, if you use it, you've got to adapt to it. So it seems you've done a very good job at getting at my way of working.

The designer's human-centred approach was valued by researchers. Some were surprised when they saw that their ideas and comments were incorporated into models, prototypes, etc., and that these were then held up for criticism. One researcher said:

> I think it's been your way of approaching it which has captured the imagination – certainly my imagination, and I know my colleagues' . . . your approach has epitomized the treating of us as people, of listening.

Another researcher added:

The way you've interviewed, the way you've got information, the way you've actually managed the summaries of what's been said, and the understanding of the actual comments [made by me] has been very good.

*Implications for analysis*

Most researchers felt that analysis has been constrained by mechanical tasks 'which only serve to dull creative insight', and the introduction of a well-designed system should enhance the process. One researcher felt that she might need to get her 'hands dirty' by manually cutting and pasting, and she suspected that the machine's presence would always seem intrusive.

Researchers were enthusiastic about the hierarchical organization provided by the system. Several researchers were interested in taking the idea beyond simply being able to restructure the data organization. They wanted to explore multiple organizations of the same data by having more than one map. The lattice model provoked a similar response. One researcher was very interested in taking multiple organization and combining it with more than one lattice for each piece of data, to investigate 'multiple views of actions'.

Another idea discussed was that of 'undoing' analysis. The system model represents analysis as forming paths (each path may consist of many text–summary or text–abstraction links) through the lattices. Conversely, undoing analysis means retracing the steps made with the system back along each path, one-by-one in reverse order. As far as the system is concerned, as soon as a step is undone, it never existed. As far as the person using the system is concerned, however, knowledge of that step and why it was undone will influence the rest of the analysis to some degree. Researchers were interested in performing 'experimental' analysis, exploring possible 'routes' ahead and being able to undo those which didn't work out. A distinction was drawn between how researchers currently re-form parts of their analysis and how a program might be useful in aiding and extending this process. They felt that while undoing alone was not a comprehensive description of how they re-formed analysis, it would be a useful aid to the process, particularly when combined with the other facilities of the system (such as the ability to reorganize data).

*Future development*

The project investigated several concepts involved in analysis and developed a basic design which met many of the needs of a group of researchers. Anyone contemplating future development of the system should bear two issues in mind. First, tests of the design so far have not included a complete analysis. An important next step would be to build a robust system that could be given to researchers, enabling them to perform complete analyses and allowing a longitudinal study of the system's usefulness to be undertaken. Secondly, it would be essential to test future developments with researchers who were not involved with the design to date. This would ensure a view uncoloured by membership of the initial design group.

Several researchers suggested that it might be useful to develop the model of analysis further, without reference to a computer system. Although the system model is a representation of the 'machine's view' of analysis – how the system operates – and is not representative of many of the levels at which analysis takes place, the model and its various components were found to be powerful and compelling. Researchers saw in the model 'something very conceptually important'.

# PART TWO

# IMPLICATIONS FOR RESEARCH PRACTICE

The literature on computers and qualitative analysis has been somewhat preoccupied with justifications for the use of computers and speculations on what computerization may mean for the practice of the craft. There has been little comment on the programs' potential for systematizing qualitative analysis. Periodically the wider field of qualitative research, particularly ethnography, has debated the possibility of a generic theory of qualitative analysis. This would establish a comprehensive epistemological warrant for qualitative methods, define the range of analytic work feasible using such methods, and dictate norms for quality control of qualitative data. The present practice is, of course, highly diffuse, and the matters mentioned above are usually resolved according to the canons of the individual researcher's analytic orientation.

Some feel that the assumptions built in to available programs represent a hidden form of closure around a particular view of qualitative analysis. Certainly, programs are necessarily designed on the basis of assumptions about the procedures and objects of qualitative analysis, although these are more flexible than may be guessed by non-users. A key assumption is about the centrality of coding and about the ways in which this is practised. It may be that analysts of an intuitive persuasion will find such assumptions questionable. The ideas held by designers about coding do implicitly push towards more systematic and formal practical procedures. It is assumed that all data should be available to code. It is also assumed that an initial analytic hypothesis (we use the term guardedly) should be tested for confirmation/disconfirmation against all similarly coded data. The computer helps make this process very thorough.

The question is whether in doing so the programs implicitly incorporate our reasoning into a neo-positivist model carrying unconducive riders about objectivity, truth, reflexivity, methodological individualism and so on. At the very least it means we cannot get away with sloppy practices (like opportunistic citation of extracts supporting a preferred thesis and the burying of any data contrary to it). In that the ad hoc approach to analysis is arguably more widespread than the field acknowledges, we would not regard this alone as a credible criticism of computer-based work. The only victims would be those who believe that qualitative method skills

begin and end with the injunction to 'tell it like it is'. Nor is
program-based analysis free of the problem of opportunism. One of
Seidel's preoccupations is the danger of researchers being attracted
to superficial analyses whose grounding in the data is readily
apparent and hence methodologically unproblematic. In that sense
the programs offer less of a departure from the pitfalls of
conventional analysis than may be supposed.

Another response to the idea that the computer may 'take over'
analysis with a set of implicit and partial assumptions is that these
programs need to be introduced in the context of a coherent
methods training addressing the link between aims, methods and
analysis; to give a course merely on packages is detrimental to
understanding such links. That is the essence of Allatt and Benson's
approach. This is especially important in light of the problem of
making 'bad research' look good – the so-called 'they've used a
package, it must be OK' problem. Significantly, Seidel's view that
'it's simply scissors and glue in another format' is widely current
among actual users, who may feel that grander claims would be
pandering to those who refuse to come to terms with non-numeric
evidence. Allatt and Benson present a reflection on the problems
involved in using computers, and especially qualitative analysis
programs, in the teaching of research methods. They carefully
delineate the cultural context within which novices approach
computer-assisted learning, and sketch in outline the basis of an
approach they have taken to computer-based instruction. Finally,
they address some of the issues raised by the use of programs like
the ETHNOGRAPH for undergraduate teaching.

Qualitative researchers have traditionally been at the forefront of
ethical concern in the social sciences. To date, however, the
intrusion of computers into qualitative research has occasioned little
ethical reflection. Akeroyd, in her chapter, suggests that com-
placency is misplaced. The wider social context for this assertion is
the increasing number of countries which regulate in some way the
storage and handling of personal information by computer. Akeroyd
describes some of the particular problems faced by qualitative
researchers as a result of these developments. To an extent, data
protection issues may be felt to be less salient by researchers in the
United States because, relative to some other countries, their data
protection regime is relatively underdeveloped. It may be that the
running here needs to be made by European researchers (it may be
no coincidence that one of the few programs to offer an encryption
facility for qualitative data, Textbase Alpha, is Danish in origin).

# 5

# Computing and Qualitative Analysis: Issues in Research Methods Teaching

*Pat Allatt and Lynn D. Benson*

The ideas in this chapter arose from three sets of experiences: engagement in the manual extraction and sorting of qualitative data over several pieces of research, teaching research methods to undergraduates, and, for one of the authors, the frustrating and disorienting experiences suffered as a recipient of numerous introductions to computing. The chapter suggests a way of teaching computer-assisted methods in the analysis of qualitative data as part of the undergraduate research methods curriculum.

This programme of study follows the integrative principles advocated by Wakeford (1968) over 20 years ago. In our case we integrate theory, method and computing skills. The programme has not yet been tested and is bound to be modified in practice. We offer it, however, as a contribution to the debate on methods teaching.

The programme starts by providing the knowledge and skills we feel are essential to the ease with which computing skills themselves are learned. This is followed by small-scale project work through which students are taught to use the ETHNOGRAPH, a program for the computer-assisted analysis of text-based data. The aim is not only to demonstrate the value of such tools as aids to the organization of qualitative data but also to highlight the inherent relationship between concept and practice.[1]

The theoretical underpinnings of the proposal are limited. For example, we do not draw in any formal sense upon learning theory but rather bring to the fore insights gleaned from our own experience and the reported observations of others. We address, however, issues which have been raised over the past 10 years in critiques of research methods teaching and the methods curriculum in sociology (Payne et al., 1989).

**Curriculum, pedagogy and culture**

The issues fall into three broad categories: the curriculum, pedagogy and culture.[2] A recent report (Payne et al., 1989) on the state of research methods in the undergraduate sociology curricula in the public sector of higher education in Britain refers to two aspects of the problem of curricula integration. First, although research methods courses should be the meeting ground of knowledge, skills and practice, they continue to be the same ghettos of the curriculum they were 10 and 20 years ago (Selvin, 1965; Wakeford, 1968). Wakeford's (1968) programme in methods and measurement and Wiseman and Aron's (1972) book of field projects are still strangers, it seems, to many methods courses. Payne and his colleagues (1989) argue that this marginalization of methods actually divorces the practice of sociology from its knowledge base. Moreover, within the methods courses themselves qualitative methods are rendered even more marginal because of the limited time devoted to them, the limited range of qualitative methods presented, and the emphasis given to the problems of conducting this kind of research.

The pedagogical aspects with which we are concerned centre upon a second aspect of integration, the place of computing in methods teaching. This raises the twin problems of how computing skills are taught and how they are structured into the methods course. Computing should not merely be tagged on to a course, nor should it be taught to sociology students by specialists with no knowledge of the social sciences. The latter carries the same pedagogical dangers as arose when statisticians from other departments taught statistics on undergraduate sociology courses, now, apparently, a situation which occurs less frequently (Payne et al., 1989). More importantly, perhaps, the methods and tools of investigation should not be seen as existing in isolation from either the sociological knowledge to which they relate or their role in the shaping of new knowledge.[3]

*New worlds and old worlds*
The learning and teaching of computing skills cannot be divorced from their cultural contexts.[4] One context is that of language and strangeness, the other is that of gender, technology and craft.

To enter the world of computing is to enter a new and alien domain which, like all cultures, contains its own contradictions. There is the new means of communication with its own temporal patterns, the internal contradiction of speed and immediacy punctuated by frustrating halts, and the contrast of transient imagery with the solidity of pen on paper. The anxiety provoked by these contradictions is augmented by the relationship between knowledgeable users and the machine. There is, for example, the sharp contrast between the inanimate logic of the machine and the anthropomorphism whereby the machine is assigned not only a personality but one that can be unpredictable. 'I wonder why it didn't like that?' is a standard remark of the cognoscenti when, for no apparent reason, the machine fails to respond to a correctly typed instruction. Although a supervisor's few speedily and silently tapped-in keystrokes that stimulate the machine into a response may be too sophisticated for explanation at this stage, none the less, the trial and error of the approach, and the speed and the silence of the event, create a sense of helplessness and mystification. We perhaps recognize this dimension of the phenomenon in our everyday language: the term 'computer wizard' connotes not only excellence and skill but also magic. The situation conjures up visions of time wasted at a gagged keyboard, unable to convey a message to the machine should no help be available.

To enter this culture is an emotional experience. (Some, indeed, have been known to fall in love with their computer to the extent of engendering marital breakdown.) It is a world which holds out the promise of enhanced work and saved time but one which also poses threats, arousing fear, anxiety and a perverse resistance to change. Identity and status are threatened from several sources: instructors' well-meaning assurances of how simple it all is, a whole host of idiosyncratic procedures that are not and perhaps never can be formalized,[5] and the fact that learning takes place in a public arena where difficulties are visible to peers who appear to be mastering the skills with ease. This emotional element, like pain, is forgotten once the individual becomes acclimatized or the skill mastered. While it lasts, however, it ensures that some novices embark upon the most elementary of computing tasks in a high state of tension.

The second cultural context, overlapping with the first, is that of the old world. Its constraints and definitions surface in the issue of gender, creativity, technology and craft. They affect both men and women.

Paradoxically, whilst the keyboard skills of the new technology are those of traditional typing, in the computing world many men and women are two-finger typists. There is some evidence (M. Wilson, University of Durham, personal communication on teaching computing, 1984), however, that those able to type cope more easily with the preliminary stages of computing, presumably because they are faced with the task of learning one new skill rather than two. Yet some of the most ardent advocates of computing not only overlook but also deny the need for a skill which would both increase speed and lessen frustration.[6]

Like many skills, however, typing is not culturally neutral. A skill that during this century has become dominated by women, typing is now stigmatized as low-status work not appropriate for men. For example, Lyman (1984) noted that when male academics in the humanities had the opportunity to learn word processing, the gendered nature of the skill raised the fear that their work was being feminized. Paradoxically, although computing is seen as a male world, in these cases the advent of the microcomputer poses threats to masculine identity.[7]

Fear about status is not confined to men; there are parallel fears amongst women. Typing is perceived as a threat to equality. Thus some women avoid typing courses, or are advised against them by teachers, careers officers or relatives, fearing that acquisition of the skill might confine them to stereotypical women's work. Moreover, even if escaping such employment, a woman who can type is in danger of being deemed to need less secretarial support than her male counterpart.

For women, the computing world can be foreign if not hostile in other ways. Studies show that 'girls become hostile to machinery from early childhood and from then on regard technology as a male preserve' (Paczuska, 1986). Lyman (1984) also suggests that the language of computing is an aggressively masculine, technical 'language of control . . . filled with military/game slang and jargon (the machine "crashes," you use a "control," a "break," and "escape" keys, etc.)' (Lyman, 1984: 81). Such language may reinforce gender-shaped attitudes towards computing by providing a familiar ambience for men but contradictions for women. Wizards, moreover, are male; their female counterparts are witches.

Others fear that the craft and creativity embedded in the nature of handwriting will be lost (Lyman, 1984). More than this, however, there is the matter of the creative relationship between the mind and the medium – the emergence of thoughts we never knew we had until we embark upon the physical act of writing. Because writing is not a purely mechanical process, the introduction of the computer raises the question of whether the same kind of creativity will flow from mind through keys to screen as it does through the manipulation of pencil on paper. And when we turn to qualitative data analysis that employs more sophisticated packages (Tesch, 1989; 1990) than the simple aid to data organization provided by the ETHNOGRAPH, we must ask whether there will be a loss of creativity here. Will we lose those insights which arise from physically moving the data around, or those unexpected connections made when the eye can range across charts containing more data than can be simultaneously displayed on the screen?

## Social science and the computer

Notwithstanding these reservations, social science courses in the 1990s cannot ignore the computer. This is clear in the job requirements not only of those who will become professional sociologists but also for the many whose work will entail monitoring, evaluation and assessment of client/consumer responses (Payne et al., 1989). The need for computing skills is also clear in the growing pressure to incorporate 'relevance' and transferable skills into higher education curricula. To date, most computing in research methods teaching has been tied to quantitative techniques. (The issue of undergraduate numeracy is not entered into here.) As Payne points out:

> In the statistical field, user-friendly packages have now taken much of the drudgery out of data analysis. There has been no comparable technological revolution in qualitative method. Tape recorders and video cameras merely provide yet more unorganized material for analysis. In terms of achieving comparability with the perceived professional standards, undergraduate exercises in quantitative analysis are likely to be far superior to those in qualitative analysis. (Payne et al., 1989: 268)

Although it is true that the computer offers more to quantitative work, and packages such as SPSS and Minitab are now introduced on undergraduate courses, interest in the application of the computer to qualitative work has grown steadily over the last decade, demonstrated by the interest in the international conference out of which this volume arose. The development is reflected in the allocation of journal space; the 1984 Spring/Summer edition of *Qualitative Sociology*, for instance, was dedicated to an explanation of the 'new relationship between personal computers and qualitative data' (Conrad and Reinharz, 1984: 3) and *Qualitative Sociology* and *Social Science Microcomputer Review* frequently publish new work in the field (see, for example, Gerson, 1987; Hinze, 1987; Shelly and Sibert, 1986). The growth in interest has also led to the development of specialized packages such as the ETHNOGRAPH (Tesch, 1989) as well as a multitude of suggestions for the use of general word processor and database packages (Brent, 1984). While these packages do not have the sophistication of those devoted to quantitative analysis, they none the less enhance rigour and eliminate some of the tedium in the essential task of data organization. Because of this systematizing role, but also to alert students to the spurious authority mere use of the computer can provide, it is important that students discover the strengths and dangers of computer-aided analysis. It is essential, therefore, that students are not deterred from assimilating these skills. The introduction to the technique should therefore take account of their fears rather than dismiss them. Consequently, in the programme outlined below we hope to build for computing a foundation that recognizes and overcomes inhibitions.

**Integrating computing and research methods teaching**

The teaching programme is based on the following principles:

1 No assumption of prior computing knowledge, however elementary.
2 A sympathetic awareness of the anxieties with which individuals approach the computer world.
3 The need to develop confidence and new skills by building upon past learning.
4 The need to develop an awareness of the generic value of elementary computing and word processing skills.
5 The need to develop a recognition of the computer as one of the tools of qualitative analysis and not a replacement for thinking.
6 The use of teaching methods which vary according to the nature of each task – here including individual learning, small group tuition and large group supervision.

The programme falls into two parts. The four stages in part one deal in turn with the essentials of the machine, keyboard skills, word processing, and, lastly, the organizational power of the machine. In part two, in which there are three stages, skills and techniques are integrated through exercises and small-scale project work with theoretically informed analyses of qualitative data.

*Through the gate: introductions*
The principles noted above underlie all the stages but are particularly evident in stage 1. Here they are articulated round three broad themes: teaching method, the topography of the machine, and language and symbols.

As well as the cautious if not fearful or hostile attitudes to computing described earlier, the character of the student group also has a bearing upon the teaching method. A group is likely to include students who have had varying experiences of computing: some with good and some with bad introductions, possibly some with adequate skills, and some (not necessarily the mature ones) who, despite the growing use of computers in schools, have had no experience at all. Because of this range, and the importance of waylaying anxieties, the first stage is taught in small groups with opportunity for individual progression. Presentation of the material is accompanied by detailed explanatory notes and there is ample opportunity for individual practice.

First impressions matter. It is important, therefore, to incorporate elementary and apparently trivial detail into the formally presented material, thereby giving it a legitimate status – for example, the topography of the machine and its attachments, and the meanings of regularly used symbols. The aim is to enable students to find their way round this new field as soon and as painlessly as possible, and to provide enough supports to make the user be, and feel, as independent of the instructor as is feasible; to rescue the student from the embarrassment of having to ask yet again, or from fussing round the machine for a switch, or from suffering the humiliation of being surrounded by peers who apparently have no difficulty.

The substance of the teaching at this stage would, therefore, include such simple but essential information as, for example, the position of the on/off switch, the symbol denoting the return key and what this key does (a bent arrow on a large L-shaped key has little meaning in itself), the position of the space bar, and how, in the case of microcomputers, to handle and insert a floppy disk. There will also be preparation for the second stage. According to the system used, this might include learning how to format and copy a floppy disk, use a password to access a mainframe computer, and issue the commands that give entry to relevant packages.

The presentation of material is also influenced by the style of language in the computer world because for the computer-wary this language is itself a deterrent. The brevity of a command, in some cases comprising a few symbols (not even a few words),[8] coupled with the power and startling speed of the machine, can leave the newcomer metaphorically speechless. It is not, therefore, sufficient to let this type of information rest briefly on the blackboard or overhead projector. Again, lucid, detailed guides are required with instructions on what to do if a wrong key is (inevitably) pressed.

*Let your fingers do the walking*

Stages 2 and 3 focus on words, typing and word processing. Interest in harnessing the power of the computer to data in the form of words first arose amongst literary analysts and anthropologists. For the latter the need to record copious fieldnotes put a premium on typing skills. Making typing a requirement, with a place in the curriculum, may help to overcome some inhibitions surrounding this useful skill. In stage 2, graded exercises develop skill and engender confidence to tackle later parts of the programme since familiarity with the layout and functions of the keyboard enhances the sense of control and proficiency. For, while keyboard fluency is a valuable skill in itself and important for qualitative work, it is essential if qualitative researchers wish to draw upon the power of the computer to organize their data. At this stage learning is individualized, and with self-tutoring packages such as Accu-Type it is possible to acquire the skill in about 15 hours.

The next word-focused stage, stage 3, introduces word processing skills. This and the following stage rely on individualized learning within the shelter of sympathetic tutoring. Packages such as Wordstar or Wordwise are used to teach the specialized parts of the keyboard, for example function and cursor keys, and simple editing procedures such as moving and formatting text. Because students are now familiar with the keyboard, the time spent on this may be as little as four hours, and, once the first simple procedures are mastered, the understanding of the machine enables editing skills to be extended as wished.

### At the threshold

Students are now on the brink of computer literacy. They have reached this threshold with manual competence and experience of the speed and flexibility the computer offers. They will be accustomed to communicating with the machine, have accessed packages, created files, saved them, and generated copies. Now familiar skills are integrated with new ones by introducing them to the organizational power of the computer. While ability to manage computer files is helpful to those whose interest is confined to word processing, it is essential for those who intend to hand over the manual manipulations of data to the machine. Moreover, as writers of packages for qualitative data analysis presuppose this knowledge amongst their users, formal teaching of this aspect of computing is desirable. 'The ETHNOGRAPH begins where word processing leaves off' (Seidel and Clark, 1984).

However, with self-tutor packages[9] students can explore the facilities of the system at their own pace. They learn, for example, the difference between hardware and software, to create and remove subdirectories, the role of the alpha-numeric key, and of the function keys when used directly from the operating system. By the end of this stage the student will be able to make subdirectories, copy files from one disk to another and from one subdirectory to another, list directory contents, and move in and out of packages. A short assignment to conclude the first part of the programme, possibly based on data for later analysis, will reveal any need for revision or remedial work. By recognizing the importance of these skills, devoting time to their mastery, and overcoming the inhibitions with which they are approached, when computing is needed for research it is the methodology which remains central to the lecture or assignment rather than the machine.

*Time, place, and audience*
Ideally, these skills should be learned early and sustained throughout a student's career as departmental policy on computer literacy. Because such courses and policies do not always exist, and because of the need for sympathetic teaching related to the ends to which the skill is to be put, we have set out a scheme which can be incorporated into and used in a research methods course. However, whilst the teaching of computing skills might be delegated to tutors outside the methods course, the second part of the programme should remain within it in order to protect the integrity of qualitative research.

*Theory and method: a project approach*
The second part of the programme deals with the interface of theory and the organization of data. The ETHNOGRAPH is taught and used in small-scale project work and exercises which illustrate the different types of qualitative data. This part of the programme relates to other parts of the sociology curriculum in that it draws upon and contributes to the development of sociological understanding. One of the strengths of Wakeford's (1968) workbook was that students met sociological concepts in their living form. Each of his projects illustrated a feature of data collection, analytical procedures and sociological conceptualization of the real world. According to Halfpenny (1981), the uncertainty of outcome when involving students in such work is outweighed by the advantages of becoming used to tackling practical problems as they occur. Additionally, however, the organizing power of the ETHNOGRAPH could be used here to illustrate the interaction between data and theory in the production of knowledge, for example in the recoding of data and the accessing of previously coded segments as new themes arise from the interplay in the mind of the researcher.

Some teachers, however, have reservations about the role of the ETHNOGRAPH in undergraduate work. Tesch (1989), for example, in the panel discussion following the presentation of this paper, felt that the use of the computer in qualitative analysis should be introduced at postgraduate rather than undergraduate level. She argued that there are dangers in the limited amount of sociological knowledge held by undergraduates. We would argue that the tool is one way of linking theory to its referents in the real world, and as part of an undergraduate course it can be used to develop as well as apply sociological understanding.

There are three stages: first, understanding and practice in the traditional manual organization of data; second, learning the techniques by which codes are transferred to machine-mounted data and the organizing facility of the ETHNOGRAPH; and, lastly, combining all the skills learned during the programme into this small-scale project work on qualitative methods and analysis.

Because of the reservations and some misconceptions about the use of computer aids in qualitative work, it is important to include experience of traditional manual methods of data organization (coding text, cutting and pasting, etc.). This not only ensures an understanding of the limits of the machine (its inability to replace thinking and the theoretical underpinnings of the work), but also provides the knowledge for assessing the advantages and dis- advantages of old and new techniques and evaluating packages. It also provides a theoretical and methodological context for the next stage in which precoded texts are used to develop facility in the mechanical aspects of coding, double coding, nesting, and subsequent data manipulation with the ETHNOGRAPH.

The final stage is devoted to small-scale project work which uses all the skills acquired. Here students are introduced to the range of qualitative methods and types of data (for example, interviews, diaries, life histories, ethnographies, documents). A typical project would require a range of skills stemming from research questions similar to those selected by Wakeford (1968). By this stage, because of a firm foundation of computer skills and data manipulation, students should be able to move easily between the theoretical elements of coding and organization and the mechanical manipu- lation of the data. Throughout, account is taken of both theory and method, of how research, in this case qualitative research, is actually done, and of Holsti's (1969) prescription that every methodological decision should be informed by theory.

**Conclusion**

To date, research methods courses have paid little attention to qualitative methods and analysis. Although the practical learning advocated by Halfpenny (1981) – working on exercises which illustrate types of issues and problems – is valuable and creative, the process can be lengthy, uncertain and demand a degree of theoretical sophistication. The dominance of *quantitative* analysis is understandable. For, while both types of analysis require the conceptualization of codes, quantitative work is more easily reduced to its constituent parts. Moreover, the end product, a number, has the advantage of an apparent tangibility and authority. What is necessary is a training which develops the ability to draw upon and interweave the two styles according to the demands of the inquiry.

In this programme we have attempted to set out the teaching blocks for introducing the appropriate skills for computer-aided qualitative analysis. To dismiss the traditional skill of typing as irrelevant is to discard a useful resource, and merely to affirm that the skills necessary to the new technologies are simple and easily absorbed is to ignore the very real problems students have. Attitudes are both complex and inhibiting; they stem from a set of contradictions and cultural attitudes and affect both men and women. Consequently, since there is evident distress amongst students when they encounter word processing and computing, Shipman's (1979) call for an emphasis upon numeracy for sociology students rather than computing skills, while important, is not sufficient. Students need sympathetic guidance into the new technologies rather than to find their distress treated as a rite of passage. By integrating such guidance with computing procedures that attempt to reduce the manual labour in qualitative research, we can also perhaps bring qualitative analysis into a more prominent position in the research methods curriculum.

To implement such an approach raises practical questions of cost and the availability of equipment and qualified staff. The availability of knowledge raises a further issue. The emphasis throughout this paper has been twofold: on instruction in basic skills as a precursor to the use of the computer in qualitative research and on an understanding of the principles of qualitative analysis by those teaching and using this aid. We stress the importance of the latter by referring to the misuse of statistical packages such as Minitab and spss, complete with statistical appendices. The accessibility of such packages enables students to perform statistical tests on their data irrespective of any understanding of either the reasoning behind the procedures or the meaning of the results. Most do not know whether these summaries of statistical methods cite all the assumptions upon which tests are based, and their very presence deters recourse to basic statistical texts. Number crunching can replace analysis and the package conceals the user's ignorance. The associated dangers are compounded by the authority conveyed by numbers in our society.[10] It is also worrying that computer programmers with little or no connection with sociology or the social sciences may see qualitative data as a new province for exploitation and produce packages which pay scant attention to the contexts and meanings which are the essence of qualitative work. The introduction of computing into the qualitative methods strand of the research methods curriculum could provide some protection.

Qualitative researchers must address these issues and students must be alerted to them. Students are not only potential researchers and producers of knowledge but are also likely to enter careers that draw upon new knowledge. Their ability to judge its validity could affect people's lives.

## Notes

The chapter arises from work on an associated study of the *ESRC 16–19 Initiative, Family Processes and Transfers in the Transition to Adulthood*, Grant No. XC05250019.

1. Isabel MacPherson of the Health Service Research Unit, University of Aberdeen, introduced the ETHNOGRAPH to students (health service personnel and fourth-year medical students) as purely a tool to 'cut and paste'. It is vital, she feels, that the introduction of such packages is set within an overall research methods course which covers quantitative and qualitative methods, and which emphasizes their integration where appropriate. We agree. We are not suggesting that a course is given merely on computing and packages. Our argument, rather, is that research methods teachers should pay more attention to elementary computing skills amongst their students, since it is the inhibitions surrounding the computer that deter both new and experienced researchers from testing the utility of such packages and weighing their limitations and advantages. Moreover, irrespective of the ultimate decision to accept or reject the tool, it is lack of knowledge and experience amongst researchers themselves that increases the very dangers she fears: that use of a computer package will lend a spurious credence and status to any findings. (Letter to N. Fielding, symposium organizer, following the Symposium on Qualitative Knowledge and Computing, University of Surrey, 11–12 July 1989.) These difficulties and dangers are discussed later in the text.
2. The issues also reflect the recent interest in the acquisition of vocational and transferable skills at all educational levels.
3. We are speaking of methods and tools as ways of looking at and dealing with data; we do not mean to imply that tools such as the ETHNOGRAPH replace the researcher as analyst.
4. At the panel discussion following the presentation of this paper, Tesch made the following comments:

> When instructing people about computers, we don't only provide information and teach skills, but we influence attitudes. The latter are just as important as the former. People who wish to learn about computers may know little about them, yet due to the pervasiveness of the computer in our culture, they usually approach the entire phenomenon with a certain attitude.

I have found that novices frequently harbour one of two prejudices each of which has undesirable implications. They may result in either the avoidance of the computer in qualitative research or an unrealistic dependence on it.

(a) AVOIDANCE. The computer is viewed as too complicated, as a mysterious machine that is too difficult to understand and to deal with. The expectation is that a lot of knowledge and skill is required to use a computer competently. Therefore the person is afraid that learning about computers will take too long and might be frustrating. Rather than investing that much time and effort, the use of the computer is avoided, or delayed as long as possible.

(b) DEPENDENCE. Because of its power (and the computer related notion of artificial intelligence) the computer is seen as the answer to problems that are complex and demanding. The software is presumed to take over the intellectual tasks that the person might not necessarily be able to perform herself. For instance, some researchers expect qualitative analysis programs to guide them through the process of analysis or even to discover conceptual relationships in the data. The computer is depended upon for an expertise it cannot possibly possess.

Accordingly, teaching computer literacy should aim on one hand to demystify the computer, and on the other hand to produce realistic expectations. (Tesch, 1989, comments at the panel discussion on teaching about computers in qualitative research, note to the organizers.)

5. Whilst writing this chapter we have followed the instructions of the friendly feathered guide in the IBM manual:

GENTLY slide the diskette into the drive with the label side up and towards you. (IBM Corp. and Microsoft Inc., 1987; capitals in original)

Yet on some occasions the machine has not been able to read the disk. Nowhere in the guide does our feathered friend tell us to take out the disk, twiddle the central hole, and try again – as we did! Normally tricks such as this (the equivalent of kicking the temperamental television set?) are magically performed by whoever is supervising the session.

6. Clive Holtham, professor of information management at City University Business School, notes the resistance of senior managers to learning to use a computer. He suggests the reasons are to do with time, technique and a feeling that it is unnecessary because it's not really their job. Interestingly, Anne Leeming, who runs the City University Business School's course in IT management, 'stresses that you don't have to be a keyboard wizard to benefit from a computer course: "You can find your way around with two fingers"'. (Golzen, 1989)

7. On courses where only typed assignments are accepted, some male students prevail upon female students to type their work for them.

8. Work is now being done on simplifying man/machine communication, particularly in the field of educational software. For example, new versions of operating systems use pictures (icons) to represent programs and procedures. These are selected on the screen by manipulating arrows, thus removing the need to remember an exact command. Other packages, for example the ETHNOGRAPH, are menu driven. This and its comprehensive manual make the ETHNOGRAPH a good educational tool.

9. Tutor.Com, for example, is a self-tutor package which introduces users to the MS-DOS operating system. It is available on a share-ware basis from Computer Knowledge, PO Box 91176, Los Angeles, USA.

10. MacPherson views as serious the 'spurious "scientific" kudos given by having used computer packages in handling qualitative material'. She comments, 'It's my experience that certain professions, in particular doctors, find it hard to come to terms with reports not conforming to the "BMJ" style and lacking frequencies and Chi-squares!' (letter to N. Fielding, symposium organizer, following the Symposium on Qualitative Knowledge and Computing, University of Surrey, 11–12 July 1989).

# 6

# Personal Information and Qualitative Research Data: Some Practical and Ethical Problems arising from Data Protection Legislation

*Anne V. Akeroyd*

Data protection laws in several countries now regulate matters relating to compilations of personal data when these are held in automatic data processing (adp) form and sometimes also in manual records. They provide rights and safeguards for the natural persons (and sometimes also legal persons) to whom they relate by imposing controls and requiring specific procedures in respect of the collection, holding, use and destruction of personal data. The impact of these laws has so far been limited and mainly confined to Western Europe. Why, then, should it be argued that all social scientists, and especially qualitative researchers, need to apprise themselves of the legal conditions and the actual and potential effects of data protection laws, and, in some countries, of privacy and analogous laws? This chapter addresses the reasons for this and like Akeroyd (1988) is intended to encourage experts in qualitative social scientific computing to develop technical solutions to alleviate some of the problems the laws present for social researchers.

## Personal data, information and qualitative research records

Most qualitative social research techniques involve the creation of textual materials, though audio-visual (sound–image) records may augment notes or be the basic records for analysis. The complexity of the materials is considerable and the quantity of text may be huge, ranging from about 5,000–7,000 words for a single interview to the 10,000 typewritten pages collected by 29 fieldworkers in a multi-method, multi-site project (Podolefsky and McCarty, 1983). Developments in information technology offer an easier and more efficient handling of such a large corpus of disparate materials. Just as quantitative sociologists and variable-oriented research in the

1960s benefited greatly from the development of computer statistical packages so, too, in the 1990s will qualitative researchers and case-oriented research[1] similarly benefit in respect of data handling and analysis, especially from developments in microcomputing, general software packages for text handling and specialized software and techniques for qualitative computing (see Conrad and Reinharz, 1984; Pfaffenberger, 1988; Anderson and Brent, 1989; Blank et al., 1989; Tesch, 1990);[2] though Tesch (1989) has suggested that the positive impact on computer-assisted qualitative analysis may be slower than previously estimated. Take but four recent developments. A genealogical database, ROOTS III version 3.01, can handle up to 65,535 individuals extending over 95 generations, has extensive searching and analysing routines, can print 12 different categories of charts and link text and graphic files (O'Neil, 1990). SONAR PROFESSIONAL, a Macintosh program combining text retrieval, Boolean full text searching and automatic hypertext linking capabilities, can search, analyse and index freeform text in multiple files at a speed of up to 4,000 pages per second (Garson, 1989b: 100–1). The shared Virtual Notebook, a repository of data, hypotheses, notes and patients' information, offers a very advanced version of shared fieldnotes (Shipman et al., 1989). The DISCAMERICA database contains 100 million residential and business names, addresses and telephone numbers (Garson, 1989c: 554).

The euphoric (Finlay, 1987: Ch. 1) possibilities of information technology develop apace, offering new opportunities for data collection, data sharing, analysis, simulation, interactive collaboration, new research fields and modes of publishing (Marx and Reichman, 1984; Rogers, 1987; Etzkowitz, 1989; Anderson and Brent, 1989; Garson, 1989a; Lyman, 1989; Ragin and Becker, 1989; Macfarlane, 1990). Few proponents pay detailed (if any) attention to dysphoric concomitants and consequences of computerization (though see Lyman, 1984 and 1989). This chapter draws attention to one such factor, raising drawbacks but ones which arise from a 'good cause': the need to safeguard the interests of the referents of personal data records. For, paradoxically, as this 'new world' is opening up to the innovative and technologically minded qualitative researcher, so developments in the legal domain which were stimulated in great part by adp technologies now constrain its exploration.

Information science regards data as 'facts' which are transformed into information which can then be used, though there is slippage in the deployment of these concepts. In discussing data protection law 'the two terms are unavoidably used synonymously' but 'data' can be regarded as 'potential "information"'' (Wacks, 1989: 25). Langefors considers that 'data as representation of information' or as 'signs' differ from 'information as knowledge conveyed by data (or by observation of (other) phenomena)', and though data pro- ing is carried out on signs, information is 'created from data and pre-knowledge. Hence, information is always an increment to existing knowledge' (Langefors, 1987: 89). What is needed to use data are 'observational pre-knowledge' for interpretation and knowledge of the facts, which must be taken into account in database design, and 'conclusional pre-knowledge' to allow the drawing of conclusions from the facts (Langefors, 1987: 90).

Fieldnotes may be similarly differentiated. For Lyman, fieldnotes as *data* are 'a sequence of bits of information which must be organized in categories to have significance' (1984: 84); as *in- formation*, they form 'a text containing latent form, then coding must describe the form and index it' (1984: 84); and as *knowledge*, they are 'a text which does not need to be organized because it is a form of knowledge which is whole in itself' (1984: 84).

Much information gathered by case-oriented, qualitative re- searchers and recorded in fieldnotes and other records directly relates to individual persons – their social interactions, personal relationships, behaviours, beliefs and opinions. Researchees may be named, often without pseudonyms and not identified by code numbers; described in personal or status/role terms and by various kinds of identifiers; and references to them may include various 'identifying particulars'. They are 'captured' in census forms or personal records, genealogies and audio-visual recordings, and reflected upon and sometimes apparently disparaged in explanatory notes and methodological comments, and so forth.

Qualitative records, particularly when heavy reliance is laid on key informants, often contain personal information collected deliberately or contingently acquired but which has neither been obtained from nor verified with the referent.[3] They may contain inaccurate information or at the least 'facts' whose accuracy is potentially challengeable, or details of events which the individuals to whom they relate have long forgotten.[4] Much information may have been open and known to all, some confidential and restricted, and some 'known' but not openly stated or acknowledged. Verbatim notes or interview transcripts may be supplemented by personal data gathered in informal chats or during what the layperson thinks is not 'research time', and may be contextualized by observations about non-verbal behaviour, surroundings and the like. Ethnographers are never 'off-duty' even though researchees usually fail to remember, perhaps even to realize, this; and even a sharply delimited project may not contain their propensity for 'trawling'. Finally, fieldnotes are expanded and augmented by methodological and analytical comments.[5]

Fieldnotes, though, are more than 'mere records'. For Bond, they 'are an anthropologist's most sacred possession. They are personal property, part of a world of private memories and experiences, failures and success, insecurities and decisions. They are usually carefully tucked away in a safe place' (1990: 273). Their functions (like those of other qualitative research records) vary according to whether they are read as data, information or knowledge, and according to the purposes of the researcher. Similarly, whether the researcher needs to be able to read (or to retrieve) the real identities of researchees will vary – for long-term studies this is essential. Fieldnotes may provide shorthand statements and aides-mémoire of the past (Bond, 1990: 286) or case examples (Pfaffenberger, 1988: 25); but their 'personalized noise' may sometimes have to be removed to facilitate social analysis: 'categories . . . are also techniques for suppressing observations and ridding ourselves of people and their petty activities. . . . It is not so much a matter of analyzing all that data as forgetting all those people and happenings' (R.F. Murphy, 1972: 40).

For the researcher, then, fieldnotes have very different meanings and purposes from those attached to the 'data' and 'information' of personal data records held by government agencies and commercial organizations. Despite their often personalized content and the inclusion of identifiers or 'identifying particulars', fieldnotes and other forms of qualitative data records are not conceived of or treated by – and probably not perceived by – researchers as compilations or records of personal data pertaining to individuals in the sense that the data protection laws conceive of these. They are also concerned with collectivities, whereas the laws have no interest in safeguarding the rights and interests of these. A crucial difference is the ends to which research materials are put and the relevance of the 'personal' factor therein. As Bing points out, research files 'are not used to make decisions about individuals, though they may be pertinent to larger groups of people. Therefore the data protection interests of the data subject are not pronounced' (1985: 11).

Different though they may be in some respects from commercial and governmental records, social research records do not fall outside the scope of data protection law. At best their specific characteristics and uses may justify some very limited form(s) of exemption from the provisions of the law.

## Data protection and privacy legislation

Legislation protecting personal data and/or privacy has been spreading during the past 20 years, reflecting three main concerns: human rights and personal privacy, open government and freedom of information, and national economic security (see, for example, Bing, 1985; Burkert, 1986; Flaherty, 1986; B.M. Murphy, 1986). Most laws have been enacted in Western Europe, but states in all continents are now concerned. By February 1990 there were national data protection and/or privacy laws in 21 countries, sub-national laws in six, constitutional provision in five and draft national legislation or guidelines in preparation or under consideration in another six (TDCR, 1990a). Some laws have been revised; new legislation incorporates the lessons learnt by predecessors; and continuing changes take account of new technologies (such as developments in free-text retrieval and word processing systems, computer networks and computer matching) and the dangers which they present. In second-generation legislation a wider range of material is covered (mainly in manual records), sectoral differentiation has increased (for instance according to the sensitivity of data and their purposes), and there is a trend towards self-regulation as well as an increased use of informal and civil sanctions to enforce compliance (Walden, 1988: 12). Transborder data flow issues are now receiving more attention, and artificial intelligence will be the next major issue for data commissioners (TDCR, 1989b: 5–6).

The laws are mainly based on the OECD Guidelines (OECD, 1980) or the Council of Europe Convention (CoE, 1981). However, the United Nations has now produced the *UN Guidelines Concerning Computerized Personal Data Files* establishing minimum guarantees to be incorporated into any national legislation (TDCR, 1989c). These differ in some respects from the Convention/OECD Guidelines. In particular, they contain no mention of research data nor any reference to an exemption for files used for statistics or scientific research under 'Principle 6 – Power to Make Exceptions', which is provided for in the Convention. This is particularly important for social research since the UN Guidelines (like the Convention) require that certain categories of sensitive data (such as information on racial or ethnic origin, sex life, political opinions, trade union membership) should not be compiled subject to the cases of the exceptions.

The USA has passed a number of acts concerned with personal (and other) data, notably the Freedom of Information Act of 1966, the Privacy Act of 1974 and the Privacy Protection Act of 1980, which apply mainly in respect of data collected by federal agencies. Privacy legislation has been updated, as have other laws concerned with agencies (mainly governmental) which acquire and hold personal data (see Bigelow, 1986; Laudon, 1986: Ch. 15; Freedman, 1987), though users may not realize that the Privacy Act applies to microcomputer applications and their privacy guidelines need revision (Bergin, 1989). Other acts include the Electronic Communications Act of 1986 and the Computer Matching and Privacy Act of 1988 (which applies to federal agencies) (TDCR, 1990c: 16–18). The US laws are not directly comparable to the European data protection laws, though there are some similarities – under the Freedom of Information Act individuals have some possibilities of access to information about themselves, and the Privacy Act entitles individuals to know how data collected about them will be used (Chambers, 1980: 331–2) – but they offer very little protection against activities in the private sector. There has been considerable unwillingness in the USA to develop legal provision for data protection and for privacy protection in the private sector (TDCR, 1989b: 7, 1990c: 10–11); and American commercial interests generally favour the 'free flow' of information and oppose controls on transborder data flow. However, growing concern over the increasingly invasive capabilities of information technology (see, for example, Marx and Reichman, 1984; Gray, 1989; Southward IV, 1989; TDCR, 1990c) and the need to protect its commercial interests (TDCR, 1990c: 10–11) may yet force the USA to conform.[6]

**Content and scope of the laws**

The data principles underlying the laws reflect interests in adequacy of personal data, in confidentiality and in openness (Bing, 1985: 7–11). Through the 'right to know' and the 'right of subject access' expressed in the last, data subjects can exercise or reinforce their rights and interests in the other two. The laws are concerned with matters of *privacy*,[7] *confidentiality, identifiability* and with *data protection*. Once data are depersonalized, data protection laws have no interest in them.

The laws regulate some or all of the following matters:

- the collection and/or holding of data referring to identified or identifiable individuals;
- the content, nature and quality of the data held;
- the purposes for which data are held, and their uses;
- the time period for which they can be retained;

- the security conditions and protection against risks, unauthorized access or unlawful disclosure, loss and destruction;
- publicity about the holdings;
- the right of access of data subjects to data about themselves;
- the disclosure of data to third parties;
- the transfer of data across national borders; and
- the accountability of the data controller in respect of these principles.

They vary considerably, differing *inter alia* according to whether they:

- protect any and all personal information or only certain data;
- grade personal data by level of sensitivity and restrict the holding of certain categories of data;
- apply only to human (natural) persons or also to legal persons;
- cover both public and private sector files;
- cover automated files only or also include manual files;
- require the data always to be accurate and up to date;
- impose time limits on data retention;
- impose controls on transborder data flows (TDF); and
- allow some total or partial exemptions from registration or licence and, especially, whether research and research data are privileged in any way.

**The implications for social research**

In an earlier paper (Akeroyd, 1988) I discussed actual or possible legal, technical and ethical problems that the laws posed for social researchers. I concluded that modifications to social research practice would increasingly be needed, depending on which activities were under consideration and under which legal jurisdiction(s) the researcher's data collection, processing, holding and applications fell.[8]

The most important factor is whether controls are imposed over the collection of data or only over the handling and use of records and the data/information contained therein. *Research methods, research data* and *longitudinal studies* will be most affected where a licence or concession is necessary for the collection of data and/or where restrictions are imposed on the types of data which can be compiled. Controls affecting the usage, handling, security, dissemination and the like of data and information and of printout are most likely to affect *data handling, data analysis* and *secondary (re)analysis*. An additional problem is that research records relating to one project may have different legal (and security) statuses, as is the case under laws which treat differently manual files and adp files and their printed output.

Special provision may be made for data held for research or statistical purposes, mainly exemption from access rights subject to conditions such as the common proviso that the results must not be published in a way which allows the identification of a data subject or subjects. If these cannot be met then data subjects who request access have to be provided with a comprehensive copy of the data/ information held about them, but which should not normally include information identifying a third party.

I take up here only two of the factors affecting qualitative social research records: identifiability of personal information, and data security and integrity.

*Identifiability and retrievability*

The key to identifiability and retrievability of personal information is the way a link between a data item and an individual can be made. 'Identifiability' here has three aspects: first, the *criteria or identifying particulars* on which it depends; second, the question of *retrievability*, and third, the *exemption conditions* in respect of publications.

In all the laws the critical factor making an item 'personal information' is whether or not there is a link between the data item and an individual. There are differences in the strength of the linkage required and in the technical ways in which the connection is established.[9] For example, there are differences according to the degree of 'transparency' required in the record; whether an immediate identification must be possible or need only be very indirect, as under the US Privacy Act which allows for the concatenation of trivial items ultimately adding up to only one particular individual. The Council of Europe has recently decreed that 'An individual shall not be "identifiable" if identification requires an unreasonable amount of time, cost and manpower' (TDCR, 1989a: 26),[10] which has introduced a new factor into the debate.

Identifiability is essentially linked with retrievability; but retrieving personal information from data systems is extremely difficult. This is exacerbated if the systems combine hierarchical, relational or deductive database(s) and freeform text, since they will include not only explicit and implicit (inferable) information which is retrievable with a greater or lesser degree of difficulty, but also the latent information in freeform text which is only discoverable by accident or by exhaustive search.[11]

An individual may be tracked through a relational database (see Winer and Carrière, 1990: 218); but for freeform text general and disciplinary-specific developments in software for searching, indexing and analysing freeform text files may help considerably (see Tesch, 1990; Pritchard, 1990). So, too, may hyper-semantic approaches to data modelling (Potter and Trueblood, 1988). Hypertext systems might assist in tagging and locating fairly 'transparent' personal data, explicit and implicit or inferable information, and (at least some) latent information, and markers can be used to link related units and create an 'associative trail' which can be saved and reused (Conklin, 1987; Pfaffenberger, 1988: 43).

The technical difficulties that subject access would present will be clear. Qualitative data and research records identify individuals in numerous ways and may contain many other items which singly or in concatenation could act as surrogate identifiers. They are primarily text-based, for which different types of storage and retrieval systems are both suitable and may be needed for retrieval and analytical purposes. Paradoxically, however, the identifiability conditions under which exemption from subject access may be granted (the main though not always the only ground for this) raise one of the most troublesome issues that qualitative researchers commonly face, that is, how to ensure in publications the anonymity and non-identifiability of research participants. As Bing comments, the key question is 'to whom should the identification be possible – the general, uninformed individual; the persons in the family of, or close to, the data subject; or the data subject himself' (1980: 77). This is well-worn ground for qualitative researchers, especially ethnographers. Some examples of participants' reactions to the publication of disguised but still 'recognizable' persons or office holders are enshrined in the sociological collective memory, such as the Springdale *cause célèbre*, and examples of participants' reactions continue to be recorded.[12]

Qualitative research products might now include the electronic book envisaged by Lyman (1989: 17) as combining optical disks and hypertext which readers could interact with and even annotate. Would the electronic equivalents of the marginal notes identifying citizens found in their city library's copy of *Plainsville* and which outraged residents (Gallaher, 1964) mean that the researcher had obviously breached the non-identifiability condition? Would the researchees, too, be happy with such public exposure; would they all give their informed consent and, if not, how could the refusers be 'deleted' (digital retouching might come in handy here!); and how constraining might statutory, administrative and personal guarantees of confidentiality and privacy be? Claiming exemption from subject access rights would hardly be feasible either in this scenario.[13]

Social science disciplines and individual practitioners differ markedly in the techniques used to hinder identification and protect privacy and confidentiality, and in the extent to which these are deployed as protective devices in fieldnotes and other records, data processing and publications. It is often assumed that pseudonyms (or numerical identifiers) will achieve this, though there is little discussion of the technical and practical issues involved (see references in Akeroyd, 1988: 202–5). Disguises, distortions, omissions and fabrications might affect features critical for the analysis, and may create other problems of validity, reliability and replicability. Some pseudonymizing or anonymizing techniques present difficulties for the reader; sometimes anonymity may only be achieved at the expense of truth and accuracy (Cavendish, 1982: vii–ix; see also Hedrick, 1985: 135). In some cases the problem might be *repersonalization* of text and/or fieldnotes (see Fielding, 1982: 92–3).

Computers may facilitate such data transformation for deidentification and repersonalization; but in relation to the data protection laws the satisfactory achievement of this may be much less easy and more tedious in some cases than Becker et al. suggest (1984: 18). Digital or electronic retouching could help in the anonymization of audio-visual records, but might also reintroduce linkage problems; and if this 'created' individuals who looked like others in the field setting, the question of 'identifiability' might also reappear.[14]

Though anonymous data are the opposite of personal data, Bing considers they are not discrete categories but the ends of a continuum, and that data become anonymous when the identifying particulars are removed and 'the individual is included in a group sufficiently large for the data subject to get lost in the crowd' (Bing, 1986: 86). Variable-oriented research has well-developed procedures for 'losing' the individual respondent, though there are difficulties in successfully achieving this;[15] but how does the qualitative researcher achieve this in the (usually) small 'qualitative crowd'? Key issues are what would constitute adequate non-identification in published accounts and fieldnotes and the technicalities of achieving this in computerized qualitative records.

*Security issues*
Issues of identifiability and retrievability are partly related to issues of security, matters which are safeguarded by the acts. For example, personal data/information must be protected from unauthorized access and unlawful disclosure, and the products of data processing (printout, screen displays and machine-readable data) must be safeguarded by appropriate security measures, safe storage or destruction.

Data integrity and security are often technically difficult matters to effect; and some awareness of the general problems and the in-built protections and vulnerabilities of different computer systems is advisable. Many social scientists may use computers without being fully aware of either legal or technological hazards: most discussions of security matters are in relatively inaccessible information technology and computer science journals.[16] Information scientists, of course, are not concerned with protective measures transforming the data other than cryptography: their discussions are about *computer security*.

> Its concern is secrecy (protecting information from unauthorized disclosure), integrity (protecting information from unauthorized alteration), and availability (protecting systems from denial-of-service attacks). (McLean, 1990: 10)

Smith contends that electronic data are at *greater* risk than other forms of records (1989a: 205), and provides a helpful short overview of weaknesses in computer systems (see also Smith, 1989b; Longley and Shain, 1987). In devising a balanced, appropriate and cost-effective solution, 'risk analysis . . . is the final piece in the jigsaw of computer security' (Smith, 1989a: 210).

Ensuring privacy of data is essential for the collaborative use of multi-user systems such as distributed file systems; but many procedures and devices in mainframes, networks and workstations are beyond the control of users, and the safeguards they offer vary considerably, as does their vulnerability to viruses, hacking and other disasters (McLean, 1990; Rohde and Haskett, 1990; Satyanaryanan, 1990). Access rights and the right/ability to view or to alter files can be restricted to defined categories of users having different privileges and access to data at different levels of security, though files and databases are not necessarily thereby secured against intrusion or misuse, and workstations may be in public places. Even choosing a secure password is no simple task (Highland, 1990). Some operating personnel will necessarily have overriding access rights – but are you certain that your IBM mainframe files are safe from casual or unauthorized use of the Superzap override control (Wood, 1990: 15)? Data transmitted via telecommunications may be very vulnerable (Menkus, 1990).

Microcomputers are usually more immediately controlled by users, though networking is becoming common. They present considerable security problems, but protective devices are increasing, partly as a result of data protection law, partly from commercial fears. Klopp (1990) describes American products providing, for example, access controls, audit trails, encryption techniques, backup systems, anti-theft devices, protection against viruses, accidental file-overwrites and other disaster conditions (see also Rohde and Haskett, 1990).

The social science literature on such matters is surprisingly sparse.[17] Blank stated that 'All case-oriented fieldwork has an inherent problem of protecting the confidentiality of subjects' (1989: 7) but drew no conclusions in respect of computerized data. Rogers (1987: 306–7), discussing computer-monitored data as a research resource, pointed out that 'the privacy problems associated with the sensitive nature of much computer communication data are one of the special difficulties created by the new data' (1987: 307), and mentioned various solutions to the privacy problem but did not discuss data security. Gerson cited two factors posing increased threats to confidentiality, the fast, cheap and easy replication of files and the use of telecommunication facilities to access files, asserting that 'The solution to this problem lies in careful procedures designed to minimize the possibility of occurrence, just as it has right along' (Gerson, 1984: 73). Becker et al. (1984) referred briefly to a few precautions suitable to the level of confidentiality required, such as passwords, restricting access to project members, and the use of global search-and-replace facilities to alter names and identifying details.

In the 1990s such statements, though, seem slightly complacent given developments in cheap mass storage systems for micro-computers, in computer networking, in distributed databases and file access, in computer-matching and computer-profiling software, and episodes of hacking into mainframes and virus infection in those and pcs on an international scale.

Security and legal issues are extremely important for qualitative researchers given the text-based nature and often sensitive content of their materials. Remembering to lock up floppy disks holding confidential data (Becker et al., 1984: 18, 25) is still necessary, but so now is thinking carefully about what is cached on the unsecured hard disk of the pc. If files can be read they can be copied, downloaded or printed; electronic data are not normally deleted when a file is deleted and can thus be retrieved from mainframes, hard disks, floppy and cd-rom disks, and the last two are also vulnerable to theft. It may be necessary to use encryption to protect sensitive and/or confidential data – but if they are to be analysed and used they must normally be decrypted. Could encrypted data be used in qualitative text retrievers or text analysers?

Social researchers need to consider more fully what specific precautions are needed to safeguard their data, within a computer system and through back-up procedures and safe storage facilities, and in respect of data sharing and dissemination of data/information. They should take account of general security-related developments but should also open up their own technical debate on the protection of social science data in the electronic age.

## Law, ethics and computers in qualitative research

Concern for the well-being of researchees has been at the heart of much of the long debate on ethical issues in social science. The risks for the researcher, though, should not be ignored, as Brajuha's experiences demonstrate (Brajuha and Hallowell, 1986); and data protection and privacy legislation have added a further dimension by imposing legal obligations on the holders of personal information and providing for legal action in the case of breaches.

It has been held that *data* in themselves are not necessarily sensitive, damaging or potentially harmful; the possibilities for damage arise from their use(s) and the context(s) in which they are transformed into information (Sieghart, 1982: 103). Wacks argues that what is altered by a change in context is not the quality or nature of personal, sensitive information but the attitudes towards its use held by the person to whom it relates (1989: 181). But, given the vastly increased invasive capacities of electronic technology and its potential for controls over persons, it has also been suggested that 'no personal information is in reality irrelevant, and to that degree all data can be seen as "sensitive"' (Walden, 1988: 13).[18]

It is easy to exaggerate the threats posed by research data; their invasive possibilities and the potential harms they pose for researchees can hardly match those of government and commercial databanks and activities, as invasions of privacy afforded by telecommunications (TDCR, 1990c: 15–16),[19] computer profiling and matching (Marx and Reichman, 1984) and the operations of credit and marketing companies demonstrate. But they should also not be underestimated – the potential for smaller-scale and more localized damage can be acute, as discussions about subpoenas (for example, Brajuha and Hallowell, 1986), governmental audit (Trend, 1980), and public interest arguments (Peterson, 1984) attest. Chambers' (1980: 332) reminder that public and individual access under the Freedom of Information Act may be had to fieldwork data from federally-funded projects, a matter especially important for those working outside the academy, is highly pertinent here. So, too, is Brajuha and Hallowell's suggestion that 'researchers should give thought to what elements of their data they consider confidential and/or private. Perhaps thought must be given to organizing data files and field notes in this way' (1986: 474–5).[20]

If access were obtained legally or illegally to computerized research data and/or these were subjected to computer-matching or -profiling techniques, what additional threats to researchees might thereby be entailed? If the highly complex safeguards used to protect survey respondents can be defeated by 'back-door identification techniques' (Bing, 1986: 86) or by a detail or combination of details which could reveal identities of individuals or organizations (Raffe et al., 1989: 22), how satisfactory are the pseudonyms used by qualitative researchers? How complex need the precautions be to ensure confidentiality and data security?

Social researchers are also surprisingly silent about the legal and ethical issues arising from the use of computers for research and the impact of data protection laws in particular. Barnes (1979: 166–8) drew attention to the ethical hazards of social science databanks and referred to data protection and privacy legislation (then in its infancy), pointing out that legislation is more likely to be satisfactory where researchers are well informed about the social and political implications of their work (1979: 182–4). His prediction is partially confirmed by the Norwegian experience, but qualitative research practices do not conform to the criteria for concession to establish a research register (Øyen and Olaussen, 1985: 23–5). Most discussions are about statistical or quantitative and survey-based research, especially the use of administrative data for research purposes (for example, Bazillion, 1984; Mochman and Müller, 1979; Simitis, 1981), and the most detailed accounts refer to Scandinavian laws, which are particularly restrictive. After an initial flurry, comment has almost ceased, but Raffe et al. (1989) provide a good account for survey research in Britain, which is just feeling the impact of data protection law. However, there is still virtually no acknowledgement that qualitative social researchers might use computers.[21]

In the USA social scientists are well versed in matters associated with the now taken-for-granted federal research regulations, although not all the consequences have yet been realized (M.D. Murphy and Johannsen, 1990) nor may the full effects ever be known (Chambers, 1980: 338). Discussions of legal contexts are far fewer and the contributions of qualitative researchers are limited. Many accounts are concerned about privacy and confidentiality issues in respect of research data, a complex matter given the number of laws involved, and how to protect researchees against threats posed by subpoena of research data or demands by government agencies, the use of federal records for research and the legal liabilities of the researcher (for example, Trend, 1980; Peterson, 1984; Reynolds, 1982: 112–23; Boruch and Cecil, 1983),[22]

and the legal problems of data-sharing (Fienberg et al., 1985).
Chambers' (1980) survey of us laws (and Trend's, 1980, experiences)
might indicate that ethnographers are much less knowledgeable
about the legal situation. Chambers also drew attention to the
increasing knowledgeability of researchees about their legal rights
and their growing sensitivity to being researched, the interests of
sponsors and clients and the growing interest of the courts 'in issues
where the rights of free enquiry are presumably in conflict with the
rights of the individual and society' (1980: 341).

Discussions of electronic technology and research matters are
fewer still. As Americans have yet to be affected by data protection
laws, their silence is not wholly surprising; but generally in relation
to privacy issues it might also suggest that the euphorization of the
technological possibilities has been (over)dominant. Bergin (1989)
identifies research questions but only about the practices of federal
agencies. In a general paper on the electronic threats to individual
privacy in the usa, Gray cites the example of the destruction of
identifiers in a Swedish research project.[23] Though she does not
develop the implications of that case for researchers, her conclusion
involves them.

> The intellectual consensus is that it is imperative to formulate public
> policy that addresses the issue of which forms of data collection are
> necessary and which forms are unacceptable intrusions on individual
> privacy. This necessitates a rethinking of basic issues concerning privacy,
> effective government, research data, law enforcement, and freedom of
> information. (Gray, 1989: 255)

The increasing use of computers has, I suggest, further altered the
legal context in ways most social scientists have yet to appreciate.
Qualitative researchers in the usa and elsewhere must involve
themselves in the legal debate, lest the bio-medical and survey/
quantitative models common to the lay and political understandings
of 'research' dominate the discussion as they did over the federal
research regulations.

## Conclusion

Half a decade ago Gerson asserted that 'it has become increasingly
clear that the problem of using computers for processing raw field
notes is essentially solved; the remaining issues are cosmetic and
educational' (1986: 208). I would contend that this is far from being
the case: legal issues are also outstanding matters for resolution.
That the full impact of data protection law has yet to be fully
realized by qualitative social researchers, indeed by most social

researchers, arises from a number of factors, but their ignorance must be dispelled.

The resolution of some of the actual or potential complications introduced by data protection laws may throw up some very tricky *technical* problems as well as *ethical* and *methodological* ones. Although variable-oriented, quantitative research is not exempt, case-oriented, qualitative research both presents and will be presented with more considerable technical and legal problems. Qualitative researchers may have to rethink their assumptions and may need, or be stimulated to find, technical solutions to alleviate existing problems and to obviate future difficulties. The interaction of law, ethics, methods and techniques may, however, create new conflicts and compromises, as Raffe et al. (1989) have shown for survey research. Here, then, is reinforcement for Barnes' (1984) view that *compromise* is intrinsic to social research.

There is clearly also a need to broaden understanding of the methods and requirements of qualitative research in general. If social researchers are not allowed to collect the types of data that unstructured and qualitative research methodologies require, then colleagues in some countries may be prevented from producing the particular and deeper understandings of social life which these allow, as Øyen and Olaussen have argued (1985: 25). They will also fail to benefit from and to contribute to the advances in data-handling and analytical techniques which may be offered by advances in software. The divergences already noted between national 'sociologies' and 'anthropologies' (Hiller, 1979; *International Sociology*, 1989; *Ethnos*, 1982) may widen yet further, reflecting different national legal traditions. Cross-national studies and comparative approaches in some circumstances may be restricted to a very narrow methodological field.

The impact of data protection measures should not be under-estimated. At worst, they may preclude the utilization of qualitative research methods; at the very least they impose constraints and procedures to which social researchers will have to adapt. As data protection spreads round the world, so increasing numbers of social researchers will be affected. Should data protection be extended in general to manual files, as the trends indicate is probable, then even those researchers who have not advanced beyond typewriters, scissors and paste will come under their scope.[24]

## Notes

This is a considerably revised version of a paper presented to the Symposium on Qualitative Knowledge and Computing, University of Surrey, 11–12 July 1989. I am grateful to the editors for their suggestions.

1. Ragin and Becker (1989) identify two dominant strategies of data reduction in social science: the variable-oriented (usually probabilistic) approach used in quantitative research, and the case-oriented (usually holistic and non-probabilistic) approach used in qualitative, case-oriented research, but recognize that they are not mutually exclusive.

2. See Garson's regular listings in 'News and Notes' in *Social Science Computer Review* and the programs described in Tesch (1990) and in this volume.

3. I argue elsewhere (Akeroyd, 1988: 193) that this should properly be categorized as 'proxy information' and that qualitative researchers should develop methodological and ethical procedures for handling it, as have quantitative researchers.

4. The directors of Project Metropolit, a Swedish longitudinal sociological project which became a *cause célèbre* (see Akeroyd 1988: Appendix), were credited with knowing 'more about these people than these people remember about themselves' (TDCR, 1986: 24). Re-meeting a person mentioned in his sixteen-year-old fieldnotes, Bond found that

> the memory and the vignette were now mine and not his; both he and Kafa accepted the authority of my fieldnotes and memories. I had entered their personal (or individual) histories and, in a minor way, framed the events of their past. (1990: 283)

5. Compare Pfaffenberger's 'verbatim field notes' with his 'expanded, retrospective version' (1988: Figs 1 and 3).

6. The Public Service Commission, State of New York, has produced a proposal to establish principles of privacy in telecommunications. The TDCR (1990c) report includes material from a background paper by E.M. Noam: social research is not mentioned in his list of countervailing societal interests that must be balanced against privacy (TDCR, 1990c: 12).

7. The privacy problem in relation to data systems involves violations which might result in damage or distress to the data subject. Discussions of this in social research have mainly concerned the notion of intrusion by researchers resulting in harms or wrongs to researchees, mainly as a result of publication. Sensitivity, privacy and confidentiality are relative between persons, and further differentiated by class, age, gender and national legal traditions.

8. I include very brief summaries of some parts of that discussion. Whether the problems I identified were (or still are) spurious, genuine but tractable, or intractable (Teitelbaum, 1983: 13) was not then and still is not clear.

9. See Bing (1980) on the use of identifiability, referability, systematicity and technology for this purpose.

10. Council of Europe, Recommendation No R(89)2, 'To Member States on the Protection of Personal Data used for Employment Purposes', Ch. 1.3. (TDCR, 1989a).

11. See Akeroyd (1988: 205–7) for a discussion of these issues, based on the clarification of the problem by Thom and Thorne (1983) and the development of their ideas by Greenleaf and Clarke (1984).

Retrieval from multimedia databases such as those described by Shetler will be even more complicated. These use a new category of data types – binary large objects or BLOBS: 'Text BLOBS contain valid text characters . . . Byte BLOBS are binary data streams that can contain any object . . . or any digitized data. . . . a BLOB could be very large (up to 2 gigabytes)' (Shetler, 1990: 221).

12. On Springdale see Vidich and Bensman (1964). Recent examples include Scheper-Hughes (1981) and Boonzaier et al. (1985). Moyser (1988: 131–2) comments on the problems posed by elites.

13. This has been partially achieved by a Videodisc Project about the Naga which includes film sequences, photographs, sound recordings, field diaries, letters and other printed and manuscript materials referring mainly to the pre-1947 period, but excludes trivial items and those which might cause personal offence or political embarrassment to living people (Macfarlane, 1990).

Lyman's (1989) and Walsh and Gordon's (1989) discussions of electronic distribution and hypertext technologies are concerned only with academic authorship, not with the interests and rights of researchees.

14. Gold (1989: 107, n2, citing Ripp, 1987: 74–9) also suggests that digital-image processing is an answer to the major ethical weakness of visual data – their depiction of research subjects – but is not concerned about legal aspects of identifiability. Inadvertent replication should not be lightly dismissed: Appell (1978: 10) achieved this in one of his disguised ethical case studies.

15. Identification, linkage and retrievability are troublesome for quantitative researchers; and it may be extremely hard (if not technically impossible) to ensure that no one is ever identifiable through correlation, either directly or by confusing the level of aggregation (Bing, 1986: 86–8; see also Hofferbert, 1977; Bulmer, 1979; Boruch and Cecil, 1983; Raffe et al., 1989: 21–2).

16. An excellent information source for publications on this and other topics in information technology is *Computers and Control Abstracts* (Science Abstracts series C).

17. I cannot recall any security-related products in G.D. Garson's regular listings of products in *Social Science Computer Review*; and its only paper on ethics (Martin and Martin, 1989) is addressed primarily to computer professionals.

18. This was stated in the Council of Europe's third conference on developments in data protection in 1987.

19. This list of actual and possible uses by governments, companies and individuals of information about people's actions, relationships, consumption patterns, etc. provided by existing informational facilities should give everyone pause for thought.

20. This followed a statement by the US Appeals Court justices as to what a claim to scholar's privilege might include.

21. I had found puzzling the absence of comment by Swedish sociologists about the implications for qualitative research; but there are virtually no qualitative sociologists in Sweden (Emeroth, 1988)!

22. Boruch and Cecil (1983) was published in a quantitative studies series and does not discuss fieldwork and other forms of qualitative research.

23. This I presume was Project Metropolit. The matter was rather more complex than her brief mention suggests (see Akeroyd, 1988: Appendix).

24. A draft directive issued by the European Commission in 1990 set out new and tougher pan-European guidelines for data protection laws, to come into force at the end of 1992. General data protection principles will be extended to cover paper-based information systems.

# 7

# Method and Madness in the Application of Computer Technology to Qualitative Data Analysis

## *John Seidel*

This chapter reflects on my own experiences applying the computer to the analysis of qualitative data, and on the contacts I have had with other persons engaged in this task. Personally, and professionally, I have made major commitments based on the assumption that the adaptation of computer technology to the needs of qualitative researchers is positive and desirable. Yet, in the process of using this technology, and in talking with others who are currently using it (or are contemplating using it), I have also become convinced that it has a dark side. Therefore, rather than engaging in my usual tasks of proselytizing for the use of computers in qualitative research, and writing about a computer program that I am personally quite fond of, I would like to discuss what I feel is the dark side of this technological advance. I still am committed to the position that the computer can have positive effects on qualitative method and data analysis. None the less, I have a sense of how it can also lead to some interesting forms of research behavior that I shall call analytic madness. These include:

1. an infatuation with the volume of data one can deal with, leading to a sacrifice of resolution for scope;
2. reification of the relationship between the researcher and the data;
3. distancing of the researcher from the data.

Before continuing, I want to make it clear that these are not intrinsically bad things. Rather, they are things that disturb my qualitative sensibilities. Further, I am distressed to think that I have written a computer program which is contributing to what I perceive as forms of analytic madness. On the other hand, I am sure that the things I am calling forms of methodological and analytic madness are, for others, forms of methodological and analytic ecstasy.

## Technology as a double-edged sword

The conduct of qualitative data analysis has always been, to a certain extent, an artefact of the technology available to the qualitative researcher. Further, I would argue that technological innovation in qualitative research has always been a double-edged sword. For example, the emergence of the small, inexpensive audio tape recorder in the middle of the twentieth century (late 1960s and early 1970s) marked a major transition for a discipline that had, up until then, primarily based its analyses on data records produced by pencil and paper note-taking. (Some might argue that the technology of the typewriter had a significant impact on qualitative research. I would counter that it only amounts to a direct extension of the paper and pencil technology. In any event, I choose to pass by the typewriter, and also the emergence of inexpensive photocopying, and pick as my starting point the emergence of the inexpensive cassette audio recorder.)

Jack Douglas, in his 1976 book on fieldwork, takes a cautious view on the introduction of audio tape technology into fieldwork. While he does see its potentials, Douglas also recognizes its dark side.

> Recording devices are the technological invention with probably the greatest potential use in field research. Because of this potential they pose a strong temptation to the beginning researcher, one that can easily lead him astray. Some researchers have been almost transfixed by recording devices, so that they come to define their research settings and their theoretical interests in society as a whole in terms of these devices. (1976: 32)

Douglas, in addition to being concerned about how research settings and theoretical interests might become artefacts of audio tape technology, is also concerned about how it might restrict, rather than enhance, the researcher's access to parts of the social world. He specifically argues that excessive reliance on audio tape recording will mean that the researcher will begin to have access only to public data and will lose access to private data and events that people are concerned about revealing.

Whether Douglas is right or wrong about this is not an issue here. What is important is his argument that the introduction of a new technology into the research process has potentially negative consequences. I interpret his principal concern as being that research and data analysis will be determined by the technology; methodological, theoretical and substantive concerns will become artefacts of technology. I am sensitive and sympathetic to this issue.

Yet, I must confess that I personally cannot function without audio and visual tape in my research. Further I would argue, against Douglas, that the use of this technology allows me access to phenomena that would be impossible to analyze and understand without such technology. But I (and I don't think that I am an isolated case) rarely if ever reflect or consider the potential dark side of my choice of technology. I am a child of the mid-twentieth century whose first fieldwork experiences were based on tape-recorded research. I take the audio tape recorder for granted. Finally, when I look at what the audio tape allows me to do, I have to conclude that what Douglas might call forms of methodological madness are, for me, forms of methodological ecstasy.

Given this, I hope that what I have to say about the relationship between computer technology and qualitative data analysis is not taken as polemicizing, or methodological moralizing (although I do have my own ideological quirks and preferences). Rather my purpose here is to reflect on, and hopefully sensitize qualitative researchers to, issues which we generally do not bother ourselves with.

### Madness 1: Trading resolution for scope

*A fascination with volume*
In my contacts with qualitative researchers I have discovered that many seem to have become infatuated with the idea of collecting and managing large volumes of data. For better or worse, the application of computer technology to the analysis of qualitative data has become a means of aiding and abetting this infatuation.

I will not condemn the collections of many thousands of pages of transcribed interviews. In some cases this may indeed be an appropriate thing to do. But sometimes I become concerned when a graduate calls me for information about the ETHNOGRAPH, and then describes an interview study involving 60 one- to two-hour interviews over a six-month period.

When I hear this type of story, two questions come to mind: (1) How carefully can a person read and meaningfully understand this volume of information? (2) How will the analytic approach be shaped by the sheer volume of data? My concern is not with whether or not the researcher should do this. Rather, I am concerned about how the nature of the task will influence the analytic methods of the researcher and the ultimate insights that the researcher may be able to derive from the data. I believe that the volume of data will drive the analysis and that the researcher will end up missing interesting and important things in the data. This can have serious consequences for the ultimate analysis of the data.

Finally, and perhaps most importantly, I am concerned that maybe the student selected this approach simply because the technology now makes it feasible.

Again, let me emphasize that I am not saying that people should not be working with large volumes of data, nor am I saying that we cannot learn useful and interesting things from large-scale investigations like this. My concern is what will happen if computer technology shifts the overall thrust of qualitative data analysis in this direction.

*The hegemony of the distributional perspective*
I am confronting this dilemma in my own work, which involves the videotaping of interactions between nurses and women during the second stage of labor. In this work I go into labor and delivery rooms and videotape the final work of women giving birth to babies. Such labors can be very short, lasting only five or ten minutes. They can also be very long, taking up to four hours to complete. Most of the labors in our sample take between one half to two hours. So far we have collected over 20 tapes, of which we are intensively analyzing 10. Our transcripts of the audio portions of these tapes are between 30 and 100 pages long, with most being in the 40–60-page range.

One of the games that we are playing in our research, and which I have allowed myself to be victimized by, is the volume game. Volume is unfortunately conceived in terms of numbers of labors. When you start mentioning that you have only 20 or so labors in your sample, and that you are working with only 10 of these, some people feel a little uncomfortable. One of the reasons they get concerned is that they are thinking in terms of the needs of quantitative distributional studies. (And, indeed, our study does have a quantitative distributional component.) The object of a distributional study is to discover and account for variations across large numbers of labors in several different sites. This conflicts (although not absolutely or necessarily) with a qualitative concern with the structure and organization of particular labors.

Unfortunately, when the distributional perspective prevails, extended transcripts become treated as if they were survey questionnaires or quantifiable observation guides. Instead of focusing on the intricacies and particulars of a few labors, we end up with more superficial glosses of a lot of labors. I would argue that the question is not how many labors can we observe, but how much can we learn from a particular labor?

*Understandings based on mis-understandings*
When the analytic process is driven by a thirst for large numbers of

cases, time and energy become distributed across many cases. This means that the amount of time available to read, re-read and think about what happens in a particular case is diminished. Rather than analyzing identified phenomena, we begin to be reduced to counting the occurrences of those phenomena, analyzing the numbers we have generated, and then end up simply using our data to 'flesh out' or provide examples of the phenomena. Our attention and analytic energy are spread out over a large number of instances, and little analytic effort is put into any given instance.

This can be a problem in the following sense. One of our coding units in our data is something that we call a 'mockup'. This is a loosely defined and applied concept that is used to identify times when a nurse generates verbal descriptions of things that will be happening, or have just happened, in the labor. (Things that have already happened should probably be called 'formulations', but for the present we are lumping all these types of things together. We will deal with this conceptual muddle as our work progresses.)

Currently I, and a graduate student, are directing our attention to the things *we have chosen* to call mockups. One of the things we are discovering is that mockups are not discrete events, as our coding practices assumed. For example, we identified a 'mockup' occurring at a particular point in the labor. Then, after the passage of several minutes, we identified another 'mockup'. With our initial coding rules we have two mockups. But, when we started examining these two mockups, we found that the second mockup was an extension of the first. Further, we discovered that the second part of the mockup was actually a compound mockup: part of it was indeed an extension of the first mockup, and part of it was new. We discovered this by spending an afternoon contemplating these two examples. Our preliminary conclusion is that these two mockups must be understood in terms of each other, and also in terms of the general flow of behavior within which they occurred.

Another afternoon we looked at a string of three things we had coded as 'mockups' and concluded that they also need to be treated as a unit, even though they are separated temporally and, in regard to our transcript, spatially. Unfortunately, because of our coding rules, and because of the linear character of the transcript, each was separately identified.

Now if we had not intensively and exhaustively contemplated, analyzed and re-evaluated our understandings of this bit of data, we would have glibly asserted that we had located five mockups. But intensive analysis of these five mockups led us to the conclusion that we really only had two mockups, each of which extended across time and space. Further, our analysis indicates that each mockup has interesting properties, which we are using to develop a typology of mockups, which, in turn, should allow us eventually to generate a theory of mockups. If we are lucky, our theory will eventually allow us to explain how, when, where and why various kinds of mockups occur. Now some people might object that the issue here is not really the volume of data but the initial analytic interests and problems which drive the researcher. My concern is that, because computer technology allows us to deal with large volumes of data, we will be lured into analytic practices and conceptual problems more conducive to breadth analysis rather than depth analysis. We will start trading off resolution for scope.

In the example I have just described, we spent several hours working on about four minutes of data. We have thousands of minutes of data yet to analyze. Consequently, there is a lot of pressure for us to take a scope approach rather than a resolution approach in dealing with our data. Yet if we had not opted for resolution, I believe any understandings and analyses that we had developed about mockups would have been based on inadequate and incomplete understandings of the phenomenon.

## Madness 2: Reification of the relationship between the researcher and the data

This is not a new issue or problem in the analysis of qualitative data, but it is a problem which is probably being exacerbated by the application of computer technology to the analysis of qualitative data. From my perspective the problem has to do with the assigning of code words to identify segments of text. I have long publicly regretted the use of the term 'codeword', and the phrase 'coding the data', yet I unfortunately perpetuate it via the ETHNOGRAPH.

The problem I have with this term is the epistemological assumptions that researchers bring to it. For many researchers, identifying and naming things that they find in their data is assumed to be a simple, straightforward, unproblematic process. There really are such things as 'mockups' out there in the data, and they are readily and easily identifiable. For me, things like 'mockups' are not really out there; rather they are artefacts of a strange and peculiar relationship that I am currently having with my data. They derive in part from conceptual and intellectual baggage that I have been carrying around for many years, and from practical contingencies I have to resolve in dealing with the data – the most important contingency being that I must start making some kind of sense of the data.

Some of the people who have expressed an interest in using the ETHNOGRAPH have a completely different notion of what it means to 'code' their data. They really think that there are things out there that are simply waiting to be identified, collected and counted. These researchers seem to believe that they do not need to scrutinize, analyze and critically evaluate these things that they have collected and counted. They take the presence of these things in their data as significant just because they are there in certain quantities or proportions. This is a problem that I have encountered in my current research.

Jacqueline Wiseman, in her methodological appendix to *Stations of the Lost* (Wiseman, 1970) is one among many who has addressed this issue. Many times a single occurrence of something is more important, theoretically and analytically, than multiple occurrences of something. Further, the number of times something is identified as being 'out there' is problematic, as the discussion in the previous section indicates.

While working on the next version of the ETHNOGRAPH, I have been developing a feature that allows the researcher to generate quasi-frequency distributions and cross-tabulations of the occurrence and co-occurrence of codewords within and across files. I have been testing this new feature on my current data. One test was particularly interesting. One piece of conceptual baggage that we have developed is a distinction between 'responsive' and 'regulatory' behaviors on the part of a nurse during a uterine contraction. We have one videotaped labor where, based on viewing the tape, we had judged the nurse to be operating in a primarily 'responsive' mode, and felt quite secure about that assessment. The nurse did exhibit some instances of 'regulatory' behavior, but these seemed to be secondary to her general forms of behavior. I decided to do a frequency check on the number of 'regulatory' versus 'responsive' forms of behavior we had identified and discovered, much to my dismay, that there was about a 50–50 split. Both forms occurred with equal frequency!

Now suddenly we have an interesting measure. One inclination is to start looking at the gross distribution of 'regulatory' and 'responsive' forms of behavior across a large number of labors. Some would be 'high regulatory', some would be 'mixed', and some would be 'high responsive'. This seems like it might be a promising and potentially useful thing to do. But at this point we need to stop and think for a minute. The thing we need to think about is exactly how did some things become identified as being either 'regulatory' or 'responsive'. By taking a resolution approach to the data, we are beginning to discover that our ideas of what counts as being regulatory or responsive are problematic. In fact, we have been biased in our 'coding' of segments as 'regulatory' or 'responsive'.

Some of our identifications change when we change the coding rules. We have also come to identify new forms of pushing sequences which had previously been 'coded' as examples of either 'responsive' or 'regulatory' pushing sequences. These new forms have been identified and coded as 'negotiated' and 'mixed' pushing sequences.

The point here is that we must be very careful about how we treat the coding process and what we do with 'coded' data during the analytic phase. My perspective is that the things we identified in our data are artefacts of a relationship we have with our data. The danger is that we will start taking these things for granted. We will reify these things as objects and then base our understandings of the phenomena on these reified objects and, in the process, lose the phenomena.

**Madness 3: Distancing the researcher from the data**

The final form of madness that I want to address has been partially addressed in the previous two sections of this chapter, but I also feel that it deserves some attention in its own right.

Recently I read a paper that told about the author's use of the ETHNOGRAPH. One concern expressed by this author was that the use of the computer had separated him from his data. I was quite shocked. The design of the ETHNOGRAPH is intended to keep returning the researcher to the data. The researcher has initially to read a hard copy of the data to begin the sense-making process. Once a coded scheme has been developed, that coding scheme reorganizes the reading process by generating new collections of parts of the data file that still have to be read and analyzed in order for the researcher to get on with the work. Given this, I had envisioned that the ETHNOGRAPH would be a vehicle for enhancing the researcher's relationship with the data. But this researcher felt that it had been diminished. Quite frankly I was distressed.

Another researcher called me up and said that he missed having his piles of xeroxed copies and note cards lying around. He felt that he was missing something. I told him not to worry. The program did not eliminate or reduce the number of piles of paper. Rather it simply organized and multiplied them. In no time at all he would be swimming in paper.

The point here is that many qualitative researchers really value close involvement and interaction with their data. And some computer programs do in fact diminish this relationship. Further, the next incarnation of the ETHNOGRAPH will aid and abet this process with its limited quasi-statistical capabilities. I have already suggested some of the problems with this type of feature in the previous sections.

Yet others see that one of the advantages of the application of computer technology to qualitative data analysis is its ability to do data reduction for them. In particular, Ray Padilla has shown me some very interesting work involving generating cross-tabulations of the coding of transcripts of focus groups. To me, this is a form of madness, but to these researchers this is a form of methodological ecstasy. It allows them to move forward in new directions and reach new understandings.

I have no objection to this. My concern is that qualitative data analysis might get reduced to this, and that qualitative researchers might start working in this manner, not because it is the best or most appropriate way to proceed, but because the technology makes it easy for them to work in this way.

## Conclusions

My concerns are not unlike Jack Douglas's concerns over the introduction of audio recording technology into the conduct of qualitative research. Douglas did not condemn this technology; in fact he saw many potential benefits from its use in qualitative research. His concern was not that it would be used, but that people would become so infatuated with it that it would drive the research rather than serve the research, and that parts of the social world and social phenomena would be lost because of this.

I have to confess that I have become a researcher whose work has been dominated by audio tape technology. I cannot function without my tape recorder. I am not a skilled note-taker and fieldnote writer. What I work with is mostly what I can capture on audio and video tape. In this sense my work, my analytic interests and my conceptual concerns are dictated by technology. Yet I would argue that this technology has opened parts of the world that would otherwise have been closed to me. On the other hand, as Douglas has correctly pointed out, it has probably closed off other parts of the world which, if I had access to them, might cause me to change my analysis and understanding of the world that I study.

Similar questions need to be asked about our application of computer technology to the process of qualitative data analysis. I believe, and have based a substantial professional and personal commitment on this belief, that a lot is to be gained by putting computer technology to work for us as ethnographers. But I am also acutely aware of the dark side of this technology. Periodically I stand back and take a look at myself as a glassy-eyed person who is too easily impressed with what this computer program can do for him in his work. And then I think about what it might be doing *to* me, instead of *for* me. This does not mean that I am going to stop what I do. Nor does it mean that I do not have hopes for this technology and the contributions it might make to the process of qualitative data analysis. However, it does make me stop and think about what it might be doing to me and my work, and to the work of others, and whether or not, in the long run, I, and the people who use this technology, will really be better off. On the other hand, I know that the things I see as simply dark clouds have silver linings for other qualitative researchers. My hope is that the things I view as ecstasies do not become lost and transformed into forms of madness.

# PART THREE

# QUALITATIVE KNOWLEDGE AND COMPUTING

There has been a recent and significant move to harness developments in knowledge-based systems to qualitative analysis. Fischer and Finkelstein (this volume) drew on techniques from artificial intelligence, system specification, anthropology and formal semantics in their attempt to develop a computer-based formal method for the description of social behaviour. Using such methods they tried to analyse the social processes involved in arranging marriages in urban Pakistan. Fischer and Finkelstein argue that computer-based methods can help to overcome the difficulties in observing, recording and coherently representing social knowledge. Formal methods allow the representation of both declarative and procedural description within systems in which multiple agents engage in complex temporal behaviour.

In recent times the issue of formalization has been aired in debate over the systematization of qualitative analysis, where formal logic, mathematical sociology and rational choice theory have been applied to narrative descriptions based on fieldwork techniques. This has excited a concern with modelling human action, represented in this volume by the work of Heise, and elsewhere by that of Abell (1987) and others. Such interests are also apparent in Agar's work on inference from ethnographic data and on criteria of adequacy in their application. It would be fair to say, however, that practitioners remain sceptical, and much of this work receives closer attention in artificial intelligence, sociolinguistics and economics than in sociology.

Another recent development in computing has been the emergence of hypertext systems. Hypertext is a database management system that allows the user to 'connect strings of information using associative links' (Fiderio, 1988). Hypertext treats information in a non-linear way. Hypertext systems allow users dynamically to link information sources of various kinds and to move between them rapidly. The dynamic, associative and non-linear character of hypertext probably mimics quite well the heuristic and iterative processes typical of qualitative analysis. An ethnographer might wish, for example, to link together fieldnotes, interview transcripts, genealogical data, survey data and visual material, moving back and forth from one source to another as the analysis proceeds.

Hypertext is a potentially exciting development in the field of qualitative research, but one whose potential is only just beginning to be realized. Cordingley discusses the development of KANT, a hypertext environment. She describes the advantages of such a system while also undertaking the useful task of providing an assessment of the 'downside of hypertext tools'.

Agar, a pioneer of computer-based anthropological analysis and proponent of systematic discourse analysis, discusses in his chapter his strategic decision to postpone formalizing and testing a set of theoretical schema using a program he developed. This decision was based on both the epistemological and technological shortcomings of existing programs. Agar's argument suggests that we do need to be alive to the dangers of building rigid programs around partial assumptions and of retailing them as the advance to formalism that would gather all qualitative analysis under some consensual theoretical banner. However, it would be unwise to conclude that the programs do nothing to change the craft of qualitative analysis, and careful attention must be paid to the theoretical assumptions embedded in them.

# 8

# Social Knowledge Representation: a Case Study

*Michael D. Fischer and Anthony Finkelstein*

This chapter outlines the development and application of a computer-based formal method for describing social behaviour – and theories about that behaviour – to an ethnographic field study of the arrangement of marriages in an urban Punjabi community near Lahore, Pakistan. We suggest that by adapting techniques drawn from distributed artificial intelligence, system specification, anthropology and formal semantics it is possible to avoid the triviality often associated with formal descriptions of social domains on the one hand, and arid abstraction on the other. The chapter outlines some of the limitations and the horizons of the use of such methods in anthropology.

Arranging a marriage is one of the most important activities for the residents of Greentown, a community in Lahore, Pakistan. It is a complex and risky problem-solving enterprise with no obvious 'correct' or unique solution. There is no deterministic solution, and it is difficult to consider even an optimum solution. The outcome is not the product of a single individual; it is the joint result of interaction of a large number of people who share an interest in the outcome. Our research[1] over the past two years has sought to establish the resources available to solve this type of problem in general, and how these are combined and adapted to resolve specific instances of the problem.

There are an enormous number of ways in which people can solve a specific complex problem such as the arrangement of a marriage, and most are 'correct' even when they fail to correspond closely to a norm. The events of arranging are themselves embedded in a vortex of other events, some directly related to the activity, others having effects which are unexpected. Although we can give general accounts of how specific arrangements are undertaken, we cannot, and suggest that we can never, 'predict' how a specific case will develop for more than a short time. The indigenous experts fare better, but they too have a short horizon of prediction. Although the goal may be known in advance – arranging a suitable marriage –

the process of achieving this goal is dependent on the unfolding of events, both those precipitated by the actors, and those which occur incidentally.

**Why formal representation?**

When focusing on the relation between social behaviour and social knowledge, it is crucial to record the knowledge that people use for both the creation of their own and the interpretation of others' social behaviour. Unfortunately, knowledge is perhaps the most difficult aspect of social behaviour to observe, record and represent in a coherent manner. Inconsistencies, distortions and simple errors are common in descriptions of social knowledge. There are many reasons why these problems arise. The ethnographer may fail to note, observe or ask vital information. Indigenous consultants give either very specific case-related accounts or very general statements that apply to no specific cases. Consultants may be uncertain or unable to express their knowledge clearly and change prior statements without notice. Ethnographers may misunderstand what they are told. Understanding a complex social behaviour – the prerequisite for interpretation or production – is an inherently difficult task and serious problems arise from these difficulties, and lead to ambiguous, incomplete and inconsistent descriptions.

Although we can never describe any social situation fully, there is no reason why our *models* of social situations cannot be completely defined and the statements we make about these models derivable from the model and its definitions. Formal techniques based on the use of discrete mathematics and logic for building descriptions should enable us to overcome many of the major difficulties currently encountered in the building of an accurate picture of social knowledge: to resolve, or at least acknowledge, ambiguity in statements by reference to a formal semantics; to test a description for incompleteness and inconsistency in statements; formally to verify a description; to trace back components of a description to the originating statements and hence to provide a means to modify and validate a description at later stages of work.

Because of the enormous impact of the above problems, and others, in descriptions, one might expect that formal description techniques would be an accepted part of ethnographic practice. But this has not happened. Are social anthropologists irrationally conservative? Do they feel threatened by methods many of them do not understand? Or are there genuine problems with adopting formal techniques as part of an anthropologist's pragmatic armoury?

## Problems and pitfalls in formal representation

The bulk of work on formal representation applied to social science relates to information that is relatively easy to categorize and interpret. But most existing information about social phenomena is too complex to organize effectively in this manner (Donnan, 1988). The primary reason formal representation appears to have failed in social anthropology is the lack of a suitable match between the complexity of the system to be described (and the absence of adequate models for that system) and the expressive power of the formal language chosen. Also, some description languages are said to be 'formal' merely because of their use of mathematical symbols, not because they have a formal semantics. A descriptive system ought to be soundly based; otherwise there are few benefits in its use and many disadvantages.

The most serious shortcoming of past applications of algebraic- and logic-based descriptions to anthropological material is that these have largely ignored process. Social processes are responsible for people's knowledge (they are the evidence from which individuals form their knowledge), and are the medium of expression for this knowledge by individual agents. It is process which connects the various kinds of knowledge together. Any formal treatment that cannot represent process ignores a central problem.

Although applying a formal description technique requires considerable technical competence, it should be achievable by all intelligent and analytically minded people. The prerequisite of learning a formal description technique should not be that the practitioner be a creative mathematician. Equally, formal methods should be used to communicate practical techniques, not to make difficult techniques palatable. The act of introducing the description techniques and the training of new practitioners is an important point at which people may be discouraged from their use. To prevent this a well-planned strategy for technology transfer is essential.

Most people have no more intuition about understanding very complex social domains and writing lengthy formal descriptions of them than they have about writing error-free computer programs; they need guidance. The basis of such guidance should be a method – a set of rules for guiding and organizing the activity by which a formal description can be produced from observations. A method helps a practitioner to get from one point to another rather than simply describing how wonderful the end point (a formal description) will be when it has been reached. It must not, however, stultify; it should stimulate understanding by promoting a conscious approach to formal description.

Descriptions are written not as a self-contained activity, but as an integral part of the process of social interpretation. It should, therefore, be possible to establish ways in which formal descriptions can be used to initiate subsequent analysis. If the units of description or mode of presentation seem inappropriate, the description will be ignored. It is, however, equally dangerous to allow the description to predispose an interpreter to a particular interpretation strategy or embody premature interpretations.

## Requirements for formal representation schemes in ethnography

Ethnographic research involves the collection of rich and complex information. The level of complexity which the anthropologist desires to maintain compounds the problems of a formal description. We believe that formal description in anthropology can be made practical with the development of specific computer-based tools and guidance.

For anthropology it is not enough to go to the field to collect data, and then return home to attempt our formal analysis. Fieldwork is expensive and time consuming, and in general not repeatable. If our goal is to improve ethnographic description by adding formal description to our other established tools, the use of this new tool must begin in the field. This introduces a problem, since the constraints of fieldwork limit the amount of analysis that can be performed at the expense of data collection. At the same time we must ensure that we are not aimlessly collecting information.

The use of computer-based methods while in the field can diminish this problem. In devising a computer-based method for the formal representation of ethnographic data as they are collected, the method in practice must meet several criteria. During the collection phase the problem under study is neither well formed nor well understood. Methodological considerations demand that any formal or semi-formal representation and associated computer-based tools have at least the following capabilities:

1. It must have a mechanism for identifying and evaluating variation and non-exclusive alternatives.
2. It must be extensible – easy to add new facts and propositions and modify old facts and propositions.
3. It must not 'fail' despite conditions that are fatal to a deductive analysis of the represented information.

4. It must assist in the identification and representation of contradictions and conflicts within the model. Although many conflicts are a consequence of error by the ethnographer, many are not errors, and must be maintained in the knowledge-base. Conflicts and contradictions are what give form to a system, and there always appear to be competing models in a culture, even within a single individual of that culture.

In essence, we require a model which incorporates a large number of 'facts', 'rules' and other models of information, where each of these can be acquired and modified independently of each other – distributed, local models (local in the sense that their immediate domain is fairly specific and localized, and they are only implicitly dependent on other models). What is needed is a formal system within which both declarative description ('knowledge of') and procedural description ('knowledge for') (Geertz, 1976) can be represented, which can be reasoned in, and which can represent complex temporal behaviour by multiple agents.

**Ethnographic setting**

The research for the case study was carried out in Greentown, a peri-urban community in Lahore, Pakistan. Greentown is a relatively new community, growing from a few hundred people in 1974 to 20,000 by 1983, and an estimated 40,000 by 1988. About half of the population originate from 'katchi abadi' ('squatters' settlements') within Lahore. They were relocated to Greentown by the government to clear land for building. The government offered each of the residents a house and in some cases a government job, which are highly prized for their security.

The lives of these people were transformed: suddenly they had acquired the attributes associated with much higher status than their backgrounds would suggest – secure title to land, government jobs, improved secure incomes, piped water, sewage, and electricity. However, these changes were not sufficient to entail a rise in status. Increasing status requires repositioning oneself in many other areas: education, the conduct of women and children, various levels of political influence, one's real or constructed history, and the extension of these to the groups to which one belongs.

There are two fairly simple operational 'tests' or measurements for status: whom one is 'friends' with, and whom one can marry. The most noted aspect of social organization in South Asia is the Hindu caste system, which is generally interpreted as a hierarchical arrangement between groups. In Muslim South Asia, and Pakistan in particular, there are caste-like categories, called 'zat', which appear to have a ranking relationship between them, though nothing like the rigid hierarchy reported for Hindu caste.[2] Intragroup hierarchy appears to be the underlying structuring principle (Fischer, 1991). Rough inter-group rankings can be derived from intra-group rankings, but intra-group rankings cannot be derived from the inter-group rankings. Besides zat, there are other types of groups ranging from a household to a large cognatic kin group, all of which exhibit the internal/external structuring principle. This principle appears to be applicable at the macro-political level in Pakistan (Sherani, 1988).

In previous work in Greentown (1982/3) this problem was approached at a low level, using marriage as the focus. An attempt was made to relate the symbolic models of arranging marriages to the practical application of those models in Greentown. Data were collected about past, present and planned marriages, as well as less structured data about marriage and arranging marriages. The analysis of this 'low-level' material was relatively straightforward in anthropological terms, and formed the basis of an 'expert system' (Fischer, 1986a) which made reasonable predictions about the suitability of candidates for marriage. This research suggested that the transactional structure and values underlying arranging marriage are replicated throughout the economic and political structure of Greentown (Fischer, 1991). Marriage is not only the basic reproductive act of a social unit, but the prototype for all social relationships. Specifically, inter- and intra-group hierarchy should be derivable from the set of marriages contracted; the historical sequence of marriages is evidence for the evolution of group dynamics in the community.

This analysis was the motivation for the present study. It suggests a model of the society as a system, not a model of the society from the vantage point of one or more of its participants. However, if we assume that it is more than an artefact of individual agent activity, we should expect to find evidence in individual marriage arranging events to support this conclusion.

## The representation language

The formal scheme we have used in our case study is Modal Action Logic (M[A]L) (Maibaum, 1986), developed as part of the UK Alvey strategic initiative on software engineering – FOREST project. FOREST (Formal Specification Techniques) has concentrated on the specification of so-called real-time embedded systems such as lifts and intensive care patient monitoring. A real-time system is a system in which timing plays a critical role in its operation (it does not mean a system in which things must happen quickly). An embedded system is a system which operates in the context of, or is embedded within, other similar systems. Thus most social action, and hence the application of much social knowledge, is typically real-time and embedded.

M[A]L is a formal language for describing situations both in terms of structural relationships and in terms of the effects of actions by agents on those relationships. The latter capability is not common to most formal languages, but makes it ideal for describing the relationship between functional and structural models. Also, because actions are explicitly represented, computer simulations of a purely qualitative nature can be implemented, which permits a form of experimentation with the information in the representation. A description in M[A]L consists of a set of axioms and declarations. Axioms take the general form:

Pre-condition → [Agent, Action] Post-condition

This can be read as: 'If Agent performs Action and Action terminates, then given Pre-condition is true prior to Action, Post-condition is true afterwards (any state not mentioned in Post-condition is unaffected by Action).'

Thus for example (ignoring some details of quantification) we might express an axiom derived from our case study:

in_public(girl) → [girl,singing(suggestive(lyrics))] bad_habits(girl). (if the girl is singing suggestive lyrics in public then the girl has bad habits)

Classical axioms can also be used; for example:

bad_habits(mother) → bad_habits(daughter).
bad_habits(girl) → NOT marriageable(girl).

The logic is extended with deontic operators. Deontic operators are modal logic operators which express permissions and obligations. They have been extensively used to express legal rules. The operators are of two basic types, *permission/non-permission* (per) and *obligation* (obl). The operators have a precise formal meaning. An example of the use of permission is:

married(man) and less_than(wives,four) → per(man,marry).
married(woman) → NOT per(woman,marry).

Deontic operators can also be used in post-conditions. For example, the use of *obligation* in:

handicapped(child(sibling)) → [sibling,requests(marriage)] obl (agree(marriage)).

Interval temporal operators are used to associate actions with intervals of time and to express relations between those intervals. For example:

after(family(boy),formal_visit) → per(family(girl),formal_visit).
before(family(girl),formal_visit) → obl(family(boy),formal_visit).

A further operator ('big obligation') OBL (Agent, Action, Formula) is used to oblige an agent to perform an action prior to a logical formula becoming false. For example:

after(formal_visits) → OBL (father,consult(relatives),object (relatives)).

Refinements to M[A]L include the ability to combine actions in series, in parallel and non-deterministically.

Associated with M[A]L is an elicitation and formalization method – called, with tongue firmly in cheek, *Structured Common Sense* (Potts et al., 1986). A range of graphical and tabular techniques are used to incrementally build complex formal descriptions. The method includes a basic strategy for writing formal descriptions along with hints and tips about what to do in particular situations. We have modified this somewhat for the present research, but essentially it provides a framework for isolating the agents, the properties of agents, the actions associated with agents, and the outcomes of those actions in different contexts. This agent/action analysis greatly facilitates the conception and translation of the scurce material into a form that can be modelled using M[A]L-based representations.

## Applications methodology

A large part of our motivation for undertaking the research was to assess the value of being able to examine the consistency of the information collected in the field while in the field so that further information could be collected on those areas where insufficient information existed or inconsistent information emerged. In many cases inconsistent information remained inconsistent, but we were able to minimize error on our part in these cases. By simulating the effects of rules and statements in discussing individual cases, lines of enquiry were taken that might not have occurred otherwise.

Although this research aimed to develop a methodology for using formal descriptions with ethnographic material, this was done in conjunction with existing ethnographic practice in so far as was possible.

The time allocated for fieldwork was approximately three months, from 1 July until 1 October 1988. Although this is a relatively short period of time for complex fieldwork, the task was simplified because the topic, arranged marriages, had been studied within the same social groups extensively during 1982 and 1983, and contacts made within these groups had been maintained.

Preparation for fieldwork consisted of developing a methodology for the research and preparing computer-based tools to assist in the coding of rules and observations collected in the field. Much of the methodological work had been carried out from 1985 to 1988 (Fischer, 1986b and forthcoming). The tools were developed in the Turbo Prolog language. Despite some major departures from 'standard' Prolog, Turbo Prolog was selected because it was inexpensive, featured relatively fast execution times, and had a well-developed set of predicates for maintaining databases, a useful resource since it was essential to maintain references to the source texts that were the basis of the coded rules.

The version of the Prolog program[3] used to evaluate the translated statements was cumbersome but workable. After translating and coding the material, initial conditions were set manually, and then the rules were repeatedly called. Those rules which applied to the conditions set reported themselves, and set conditions which subsequent rules could apply to. If, as was often the case, the program 'stalled' or 'cycled' (repeated the same rules with no progress) we had to investigate what further rules or conditions were needed, and either code them or gather more information. This activity, in conjunction with the agent/action analysis, was important in directing the overall research.

A number of problems were encountered in the development and use of this method of representation and the computer-based tools to support it. During the fieldwork an attempt was made to translate major propositions and assertions derived from observations and interviews into Prolog predicates and to test these against the growing proposition base to identify areas of inconsistency and insufficient information to feed into future interviews and observations. This process was only partially successful in the field; it was difficult to keep up with the information as it was collected. So, although a broad framework was maintainable, it proved impossible to deal with all the information in the field using the computer representation. Selection was necessary, and selection, of course, biases the results. None of these problems was unexpected, but there was some disappointment as the gap between material collected and material processed increased.

The methodology we used for collecting information was for the most part standard ethnographic practice. The computer-based representation assisted us with the central ethnographic problem: which questions to ask and contexts to observe. Interviewing was supplemented by modelling of two sorts after each interview – the modelling of the interview material translated into a simplified form of Modal Action Logic and evaluations of the translations within a logical system. The point of this modelling was not to create a formal or semi-formal description; the latter is a means, not a goal. The goal was to determine information required to establish the logical consistency of what people were telling us. One of the major uses of the formal translation was to establish what we did not know about what we needed to know.

For example, one domain is how the reputation of various family members influences a woman's marriage chances. If we look at the problem from a statistical perspective, the norm is fairly clear: mother's reputation is most important, followed by older sisters, younger sisters, brothers, and father. However there is a lot of variation, and the statistical norm does not really match other aspects of reputation. For example, a great deal of mother's, sisters' and female ego's reputation are derived from father and brothers, yet they are ranked lowest in the particular context of marriage chances. What is clearly needed is some information which 'explains' this apparent inversion, or at least distortion, of a ranking which in almost every other domain puts male members at the higher end. We thus required further information which related the public status of men to the private status of their women, not as mirror images of each other but as different views of the same situation which work together within the social framework of marriage. In other words, the structure is more complex in the other domains than had been suspected before. Women may derive their reputation from men, but men derive theirs from their women. This conclusion is not new, and had been strongly stated in previous work (Fischer, 1991). What is new is the significance of the conclusion. Previously we produced an analysis based on reputation as control, and the most primitive form of control as that over women. This argument is not sufficient. Women have control as well, and this is clearly reflected in the ranking given above. Responsibility and control are not concentrated with a specific role, but distributed between a number of agents. This generalization not only accounted for this case, but also leads in a new direction, reconciling some problems with control of the marriage decisions themselves. Earlier statements from consultants about how it is really the mother who decides the marriage take on new significance as well as the general analysis of the structure of control and reputation.

We are not claiming that these conclusions were not possible without some kind of formal framework, just that in a previous period of two years' research they were not found, whereas they became apparent within the first three weeks of the research of 1988. The process of attempting to reconcile differing statements by investigating specific areas of difference led more efficiently to the conclusion; it helped to frame the questions and the interpretation of the results, and helped to avoid endless detail which was not of primary importance to the problem. The methodology did not arrive at the conclusion, the anthropologist did. The methodology did help lay the problem out and expose possible areas of relevancy with respect to conflicts in the data.

## Ethnographic results

Following is a brief ethnographic sketch of information relating to aspects of arranging a marriage. It is not intended to be complete, but should give an idea of the flavour of the information that was collected and the kinds of material we are seeking to describe.

The residents of Greentown readily discuss the problem of making a marriage for their children. In general, the preferences given for marriage are based on degree of genealogical closeness. A rough order relative to the parent, the usual decision-maker, is:

1. same-sex sibling's child
2. opposite-sex sibling's child
3. parent's sibling's child's child
4. spouse's sibling's child
5. other relation
6. maximal lineage (zat) member's child
7. Sayyid's (highest-ranking zat) child (universally approved by non-Sayyid)
8. a good family, any zat of equal 'izzat' (honour, respect, responsibility) (not universally approved)

These preferences basically follow a model of degree of relatedness, and the list is a simple ranking model of the different segments of Punjabi social organization. This is further substantiated by other factors that are related to social organization, which were given but were not included in this list, such as sharing a place of origin. Further information from interviews reveals other cross-cutting factors which enter into the marriage arranging process, for example:

1. *Obligations to kin* In some circumstances there is a strong obligation to kin over marriage. Although there is no strict 'right' to FaBrDa in the Punjab, there is some obligation between siblings regarding the marriage of their children. This obligation becomes stronger if there is a need on the part of the sibling; for example, if the sibling's child is a little unattractive, or if the sibling has problems with financing a wedding. The obligation also holds between other relations, but is less.
2. *Status constraints* Ideally marriages are between equals. In practice marriages are between putative equals. Marriage has a function of validating increases in status, which is a common occurrence in contemporary Lahore.
3. *Financial constraints* Although less important in principle than the previous, the cost of marriages is an important factor in practice. Marriages are very expensive, especially between non-relatives. In Greentown marriages can easily cost one to two years' household income.

A male (and his parents) starts to think about marrying after completing his education and after getting what appears to be a steady job; 27–32 is a good age for getting married, and 25 is a young age in Greentown for getting married. Very few get married without finishing education and without a good job.

A female should be married from the age of 18 to 23/4, and should have a good education, know a little English, and good Urdu (which women have not known well in the past). Education is becoming a necessity for females as well as males. Punjabis note that Bihari girls marry much younger and without education, from 14 to 18 years old. This is confirmed from census records collected in 1982.

Some of the things that are considered in evaluating the possibility of a marriage are:

- good zat
- good people
- business
- educated family
- beauty and good health
- 'Haq mehr' (a kind of bride wealth, more like a deposit against divorce) is said to be considered only after the marriage and 'jihez' (dowry) is variable in its consideration . . . some want a lot, and some nothing at all. It is becoming unfashionable to demand jihez, but it is often expected from the bride's family.

Some young men say that, for themselves, they do not care about beauty, only that they share understanding – when he says something, she understands. He wants an education, but will accept intelligence. He thinks that education gives some security about understanding.

*Principals in involvement*
- If parents are alive, they are most concerned equally. The paternal grandparents may have considerable influence. Maternal grandparents may also have some concern.

- If parents are not alive then the paternal grandparents if they are alive, otherwise the uncles or aunts, with the paternal having precedence and males over females.

- Otherwise the elder brother/sister also sometimes as in the above clause and sometimes they take over instead of the uncles or aunts.

- Father's younger brothers and older brothers have the formal right amongst collateral relatives of the parents, but sometimes the mother's brother (MoBr) is left in charge. MoBr that are also in the patrilateral line are especially prone to this favour, and especially if the MoBr is the older of the uncles.

*Informal visits*
This is a part of the initial search for a candidate for marriage to one's son or daughter. It would not take place between close relatives, but as described may be undertaken not with the intention of finding a spouse, simply as a consequence of a social visit. Women, who visit around the neighbourhood, keep a look out for suitable spouses. Sometimes these informal visits are made with intent, and the introduction is made via a neighbour or other intermediary. Sometimes they are chance meetings. If such a meeting is fruitful, then the corresponding mother tells the intermediary that she is suitably interested, and a similar meeting is made by the other mother, on an equally informal basis. If no more is said, the matter is dropped.

*Formal visits*
Two formal visits are made shortly after the informal visits (if they are required). If the prospective mates are close relatives, then the visits are not necessary and probably do not occur. The first formal visit is from the boy's family to the girl's family. The boy's group is obliged to consist of mother and father, if alive, and often the

grandparents, both paternal and maternal, and the sisters. The uncles and aunts may go, but only as observers. Some report that they are bad, and talk too much. It seems, though more will have to be done on this, that the relative may use this as a deliberate ploy to stop the marriage. Consultants suggest this is either for reasons of jealousy, or to save the child for their own child, although there may be a slight fissure between them. However, it is unclear how the relative manages to go if such a problem is known to exist. Sometimes the younger brother will go as well, and he too is a passive participant. The elder brother and the prospective groom do not go. The maternal grandparents are sometimes necessary, but not always. If they go they are active. If ego is male and there are no sisters, then no replacement need be made, unless the mother is dead or too old. In that case an aunt and/or older female cousins will be sent. On the receiving side are the Mo,Fa,FaFa and FaMo if in the home, the ElderBr (or Br if no ElderBr), the ElderSi (or Si if no ElderSi), and any others including friends and neighbours.

The questions asked in the formal visits are fairly standard, principally about their clan membership, the educational qualifications of the family and the prospective mate, the jobs of various members of the family, the housemaking skills of the girls, and, possibly most important, the kinds of marriages already contracted by the other family. There is also information which is observed rather than asked: is the home clean or not? Are people wearing clean clothes? How do they respect us? How do they serve food and tea? Were important relatives not present?

Other information is gathered from the neighbours and friends of the family. The purpose is to confirm the information of the interview, to get the neighbours' opinion of the girl, her qualifications, her respectability, and on the habits of the family; for instance, are they a religious family? Some of the extra information that could have an effect on the proceedings includes confirming the zat and background of all family members – have any of the sons given 'talaq'[4] divorce, do they smoke hashish or drink or gamble? People place great importance on making sure the women of the family are considered respectable, with different importance placed on different categories of female role (mother, sister, etc.).

The second formal visit is from the girl's people. The parents and both grandparents have the same role. The elder and younger brothers must go, and are active. The sisters may go, but are not active. Ego is present, of course. The uncles and aunts have the same role. Further informal visits may be made in any order. They are primarily for sizing the families up.

**Conclusion: exterior knowledge**

Arranging a marriage is not picking someone off a list. Although there is an elicited ranking order for marriages, any of the marriages on the list can be later defined as a 'good' marriage within the proper context. This context is not static, but negotiated, not only between the parties exchanging children but within the kin group as a whole, and especially between the parents of the child. Each takes what is essentially the same set of categories, with roughly the same set of abstract values, and finds different interpretations when applied to a specific situation. There is no one correct choice, although in most cases a 'correct' choice will emerge.

Most forms of long-term male/female socio-sexual liaison appear to converge to a single process: location of a suitable candidate, research on the suitability of the candidate, informal negotiation between the respective families, and formal negotiations. Possible exceptions are marriage by capture and marriage by elopement, for which it was difficult to gain access to enough expertise or examples, both forms being very rare for first marriages, and both forms being founded on principles that are more or less inverse to those of other forms. All of the stages in the process appear to be oriented to establishing to a refined degree the match between the two candidates with respect to status, background, economic criteria, family custom, expectations of the candidates and families, and temperament, among others. This evaluation is a very complex problem, and is the central research problem from this study. The convergence appears to hold for low-, middle-, and high-status groups, although there are minor variations in timing, ritual and weighting of criteria for the different status groups. In general, all potential liaisons are evaluated as if the criteria for a legitimate engagement were to be met – to the extent that in cases of proposed informal socio-sexual liaisons the opinions of the family and parents about the potential candidate are sought, although the motive is not revealed and thus the negotiation stages are omitted. However, these liaisons can be converted into marriages, so this omission can be interpreted as an interruption of the general process.

This last conclusion was a good example of arriving at a conclusion in the field which we are fairly certain would not have been suspected until after returning. The opportunity to talk to people engaged in cohabitation without marriage had not been available in prior research, so the topic was pursued with some interest. The initial assumption was that this act of deviance might represent a new attitude in the middle-status groups (all the consultants in this case were university students). However, in doing the agent/action analysis it became apparent that, while it was deviant in terms of local definitions, it was not deviant with respect to the primary principles underlying engagement and marriage; in this case the participants simply took on more of the roles themselves, since the arrangement could not possibly have the sanction of their families. So, although it was a very 'modern' practice from the participants' point of view, the material and methods they used in practice were drawn from the same mould as the traditional means of arranging a marriage.

As we have suggested, in the field segment of this research the major benefit was from the specification methodology, rather than the resultant formal or semi-formal translations that emerged from this specification. This is not too surprising in retrospect. Time in the field is best spent collecting new information. The purpose of the specification methodology is to ensure that there is adequate knowledge about the system to be described. A formalism is of no value to a science unless there is such a methodology, a model which allows us to connect the formal system to the rather less tidy world of events and symbols which is the object of our study. The specification method provides this connection. It provides a means of representing information so that we can make a meta-formal interpretation based on whatever formal interpretation emerges; it ensures that, however badly we distort the information that we encode, we have a record of that distortion, and can adjust our interpretation accordingly.

The formal model that we were attempting to use helped in the research more for what it demonstrated to be lacking than for any positive inferences derived from the formal representation. If we assume a consultant's view to be basically correct by definition (and this is by and large the attitude in social anthropology), then the gaps in a formal model of these views must represent areas of enquiry; these gaps must be at least partially filled before it is productive to proceed.

Finally, we will make a few comments on the future directions this research suggests. The theoretical position at the beginning of this research viewed human problem-solving in social situations as a social activity – different people coordinating to solve a problem, each with their own interests that were somehow joint in a particular context. Because of the differences, it was assumed that the systemic view (the analytic view) would vary from the views of the participants in the situation; they would not be entirely aware of the situation they were jointly creating with others. However, it was implicitly assumed that each individual had a more or less complete view and more or less complete knowledge about their own activities. One of the consequences of a social knowledge-based orientation was that we had to examine the knowledge that people were bringing to solve the problem under scrutiny – arranging a marriage. In examining this, by the end of the fieldwork it became apparent that the situation was rather different from that which was assumed. It was true that many different individuals contributed to the solution. What appeared to break down was the assumption of complete knowledge. A great deal of the activity that people engaged in was the use of other people's knowledge (or their assumed knowledge) in meeting their goals, and correspondingly providing the use of their own knowledge to others. In other words, a lot of the knowledge that people appeared to mobilize was knowledge about mobilizing other people's knowledge – the use of knowledge that they did not know, but knew about.

If this analysis is correct it has profound consequences, for both formal and informal analysis. A view that has explicitly been taken in many social sciences is that of the cognitive, rational individual. Models of reasoning, problem-solving, decision analysis and cognition assume the more or less autonomous entity who has more or less perfect knowledge about a specific problem. Based on this analysis, it would appear that social groups are more than a cooperative convenience, but that many of the reasons for success depend on the distribution of knowledge as well as the distribution of effort.

Perhaps Goodenough's test of an ethnography as knowing what the indigenous experts know might be more aptly stated in terms of what they know how to mobilize in the way of knowledge than of specific knowledge they possess themselves. We must know the knowledge as well as account for the channels of use of that knowledge, whilst the native expert need only have knowledge of the channels outside their own direct competence.

### Notes

1. The research in this paper was supported under ESRC R000231113 (1988). The work has been continued under ESRC R000231952 (1989) and SERC/ESRC/MRC SPG8920734 (1990–1993).

2. Although a new study by D. Quigley (under review) suggests that the hierarchy in Hindu caste has been distorted.

3. The program implemented what is called in AI research a production system. In a production system the idea is to have a number of rules whose only direct reference to each other is through a global set of conditions. The rules match against and modify the set of conditions, which may permit new rules to be applied.

4. Literally 'I divorce thee', which uttered three times by the husband results in divorce.

# 9

# Event Structure Analysis: a Qualitative Model of Quantitative Research

## David R. Heise

In the spirit of reflexivity (Woolgar, 1988), I begin by quoting myself, and later I illustrate arguments by analyzing my past work. Whether this is indeed Escher-like reflexivity (a hand drawing the hand which is drawing) or mere egotism, it does provide materials that are useful. First the quote – a call for papers which I published on beginning an editorship.

> *Sociological Methodology* will continue to publish important papers in the established areas of quantitative analysis. In addition, however, I'll be making an active effort to expand the literature on methods of social taxonomy and on techniques for analyzing sequences of social events. Methodologies for abstracting rules of organization will be sought especially, though they must be empirically oriented. Also, I'll welcome papers presenting advanced developments in 'qualitative' areas like historical methods, content analysis, and ethnography. (Heise, 1974: ix–x)

This hortation sounds my current theme a decade and a half later as I offer something like what the editor ordered: a methodology for modeling sequences of social events, which facilitates abstracting rules of organization, and which applies specifically to qualitative data.

Event structure analysis (Heise, 1989) materializes expert understandings about processes that might be impenetrable to the uninformed. Dealing with recorded incidents, an analyst defines events, defines logical relations among the events, and defines how each event enables and expends other events. The result is a grammar of action accounting for recorded incidents, and this model can be displayed graphically, employed for simulations, and compared with related grammars for purposes of contrast or generalization. This methodology is most appropriate in the later stages of a qualitative research project rather than at the beginning, because it depends on having incidents recorded in transcripts, narratives or sound–image recordings and also depends on intensive labor by an analyst with expertise concerning the incidents.

In the following section I discuss the presumptions which circumscribe the methodology's domain of application and from which the methodology gains its power. The subsequent section employs historical data to demonstrate the kinds of analyses which can be done and to illustrate an end product. In the final section, I reflect on the generalizability, utility and future of the methodology.

## Required data and assumptions

Like every methodology, event structure analysis allies with certain kinds of data and a set of assumptions in order to obtain analytic power.

### Event descriptions

The focus is on social events – more precisely, on verbalized renditions of events by a culture expert providing indigenous readings of social activity (Geertz, 1973). The culture expert might be a native member of the culture or an outside researcher who has achieved *verstehen*. Whichever – the requirement is that the expert phrases descriptions not only so that any comparable expert can recognize the events, but also with reality constraints embedded semantically so that other culture experts can comprehend readily how the events are inherently structured. The assumption here is that event descriptions represent expert understandings of what can and cannot happen in reality, and uncovering the tacit logic in the descriptions reveals the structuring of reality as perceived by experts.

### Implication relations

Event structure analysis does not actually extract logical structures through semantic analysis of the event descriptions – that would be too demanding and risky. Rather event descriptions provided by an expert are fed back to the expert in order to obtain judgments about what implies what. Pair by pair the expert reports whether this event is required for that event. Experts themselves are the instruments for recovering the logic of their descriptions.

This elicitation process is facilitated through the application of syllogistic reasoning. For example, once an expert has reported that event Y requires event X, and event Z requires event Y, then there is no need for the expert to consider whether Z requires X: Z must require X, because Z requires Y and Y requires X. Drawing such inferences is essential once the number of events exceeds ten or so because then the number of pair-wise questions about event relations explodes to burdensome magnitudes if pairings are made mindlessly without taking advantage of prior answers.

Syllogistic reasoning with a large set of propositions is not all that easy for humans to do, but computers can obtain such derivations accurately and fast, and thus these kinds of elicitations end up being computer-assisted. Indeed, once a computer is brought in to the process, it is used as well to record data (the event descriptions and their logical relations) and to draw diagrams of the logical structure which is uncovered.

*Event series*

Yet even with computer assistance, it really is not practical to have an expert specify events involved in a process and describe their logical connections. For one thing, the expert may neglect crucial events no matter how often the computer prompts for something else related to the topic of interest. Moreover, the pair-wise consideration of event relations creates an overwhelming labor despite syllogistic reasoning. So the domain of application has to be more constrained in order to achieve practicality.

Event structure analysis deals with sequences of events. That is, rather than conjuring event descriptions out of context, the expert describes events which happened in specific incidents and considers those events in the order of their occurrence. One advantage of this approach is that the expert is much less likely to forget crucial events, especially if urged to give detailed descriptions of incidents. A second advantage is that the pair-wise questions about prerequisites can be reduced drastically in number – essentially by half – when considering events in serial order. The expert never needs to consider if later events were required for earlier events because the present is not influenced by the future according to a widely accepted metatheoretical assumption.

Focusing the elicitation on serially ordered events in actual incidents makes it fairly easy to obtain a model, and in the process one also acquires data for testing and improving the accuracy of the model.

**Dynamic assumptions**

A structure in which events are verbally defined and logically linked to each other turns into a production-system model for generating event sequences with the addition of three assumptions about how events condition each other. A production-system model is an action grammar that puts constraints on the strings of events that can occur over time.

The most obvious assumption is that an event cannot occur until all of its prerequisites are fulfilled. Thus in temporal sequences, the first occurrence of an event should be preceded by occurrences of all events which it logically implies.

A second assumption is that occurrence of an event depletes conditions produced by prerequisite events so, if the event is to happen again, the prerequisite events must happen again also. Thus, two different occurrences of the same event should be separated by occurrences of all the event's prerequisite events.

The third assumption is that an event ordinarily does not repeat unless conditions which it produced were depleted by some consequence – by an event that has the focal event as a prerequisite. Thus repetitions of an event should be separated by occurrence of a consequence.

A corollary of assumption two yields a further inference about intervening consequences. The corollary is this: when an event occurs it depletes its prerequisite events, and thereafter any other event with the same prerequisites cannot occur until the prerequisite events are repeated. Now shift focus to one of the prerequisites. The corollary means that it is impossible for more than one of that prerequisite event's consequences to occur without the prerequisite repeating.

Beyond these general assumptions, we also allow that some pairs of events (which have to be identified *ad hoc*) have a peculiar relation in which each primes and depletes the other. Entering your office and leaving your office is an example of such a pair: once you enter your office, you have to leave before you can enter again; and after you leave your office, you must enter once more before you can leave again. Clearly, if an event is in such a commuting pair, then repetitions of the event have to be separated by occurrences of the other event in the pair.

### Adjusting assumptions

Typically, an implicational structure and the assumptions about event ordering constrain event sequencing so stringently that the model cannot account for sequences of events in actual incidents. Then the assumptions may have to be weakened for some events.

The first assumption – that occurrences of events require prior occurrence of all prerequisites – can be relaxed by allowing that an event may be primed by occurrence of any of its immediate prerequisites instead of all of them. In other words, required events can be treated as disjunctive prerequisites rather than as conjunctive. Then the first occurrence of the focal event does not have to be preceded by occurrence of all prerequisites, only by occurrence of one prerequisite (and its prerequisites). Similarly when applying assumption two we do not expect every possible prerequisite to occur between repetitions of the focal event but only enough to prime the focal event again.

The second assumption – that events use up the conditions which permit them – can be weakened by allowing that occurrence of some particular event does not deplete the conditions produced by a specific prerequisite. Thereby we can expect a repetition of the focal event without necessarily having a repetition of the event whose conditions still remain in force.

Weakening assumption two also weakens the corollary of assumption two. Thus, if we allow that an event is not depleted by one of its consequences, then a single occurrence of the event might be followed by occurrences of several different consequences.

The third assumption – that the conditions created by an event have to be undone by other happenings before the event repeats again – can be eliminated for some particular event in a model. Doing so allows the focal event to repeat without being depleted by occurrences of a consequence in between times.

In the current implementation of this methodology, commutative event pairs ordinarily are not specified at the outset, so weakening assumptions about commutation is not a general issue. Rather, commutation typically is brought into a model after having weakened assumption two to the point that we no longer have interesting constraints on the orderings of some event and its consequences. At that point a commutation may be identified so as to require that repetitions of the event always are separated by an occurrence of one particular consequence.

Such adjustments in dynamic principles are the usual way of shaping a model so that observed event series are consistent with sequences of events which the model can generate. Sometimes, though, no such adjustment will correct an inconsistency, or a required adjustment would be clumsy or would not make sense at all. Then attention turns to adjusting the logic structure, or to looking for errors in data, or to the possibility that the model is inadequate.

### Adjusting logical relations
A logic structure constrains event sequencing by specifying which events have to precede occurrence of a focal event and which events might ensue from occurrence of a focal event. Thus the generative

ramifications of a model can be changed drastically by deleting a logical connection between two events or by adding one. Such changes are not to be done casually because they conflict with the best judgment of the expert who created the logic structure. However, sometimes even the original expert can be convinced that he was wrong in judging that one event is required for another when he sees the problems his judgment creates in interpreting sequences, or that he was wrong in judging one event as unrelated to another when he sees the opportunities for explanation which such a linkage provides. Then the logic structure reasonably can be changed to make the model more consistent with an observed series of events.

Changing the logic structure can change the meaning of at least one event, and therefore a corresponding change in descriptive phrasing may be required, too. Moreover, once an event is reconceptualized, there could be ramifications in judging how the event logically relates to still other events.

*Adjusting serial data*
Occasions do arise when no acceptable changes in assumptions or in logic structure will fix an inconsistency between a model and the serial record of events. There still is one more way to achieve consistency: change the record of events. Such changes are adopted only within the usual criteria of historical analysis (McCullagh, 1984) that the weight of the evidence, including the expectation provided by the model itself, supports the modification. This theory of error in qualitative data parallels error theory in quantitative research: observations are fallible, and reality corresponds to expectations generated by a conceptual model, providing that the model accounts for most observations.

*Rejecting a model*
The last resort is to scrap the model entirely, a most unlikely outcome if definitions of events and their interrelations were obtained from a competent expert, but a probable dénouement if data were obtained from novices or outsiders. For example, my own attempts to make models on topics where I am unlearned have yielded formalizations of ignorance which are intractably unadjustable so as to be consistent with series of observed events.

**Analyses**

The medium for performing the intricate analyses which are involved in event structure modeling is a microcomputer program called ETHNO (Heise and Lewis, 1988). The program can be employed directly by culture experts who are literate, or it can be used in computer-assisted interviews, or the program can be used by researchers who claim expert competencies (*verstehen*) concerning their topics.

Two of the major options in ETHNO are: 'Create a structure', which carries out computerized elicitation of events and logical connections; and 'Analyze a series', which tests consistency of a model with event series and which allows a model and serial data to be adjusted for better convergence. These routines will be examined in detail below.

The end product of ETHNO analyses is a model specified in terms of event definitions, a diagram of the logical relations among events, and delineation of the assumptions which turn the logic structure into a generative system.

## Data

Having already illustrated this methodology's applications in ethnography (Corsaro and Heise, 1990), content analysis (Heise, 1988) and the study of careers (Heise, 1990), I now want to illustrate the procedure as a form of historiography. I happen to know no body of historical events (never mind historic) so well as my own work, and that is why I ruminate about my past. The product of analyzing my professional activities and those of my associates will be a model of scientific activity, and it may be of some use in the sociology of science.

A time-ordered list of events related to the development of Affect Control Theory (ACT) constitute the data for analysis. Affect Control Theory (Heise, 1979; Smith-Lovin and Heise, 1988) elaborates the idea that people avoid events which create 'tension' in affective associations. Selecting low-tension behaviors yields normative action for people in specified roles. Selecting roles (instead of behaviors) to minimize tension corresponds to social labeling processes in which identities are assigned to people on the basis of their actions. Emotion reflects the amount and kind of tension produced by an experience.

ACT's mathematical model applies the theoretic principle, operating on databases from empirical studies in order to provide computer simulations of social interaction. In the simulations, actors are verbally characterized by identities alone or by modifier–identity combinations, and settings may be specified. Results of simulations include verbal predictions about the behavior of interactants, their emotions, and the social labels and traits which they would attribute to each other on the basis of normal behavior or disruptive events.

I assembled the list of ACT-related events from my own vita, from chronicles in ACT reports and publications, and from records in my own files. This provided a framework of career events (degrees, employments, publications, external fundings, editorships) and of activities by key associates (co-authors, students, correspondents). I then added events which in my view were critical parts of the research process – events like collecting data, collating data, analyzing data, estimating equations, etc. The preliminary list of 160 events was sent to two other highly active ACT researchers, Lynn Smith-Lovin at the University of Arizona and Neil MacKinnon at the University of Guelph, Canada, and each provided corrections and expansions related to their own participation in the research program.

Exploratory analyses with ETHNO revealed that additional events (for example, within-university fundings) had to be added in order to create a logical structure, and the extra details were recalled by searching files when possible. Also, as I continued working on this project, I recalled events with low salience (like publication rejections, grant denials, and work by students who had left the program long ago). Indeed, the pool of related events seems bottomless, and I have purposely included only events which were directly or indirectly consequential in some public way.

Considerable effort was given to obtaining a correct chronological order not only by year but within years. However, records often did not provide such fine grain, and I had to resort to reasoning and reminiscing in order to reconstruct the stream of events within busy years.

The final list of 298 events is too long to provide here, but Appendix 9.1 shows the beginning and the end of the data. Note that the events are characterized abstractly enough to reveal the repetitiveness of research activities.

*Mechanics of elicitation*
Elicitation was begun by selecting *Create a Structure* from ETHNO's main menu, selecting a framework appropriate for processing historical data, and naming the domain of events 'ACT'.

Events were entered in sequence. An event repetition was positioned in the serial record by entering the event description exactly the same as the first time or by entering the event's abbreviation.

In response to each non-repetitive entry, ETHNO asked questions in order to determine the logical relations between the last entered event (call it Event L) and prior events (for example, Event P). The question always had the same general form: Does *Event L* require

*Event P* (or a similar event)? An expanded phrasing of this question would be: Does an initial occurrence of Event L require the prior occurrence of Event P or of some other event which can serve as the functional equivalent of Event P? A 'yes' answer established a logical link between Event L and Event P. The program immediately assessed implications of this logical connection in order to reduce the number of subsequent questions.

An updated diagram showing the current logic structure appeared on the computer's screen as each event was processed.

After the logical relations of every distinct event were defined, ETHNO filed the event descriptions, the logical linkages and the event series for future use.

### Elicitation concerns

Appendix 9.2 illustrates dialogue with the computer during the elicitation phase and the kinds of thinking I did in order to answer questions about prerequisites; it also includes comments about ETHNO's operations. I purposely show a portion of my first effort (rather than the final elicitation which led to the model displayed later) in order to demonstrate how a model evolves during its construction: the 'Revision' notes focus on changes.

Entries into ETHNO were the phrases in the 'Action' column of Appendix 9.1 preceded by R (for researcher). For example, the first three events were:

R read
R funded locally
R contributed funding.

The terse phrasings, which were convenient during ETHNO analyses, are expanded to the semantic forms that actually influenced my judgments in Table 9.1.

Some of my initial phrasings of events were superseded because systematic processing of the data refined my conceptualizations about research (Appendix 9.2 gives some examples). In other cases, phrasing stayed the same but interpretations changed: for instance, initially university support for computer usage was included as an aspect of local funding, but that interpretation was dropped when it became evident that computer funding occurred automatically whenever needed and so it need not be noticed.

The final list of events includes some events that were not in the initial list at all. These eventually were added in order to account for complexities in incidents that were not obvious at first. For example, 'R wrote report' eventually had to be added in order to deal with intricacies of co-authorships.

I ultimately deleted a few events entirely; for example: 'R affiliated with ACT research program'. I never could decide when this event happened for other people, and I could not figure out how the event applied to myself. I finally decided that this was a projection I made onto other people when they initiated projects related to ACT rather than a decision others themselves made, and I removed the event from the corpus.

When answering questions about prerequisites, I typically recalled the specific incident and wondered what would have happened if the focal event had not been preceded by the specific prior event, and I decided that the prior event was not required for the focal event if I easily could imagine the focal event occurring in the circumstances even without the prior event. When unsure about the necessity of the prior event, I recalled other experiences in which the focal event occurred – including the communicated experiences of other researchers – to see if the prior event always preceded the focal event. A single instance of the focal event occurring without the prior event (or a functional equivalent) led me to discard the prior event as a prerequisite for the focal event. Thus my own experience in operating as an expert suggests that experts judge logical relations by applying the method of analytic induction (Znaniecki, 1934; Robinson, 1951) to a corpus of experiences stored in personal memory.

Thinking about prerequisites was rapid and easy when events were phrased well. When phrasing was 'off', I frequently had to ponder whether prerequisites were functionally equivalent to each other. Phrasing also was important in keeping me focused on certain actors (for example, in reminding me that I was considering only researchers) and in differentiating contrasting objects (for example, in reminding me that there is a difference between a dataset collected for a single project and a multi-use database).

*Mechanics of series analysis*
I presumed that a series of actions by a specific researcher was explainable by a general model, and therefore I concatenated the event series for different researchers. Thus the event series which I analyzed was not a single progression but rather 16 blocks of time-ordered events, one for each different researcher, ranging in length from 145 events down to 2 events. On reaching the marker for a new series (the name ACT instead of an event description), ETHNO automatically started a new analysis, while retaining any changes in the model which were made while analyzing previous blocks.

Testing congruence between the model and the series data was begun by selecting *Analyze a Series* from ETHNO's main menu and then recalling the file containing data for the ACT research program. The logic diagram for the model was displayed on the screen with the abbreviation of the first event blinking.

Pressing the ENTER key visually marked the first event as accomplished and lit up paths to all events which became possible once the first event was done. (ETHNO's graphic representation of completed events and possible events was inspired by Clarke's, 1983, idea of penciling over completed portions of a behavior plan.) Meanwhile the abbreviation for the second event started blinking. Repeated pressing of the ENTER key stepped through the events in sequence, and, as additional events were accomplished, other abbreviations were marked as done, other lines to newly possible events were brightened, and visual marking was removed from events which had been used up by consequences.

Eventually an event was encountered which could not be explained in terms of the logical structure and the default assumptions about how events enable and deplete one another. In a superimposed window the program explained the problem – either an unfulfilled prerequisite or an event repeating without an intervening consequence – and began offering suggestions on how the problem could be solved.

After one of the suggestions was adopted, the program implemented the change and automatically reanalyzed all prior events to make sure the solution did not create problems earlier in the series. Then it stepped through more of the events in the event series.

On reaching the last event the program filed for future use the event descriptions, logical relations, assumptions applying for each event, and the complete event series. The file contained all modifications incorporated during the series analysis.

*Modifications from series analysis*
Appendix 9.3 illustrates the dialogue with the computer which occurs during a series analysis. Though the illustration is limited to the same events as were treated in Appendix 9.2, an example of each of the major types of problem appears in Appendix 9.3, and some (but not all) of ETHNO's different kinds of suggested solutions are exemplified.

In the course of series analyses I made one change in logical structure, added commutation for one pair of events, gave disjunctive prerequisites to 13 events, eliminated depletion along 37 (of 58) linkages between events, and allowed 30 of the 42 events to be repeatable without depletion.

In all, 30 items in the serial record of 298 events were added, moved or changed from one classification to another as a result of series analysis. Mostly these were cases in which I was reminded to add an event that was recalled easily when logic demanded. Once I had an event six positions higher in serial ranking than it should have been (though still in the right year). In two cases, series analysis uncovered the fact that I had recorded erroneously the kind of event which occurred: external versus local funding in one case; database measurements versus single-study measurements in another case.

ETHNO suggested the solutions which were adopted in all cases except one. In the one instance where ETHNO could offer no suggestions, I had glossed over two events in sequence (collating and analyzing a database) which are required for publishing a database study. The missing events had to be added to the event series using an ETHNO editing routine in order to proceed.

## Final model

The event structure model for the ACT program of quantitative research consists of event descriptions, a logical structure, and specifications concerning how each event's logical relations constrain event orderings.

Table 9.1 lists the events in the model, showing ETHNO abbreviations, short names used in analyses, and detailed descriptions which gave an appropriate semantic basis to the logic structure.

Table 9.1 *Event descriptions*

**Ana**    **analyzed database.** R (a researcher) extracted new information from a database through transformations of measurements or by focusing on a subset of cases.

**Cer**    **certified in profession.** R obtained a doctorate or other professional credential while not involved in the research program.

**Col**    **collated data.** R organized the stimuli used to obtain measurements from respondents, organized and verified the measurements themselves, and then perhaps computed descriptive statistics (e.g. means) which could be the basis for further analyses.

**Con**    **contributed funding.** R employed personal funds to foster research activities.

**CIn**    **contracted with publisher.** R obtained a written contract assuring that a publisher would accept a book manuscript for publication.

**Den**    **denied funding.** R received a letter from an external funding agency in which the agency declined the opportunity to support proposed research activities.

**DIn**    **denied monograph publication.** R received a letter from a publisher in which the publisher declined the opportunity to publish a book manuscript reporting research activities.

**Edi**    **edited journal issue.** R negotiated with the official editor of a journal and

Table 9.1   *Event descriptions (continued)*

|       | |
|-------|--|
|       | thereby gained editorial control over one issue of the journal for the purpose of promoting a topic or a research program. |
| Est   | **estimated equations.** R concretized algebraic portrayals of relations between various measurements by estimating equation parameters as numerical values through statistical analyses of a sample of measurements. Some collation of data is presumed to be part of equation estimation. |
| Fun   | **funded locally.** R received funds administered within a university to free a researcher from remunerative activities like teaching or to buy research materials and services. |
| Fln   | **funded externally.** R received funds from a source beyond the researcher's own university to free one or more researchers from remunerative activities like teaching or to buy research materials and services. |
| Gat   | **gathered database measurements.** R measured people's subjective responses to verbal stimuli in order to create a database. (ACT databases were created solely through survey methods.) |
| Gav   | **gave invited talk.** R was invited to speak at a conference or a colloquium outside of the researcher's own university, and the talk led to a publication about the research program by the researcher or by someone in the audience. |
| Imp   | **improved simulation system.** R made the output of a simulation system more realistic by refining the computer program, by incorporating more refined equations and rules, or by refining usage of a database. |
| Iss   | **issued simulation system.** R found a way of distributing a simulation program, with databases and instructions, so that people could operate the system on accessible computers. |
| Joi   | **joined faculty.** R obtained a professorship permitting pursuit of intellectual interests and enlistment of student researchers into the research program. |
| Mat   | **mathematized formulation.** R constructed a mathematical derivation which transformed assumptions about reality along with empirically based equations describing a process into additional equations describing another process. |
| Mlt   | **mathematized methodology.** R constructed a mathematical derivation which resulted in the definition of a complex methodological procedure. |
| Mea   | **measured responses.** R obtained measurements of people's responses to a number of verbal stimuli (presented in a questionnaire or by a computer) in order to conduct a specific analysis. |
| Per   | **performed simulation.** R employed a simulation system to enter information about social situations and obtain a computer report about theoretical predictions. |
| Pro   | **programmed simulation system.** R programmed a computer in order to implement an empirically grounded mathematical model (plus additional rules) while making use of a database such that a variety of problems could be set up easily and theoretical predictions examined readily. |
| Pub   | **published database study.** R published a description of methods and of the results of processing a database in order to address some issue. |
| P1b   | **published equation estimations.** R published an article describing how some process can be given an algebraic formulation and how numbers were found to make the equations concrete and descriptive of reality. |
| P2b   | **published methodology.** R published a report describing a generalized research procedure and discussing its benefits and limitations. |

Table 9.1   *Event descriptions (continued)*

**P3b**  **published theory formulation.** R published a statement claiming that some abstracted aspects of reality are interrelated in a principled way.

**P4b**  **published simulator results.** R published illustrative simulation results in order to communicate a theory's capacity for portraying reality.

**P5b**  **published research monograph.** R published a lengthy systematic exposition describing activities and outcomes in a research program.

**P6b**  **published math derivations.** R published a report describing how a mathematical derivation was obtained and how the results are to be interpreted.

**P7b**  **published research overview.** R published an exposition outlining the claims, activities and products of a research program.

**P8b**  **published test of theory.** R published a report defining a theoretical assumption or prediction, how the claim was examined empirically, what the results were, and how the results favor or undermine the focal theoretical formulation as well as other theoretical formulations.

**P9b**  **published edited book.** R published a collection of writings by various authors on a particular topic or research program.

**Ran**  **ran (a social psychology) experiment.** R constructed real social situations representing distinctive circumstances and assessed some aspects of people's responses to the different circumstances.

**Rea**  **read.** R consumed reports and publications regarding theory, research or research methods from within the researcher's own research program or from other research programs.

**R1a**  **reanalyzed prior study.** R performed new analyses on measurements which were collected and analyzed previously, and the new analysis addressed the same issue as the prior work.

**Rec**  **received doctorate.** R was awarded a doctorate degree certifying the person as a competent researcher.

**Req**  **requested funding.** R sought external funding from a government agency or from a foundation or from an outside research institution through submission of a proposal outlining a research plan and a budget for specific research activities.

**Sol**  **solicited paper.** R requested preparation of a report by another scholar or researcher, with assurance that the report would be published in an edited book.

**Sub**  **submitted research monograph.** R sent a book-size manuscript reporting theory and research to a publisher for possible publication.

**Tes**  **tested theory.** R used empirical data to examine the accuracy of a theoretical assumption or prediction. Some collation and analysis of data is presumed to be part of testing a theory.

**Uti**  **utilized existing database.** R made use of a collated database in order to conduct some kind of research.

**Vis**  **visited other faculty.** R visited another faculty during a sabbatical leave from his or her own faculty.

**Wro**  **wrote research report.** R prepared a report interpreting literature, describing how an experiment was conducted or how measurements were made, how statistical or other kinds of analyses were done, or how mathematical solutions were derived.

Logical connections among the events (with each event represented by its abbreviation) are shown in Figure 9.1. The topmost
entry is simply the name of the system; the tier below the topmost
entry shows events which have no specified prerequisites within the
system.

Lines traced downward from an event define the event's potential
consequences. (Gaps in lines occur when two unrelated paths cross
each other.) For example, *Contributed funding* (Con) can lead to
*Measured responses* (Mea) or to *Gathered database measurements*
(Gat). Tracing further reveals indirect consequences; e.g., *Contributed funding* may lead indirectly through *Measured responses* to
*Tested theory* (Tes) or *Estimated equations* (Est) or *Wrote research
report* (Wro).

Lines ascending from an event define the event's prerequisites,
which are disjunctive if the event abbreviation is printed all in
capitals, conjunctive otherwise. For example, the prerequisites for
*Improved simulation system* (Imp) are *Programmed simulation
system* (Pro) AND *Performed simulation* (Per); the prerequisites of
*Measured responses* (Mea) are *Contributed funding* (Con) OR
*Funded locally* (Fun). Only two events in the system (improving and
issuing a simulation system – Imp and Iss) have conjunctive
prerequisites rather than disjunctive.

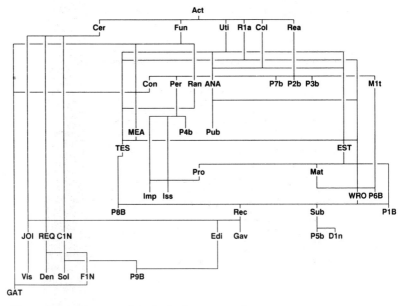

Figure 9.1   *Diagram of the logical structure of research activities*

ETHNO's diagrams ordinarily do not show a line between two elements if that line can be reproduced by tracing direct paths (for instance, there is no line between Con and Tes because their connection can be determined by tracing through Mea). I forced two exceptions in this model – direct lines indicate that gathering database measurements (Gat) can be directly supported by personal contributions (Con) or by local institutions (Fun), as well as being indirectly dependent on past contributions or past local funding. Dynamic assumptions which cannot be represented in the diagram are shown in Table 9.2.

Thirty of the 42 events had to be declared repeatable without depletion. Mostly the repeatable events have permanent products (like publications) so the designation of being repeatable without

Table 9.2  *Assumptions for the model of research activities*

### Repeatable Without Depletion

| | |
|---|---|
| Ana: R analyzed database | Pub: R published database study |
| Col: R collated data | P1b: R published equation estimations |
| Con: R contributed funding | P2b: R published methodology |
| Den: R denied funding | P3b: R published theory formulation |
| Edi: R edited journal issue | P4b: R published simulator results |
| Est: R estimated equations | P5b: R published research monograph |
| F1n: R funded externally | P6b: R published math derivations |
| Gat: R gathered database measurements | P7b: R published research overview |
| Gav: R gave invited talk | P8b: R published test of theory |
| Imp: R improved simulation system | P9b: R published edited book |
| Iss: R issued simulation system | Rea: R read |
| Joi: R joined faculty | Req: R requested funding |
| Mat: R mathematized formulation | Sol: R solicited paper |
| Per: R performed simulation | Tes: R tested theory |
| Pro: R programmed simulation system | Wro: R wrote research report |

### Require Depletion to Repeat

| | |
|---|---|
| C1n: R contracted with publisher | Ran: R ran experiment |
| Cer: R certified in profession | R1a: R reanalyzed prior study |
| D1n: R denied monograph publication | Rec: R received doctorate |
| Fun: R funded locally | Sub: R submitted research monograph |
| M1t: R mathematized methodology | Uti: R utilized existing database |
| Mea: R measured responses | Vis: R visited other faculty |

### Non-Depletive Relations

| | | | | |
|---|---|---|---|---|
| Wro to Ana | Mat to Est | P4b to Per | Per to Rea | P8b to Tes |
| Sol to C1n | P1b to Est | Imp to Pro | Wro to R1a | P1b to Wro |
| C1n to Cer | Pro to Est | Iss to Pro | C1n to Rec | P8b to Wro |
| Joi to Cer | Wro to Est | Con to Rea | Edi to Rec | Rec to Wro |
| Req to Cer | P6b to Mat | M1t to Rea | Gav to Rec | Sub to Wro |
| Ana to Col | Wro to Mat | P2b to Rea | Joi to Rec | |
| Est to Col | Wro to Mea | P3b to Rea | Req to Rec | |
| P9b to Edi | Iss to Per | P7b to Rea | F1n to Req | |

### Commutative Relation
between D1n and Sub

depletion is natural. In a few instances the designation results from a current limitation in ETHNO – the program does not stack event occurrences and count depletions; thus an event like 'analyzed database' has to be repeatable because researchers who are pursuing several projects simultaneously may do several analyses before writing up any of them.

One pair of events was put into a commutative relation: submission of a research monograph to a publisher (Sub) and having the manuscript rejected (D1n). The commutation represents the process whereby submission is made to one publisher at a time, and rejection primes another submission. Submitting manuscripts always is essential for getting the manuscripts published, and this is the case whether they are articles or books, but the model amalgamates submission and publication in the case of articles because there are so many forms of article publication that listing component steps would clutter the model substantially, and, in any case, most ACT article manuscripts were not rejected, so the detail would be of little value. Note that a commutative structure does not cover submission and denial of grant requests, first, because multiple grant requests often are made at once, and, second, because the intellectual framework and the personnel which justify a request may vanish before a re-submission can be made.

*Overview of the model*
The model presented in Table 9.1, Figure 9.1, and Table 9.2 defines 42 research-related events and specifies how ordering of those events is constrained, thereby forming a grammar of action which generates sensible sequences of action in a quantitative research program. The model accounts for event series containing 298 events by 12 associates of the program and by four outside scholars.

Five events are customary happenings in **academic** careers: *Gave invited talk, Joined faculty, Read, Received doctorate, Visited other faculty. Certified in profession* is a convenience construct which simplified inclusion of researchers who obtained their PhDs before becoming involved with ACT (and in one case was used to represent certification in a non-sociology profession which permitted applying for special funds). Thus, professional participation in the academic world is an important aspect of the kind of research which I modeled.

Another five events deal with **economic** aspects of research: *Contributed funding, Denied funding, Funded externally, Funded locally, Requested funding.* A quantitative research program based on empirical data has to attend in one way or another to research financing.

Many events in the research program relate to **publishing**. Nine events, *Published database study, Published equation estimations, Published math derivations, Published methodology, Published research overview, Published simulator results, Published test of theory, Published theory formulation, Issued simulation system,* define types of publication. Note that these events refer to kinds of statements rather than to publication of standard units like articles or chapters. It is the content of publications which relates most directly to research activities, and a single publication may contain several kinds of content, therefore amount to several events. Seven other events also relate to publishing, but their focus is on processes involved in creating books and special issues of journals: *Contracted with publisher, Denied monograph publication, Edited journal issue, Published edited book, Published research monograph, Solicited paper, Submitted research monograph.*

Events which have no further consequences within a system amount to system outputs, and publications and public presentations are the outputs of a research program, these intellectual products being exchanged with other research programs. Denials of publication also are kinds of outputs, and in a sense these foregoings are exchanged with other research programs, too. Soliciting papers for an edited book involves control of resources which also may be offered to other research programs.

Finally, 15 of the events are specifically focused on **research**. Three of these, *Gathered database measurements, Measured responses* and *Ran experiment*, are intrinsically social in social science research. (*Measured responses* is distinguished from *Ran experiment* in that stimuli in experiments are real social situations rather than printed presentations; a database study is distinct from *Measured responses* in that the sample of people or the sample of stimuli is sufficiently comprehensive that the data may be broken into different categories for various kinds of analyses.) Otherwise – in contrast to the academic, economic and publishing aspects of research – these technical activities might be implemented without engaging in much social interaction or written correspondence: *Analyzed database, Collated data, Estimated equations, Improved simulation system, Mathematized formulation, Mathematized methodology, Performed simulation, Programmed simulation system, Reanalyzed prior study, Tested theory, Utilized existing database, Wrote research report.*

The core research activities (in the center of the diagram) essentially consist of three lines of development: testing theory, developing simulation systems, and developing mathematical formulations. Because most of the events in these sequences become possible with occurrence of a single prior event (either because that event is the sole prerequisite or because it is one of the several prerequisites in a disjunctive set), the core research activities typically are 'straight-line' ventures in which one step naturally leads to another rather than occasional opportunities which suddenly open on completion of a variety of immediate prerequisites.

Many research-related events do not deplete their prerequisites, so the conditions created by events in a research program often last long enough to support several events. For example, receiving a doctorate provides a continuing resource; reading is practically non-depletable in the sense of providing permanent intellectual resources; and collation of a database, estimation or derivation of equations, or writing a research report similarly provide long-lasting resources for a research program. Thus a quantitative research program cumulates research capital over time, enhancing its durability and productivity.

### Discussion

The model presented here does not deal with every interesting sociological aspect of research programs. For example, the model shows that funding is essential for some research events, but it does not show that funding accelerates research events – an effect which is evident in the historical record and which might be formalized through a different methodology (for example, Tuma et al., 1979). Also, the model shows how research products are generated, but it does not show how different research programs are linked through the exchange of those products, though that is a common theme in the sociology of science and readily studied through application of network methodology (for example, Burt, 1990).

The model presented here inevitably is conditioned by social institutions which were in the background during the research activities. For example, publication events are important in the model, and that is because the historical record contained numerous publishing events, deemed meaningful and faithfully recorded by researchers because publishing is demanded by the academic institutions that employ researchers. Quite a different picture of research might emerge in other supporting institutions (like corporations) which promote the recording of different events, thereby changing the recorded history from which the model is derived.

The model is to some degree a product of the unique experiences of the expert constructing the model. For example, events related to simulation might not appear in the models of expert representatives from other quantitative research programs, and other researchers might distinguish more events relating to experiments and testing theory than I did. Indeed, ten years from now I might provide a somewhat different model of the ACT research program because I will have accumulated more experiences by then.

Limitations notwithstanding, the model has several kinds of utilities. First, as a scientific product, it is an object that can be compared and classified with similar objects (like models of other academic research programs and of corporate research) in order to identify differences or to abstract general features of the domain. Second, as a dynamic simulator of research events, the model might be used to socialize neophytes and to disseminate knowledge that could foster wider institutionalization of quantitative research programs. Third, the model permits 'action at a distance' (Latour, 1987) for administrators in academic, funding and publishing institutions by facilitating the anticipation and direction of events which the authorities themselves do not produce.

Event structure analysis has a close affinity with Abell's (1987; 1988) method of comparative narratives, but whereas event structure analysis is focused primarily on data analysis procedures, Abell's work on comparative narratives is focused primarily on solving related conceptual problems. Exchange might be expected between these two research programs. For example, ETHNO's abstraction routine might incorporate Abell's idea that abstraction amounts to a homomorphic reduction. Meanwhile empirical projects like this one clearly indicate that Abell's preferred homomorphism has to be weakened in order to deal with cycling, because repetition of events is ubiquitous in human action once one goes beyond the most concrete level of description.

## Appendix 9.1: Beginning and ending events in the ACT event series

| | Year | Researcher or other actor | Action | Details |
|---|---|---|---|---|
| 1 | 1961 | Heise | read | Goffman, Parsons, Lewin, Osgood |
| 2 | 1962 | Heise | funded locally | NIMH pre-doctoral fellow |
| 3 | 1963 | Heise | contributed funding | For Heise, 1965, questionnaires |
| 4 | | Heise | gathered database measurements | For Heise, 1965 |

156   *Using computers in qualitative research*

| | Year | Researcher or other actor | Action | Details |
|---|---|---|---|---|
| 5 | | Heise | collated data | For Heise, 1965 |
| 6 | | Heise | analyzed database | For Heise, 1965 |
| 7 | | Heise | wrote research report | Dissertation |
| 8 | 1964 | Heise | received doctorate | Chicago |
| 9 | | Heise | requested funding | Post-doc |
| 10 | | Heise | funded externally | NIMH post-doc at Wisconsin |
| 11 | | Scholar 1 | certified in profession | Kemper received sociology PhD in 1960s |
| 12 | 1965 | Heise | joined faculty | Wisconsin |
| 13 | | Heise | read | Gollob, Osgood, Heider |
| 14 | | Heise | published database study | Heise, 1965 |
| 15 | | Heise | contributed funding | Questionnaires for Heise, 1969a |
| 287 | 1989 | Smith-Lovin | published research overview | Smith-Lovin, 1989 |
| 288 | | Heise | published theory formulation | Emotion-labeling: Heise, 1989 |
| 289 | | Heise | published research overview | Emotion-labeling: Heise, 1989 |
| 290 | | Heise | published math derivations | Emotion-labeling: Heise, 1989 |
| 291 | | Heise | published simulator results | Emotion-labeling: Heise, 1989 |
| 292 | | MacKinnon | published database study | MacKinnon & Keating, 1989 |
| 293 | | Keating | published database study | MacKinnon & Keating, 1989 |
| 294 | | Heise | published equation estimations | Heise & Thomas, 1989 |
| 295 | | Thomas | published equation estimations | Heise & Thomas, 1989 |
| 296 | | Smith-Lovin | published research overview | Smith-Lovin, 1989 |
| 297 | | Heise | published simulator results | Heise, 1989 |
| 298 | | Scholar 4 | published research overview | Thoits, 1989 |

*Note*: The following researchers are represented in the data: C. Averett, W. Douglas, D. Heise, L. Keating, L. Lazowski, N. MacKinnon, R. Morgan, B. Smith, L. Smith-Lovin, L. Thomas, B. Wiggins, D. Willigan. Also included are some activities by four outside scholars: T. Kemper, H. Smith, S. Stryker, P. Thoits. Not included are events by graduate students whose work yielded no publications as of February 1989: C. Cassel, M. Young, L. Wood, R. Sands and S. Lerner at the University of North Carolina; I. Okuyama and M. Brondino at the University of South Carolina; T. Leowinata at the University of Guelph; M. Malone and D. Barrett at Indiana University; D. Robinson-Reeve at Cornell University.

## Appendix 9.2: ETHNO ELICITATION

### Preliminaries

*Create a Structure* was chosen from ETHNO's main menu. Asked for a framework file, I entered D̲ (for dynamic), in order to process historical data. ETHNO provided a screen of instructions and asked for the name of the structure I was going to create.

I began entering data by typing A̲C̲T̲, an acronym for the title, 'development of Affect Control Theory'. ETHNO asked for the first event. I typed: R̲ r̲e̲a̲d̲, which is the first event given in Appendix 9.1, ignoring specific details.

At that point ETHNO drew a diagram on the screen, **Act** at the top, **Rea** below it, connected by a vertical line. (Each entry on an ETHNO diagram is represented by a three-letter abbreviation formed from the second word of the entry.)

In a separate window at the bottom of screen ETHNO asked, 'Next happening?'

Henceforth I show the event which I entered and ETHNO's abbreviation for it. Then I show the questions ETHNO asked and the answers which I gave, followed by an explanation of my answers. I also provide commentaries to indicate how definitions and interpretations were revised in the course of analyses and to explain ETHNO's operations.

### R funded locally **Fun**

**Does 'R funded locally' require 'R read' (or a similar event)'?** N̲

ETHNO needed to know the logical relation between a researcher reading and a researcher being locally funded. Prior reading of research reports is not really required in order to receive funding which is administered within a university, only that a researcher be affiliated with the university (and all characters in the ACT research program had university affiliations as students or post-doctoral fellows or faculty). Thus I answered 'no'.

*ETHNO notes*:

ETHNO did not ask whether funding is required for reading because funding occurred later than reading.

### R contributed funding **Con**

**Does 'R contributed funding' require 'R funded locally' (or a similar event)?** N̲
**Does 'R contributed funding' require 'R read' (or a similar event)?** Y̲

Why do researchers use personal funds for research projects? Few prior events are available to serve as explanation in this case. I assumed that funding from a university is not essential. I said that reading is required, thereby letting the act of reading take on the extra meaning of developing enthusiasm for a researchable idea.

*ETHNO notes*:

At this point the ETHNO chart which appeared on the screen looked as follows.

This shows that events of receiving funding and reading are part of the ACT event structure. Additionally it shows that contributing personal funds for research implies reading (that is, enthusiasm for an idea). Note that reading is a *necessary* but *not*

*sufficient* condition for personal contributions: ETHNO diagrams display developmental relations, not causal relations.

### R collected database  Col
**Does 'R collected database' require 'R contributed funding' (or a similar event)?** Y
**Does 'R collected database' require 'R funded locally' (or a similar event)?** Y
Assembling a sizeable database of quantitative measurements requires money for questionnaires, computer materials, etc. So funding from some source is required. I answered 'yes' to both questions because in this particular case funding from both sources was required (I collected data on 1,000 words, and I could not have done so without my fellowship plus some personal expenditures).
*Revision*:
The name of this event eventually changed to 'R gathered database measurements' (**Gat**) to emphasize that this event refers only to the fieldwork aspect of assembling a database.

### R funded locally  Fun
At this point in the original event series there was a repetition of the event 'R funded locally'.
*Revision*:
The local funding in this case was support for computer usage, and eventually all instances of computer support were deleted from the corpus because obtaining university funding to support computer usage never was a contingent factor in research dynamics – such funding always was available (even though one had to 'apply' for it).
*ETHNO notes*:
Since this was a repetition, I entered the event's ETHNO abbreviation, whereupon ETHNO incorporated a repetition of the event into the event series but asked no questions since the logical relations of this event were already defined.

### R programmed database  Pro
**Does 'R programmed database system' require 'R collected database' (or a similar event)?** Y
I reasoned that social researchers do not develop database systems in the abstract, that a researcher has to collect a database before he would bother entering a program of instructions to a computer in order to process data, and thus I answered 'yes' to the question.
*Revision*:
The description of this event changed to 'R collated data' (**Col**) in the course of analyses, purposely eliminating reference to computer programming because there were instances where the same operations were conducted without computer assistance.
*ETHNO notes*:
No additional questions were asked about this event because ETHNO computed answers on its own. Programming implies collecting data, and collecting data implies two kinds of funding, so programming also implies these kinds of funding. Moreover, personal funding implies reading, so programming implies earlier reading.

### R analyzed database  Ana
**Does 'R analyzed database' require 'R programmed database system' (or a similar event)?** Y

Changing 'R programmed database system' to 'R collated data' modifies some interpretations dramatically, and so it is best to show my original reasoning in quotation marks.

'Durkheim, Sorokin, and other early sociologists analyzed huge databases without computer assistance, but the discipline changed just prior to my entrance into the field, and I am among the sociologists who employ a computer in order to cope with a large set of quantitative data. I answered "yes" to this question to reflect the technology and the economics of the field currently.'

*Revision*:
Since 'programmed' ended up simply as 'collated', the original reasoning is irrelevant and somewhat misleading: current research (my own included) still involves many of the same operations as classic research, though these operations can now be done more efficiently with computers. However, the logic structure remains the same for these events because analyzing data requires collating data.

Though not in the series that I analyzed initially, 'R wrote research report' (**Wro**) eventually was added as the next event. 'Wrote research report' deals with unpublished manuscripts that got incorporated into co-authored publications (or which had other kinds of consequences) and had to be included wherever appropriate once identified as part of the system.

## R received doctorate **Rec**
**Does 'R received doctorate' require 'R analyzed database' (or a similar event)?** N
**Does 'R received doctorate' require 'R programmed database system' (or a similar event)?** N
**Does 'R received doctorate' require 'R collected database' (or a similar event)?** N
**Does 'R received doctorate' require 'R contributed funding' (or a similar event)?** N
**Does 'R received doctorate' require 'R funded locally' (or a similar event)?** N
**Does 'R received doctorate' require 'R read' (or a similar event)?** Y
Original reasoning:
'Obtaining a doctorate in the social sciences usually involves collecting and analyzing data, but that is not essential. Funding events of any kind have no logical relation to granting of a degree. It is inconceivable, though, that a PhD would be awarded without the candidate knowing some of the literature in his or her field, so I answered that receiving a doctorate does imply reading.'

*Revision*:
Inclusion of 'R wrote research report' in later analyses led to quite a different structure. Receiving a doctorate requires writing a research report (a dissertation), and research reports of quantitative researchers may involve significant confrontations with data. Essentially, later analyses forced me to recognize that I was dealing not with anyone in 'social science' but only with people in quantitative research programs.

The event series in Appendix 9.1 next shows an event which was glossed in my initial analysis: 'R requested funding' (**Req**). Ultimately, I had to include 'R requested funding' in the system in order to explain how denials of funding could happen, and, once included, this event had to be placed everywhere it happened.

## R funded externally **Fln**
**Does 'R funded externally' require 'R analyzed database' (or a similar event)?** N
**Does 'R funded externally' require 'R programmed database' system (or a similar event)?** N
**Does 'R funded externally' require 'R collected database' (or a similar event)?** N

**Does 'R funded externally' require 'R received doctorate' (or a similar event)?** Y
**Does 'R funded externally' require 'R contributed funding' (or a similar event)?** N
**Does 'R funded externally' require 'R funded locally' (or a similar event)?** N
Original reasoning:
'Empirical analyses are not essential in order to receive a financial award from outside of one's university (though having done some empirical analyses might improve one's chances). Nor are prior funding experiences necessarily relevant. The implicit prerequisite is a PhD. (While some national awards are given to pre-doctoral students, they invariably require strong faculty sponsorship of the student which can be treated as a "similar event".)'
*Revision*:
In the final logic structure, external funding implies receipt of a PhD, and a PhD among quantitative researchers implies past empirical research, so external funding does imply empirical research.
*ETHNO notes*:
The abbreviation for 'R funded externally' is formed from the second word as usual, but ETHNO substitutes a 1 for the second letter of the abbreviation in order to prevent a duplication.

Appendix 9.1 next shows an event which was not included in the series at this point: 'R certified in profession' (**Cer**). This event involves a different researcher, so the event was not entered until later when the block of events involving Scholar 1 were under consideration.

## R joined faculty  Joi
**Does 'R joined faculty' require 'R analyzed database' (or a similar event)?** N
**Does 'R joined faculty' require 'R programmed database system' (or a similar event)?** N
**Does 'R joined faculty' require 'R funded externally' (or a similar event)?** N
**Does 'R joined faculty' require 'R collected database' (or a similar event)?** N
**Does 'R joined faculty' require 'R received doctorate' (or a similar event)?** Y
**Does 'R joined faculty' require 'R contributed funding' (or a similar event)?** N
**Does 'R joined faculty' require 'R funded locally' (or a similar event)?** N
Original interpretation:
'Joining a faculty requires a PhD, with only rare exceptions (covered by the "similar event" phrase). No specific kinds of research experience are universally required, and prior funding is not essential.'
*Revision*:
Anything that requires a PhD implies past empirical research experience for quantitative research.

## R read  Rea
This repeats an earlier event.
*ETHNO notes*:
The abbreviation rea is entered, whereupon ETHNO logs the event into the event series but asks no questions since the event is already positioned in the logic structure.

## R published database study  Pub
**Does 'R published database study' require 'R analyzed database' (or a similar event)?** Y

**Does 'R published database study' require 'R joined faculty' (or a similar event)?** N
**Does 'R published database study' require 'R funded externally' (or a similar event)?**
N
**Does 'R published database study' require 'R received doctorate' (or a similar event)?**
N
A researcher (or someone under the researcher's supervision – a similar event) has to analyze a database in order to publish statistics and interpretations based on the dataset. Publications are not dependent on other career events of any kind since both students and non-academic researchers publish.

***ETHNO* notes:**
Observe that ETHNO asked no questions about the relation of 'R published database study' to 'R read', 'R funded locally', 'R contributed funding', 'R collected database', or 'R programmed database'. The answers to the relational questions concerning these events were derived syllogistically from the fact that publishing a database study requires analyzing a database.

R contributed funding **Con**
***ETHNO* notes:**
This repetition of a prior event was entered by typing its abbreviation in order to place it in the event series. The program asked no questions since the structural position of the event was already known.

## Appendix 9.3: ETHNO series analysis

After I selected the *Analyze a Series* option from ETHNO's menu and entered the name of the file, the program displayed the logic-diagram on the screen with the abbreviation for the first event blinking to indicate that the event was 'occurring'. I pressed the ENTER key, and the blinking item changed to the abbreviation for the second event. I proceeded through the first seven events this way without ETHNO noting problems.

**R read**
**R funded locally**
**R contributed funding**
**R collected database**
**R funded locally**
**R programmed database system**
**R analyzed database**

The eighth event, though, caused an interruption.

**R received doctorate**
**Problem! Conditions for this event are not fulfilled.**

Getting a doctorate requires reading, and ETHNO assumed that the researcher's reading got used up when he contributed funds for research because making a contribution also depends on reading. The default assumption is that events deplete their prerequisites.

Having stated the problem, ETHNO began possible solutions.

**Is 'R read' *not* required for:**
  **Rec 'R received doctorate'**

**Con 'R contributed funding'**
**Enter abbreviation of non-dependent event.** Skipped.

ETHNO suggested two ways to change the logical structure so that a problem would not exist here. If reading is not required for getting a doctorate, then it would not matter that the reading was used up – getting a doctorate does not depend on it. On the other hand, if reading is not required for a funding contribution, then the contribution would not have depleted the reading, and the reading still would be available for getting a doctorate.

I decided that I made no errors in specifying the consequences of reading, so neither of these solutions was acceptable, and I skipped to ETHNO's next offered solution.

**Can 'R contributed funding' happen without depleting 'R read' (y or n)?** Y

This indeed is the solution, and the rest of the implementation follows below. First, though, consider ETHNO's final suggestion.

**Rea 'R read' might have happened – unrecorded – just before 'R received doctorate' (y or n)?** Skipped.

Maybe the original reading got used up by making a contribution, but then some more reading was done in order to get a doctorate. If so, then ETHNO could insert another reading event to correct the data record. This is not the desired solution in this case, but the idea is applicable in some cases.

Now, returning to the actual solution: after I typed Y ETHNO wanted to know what event does deplete reading, and it offered all the other consequences of reading as possibilities.

**'R read' is depleted by 'R received doctorate' (y or n)?** N
**'R read' is depleted by 'R verbalized formulation' (y or n)?** N
**'R read' is depleted by 'R published methodology' (y or n)** N

I answered 'no' to all of these questions because in my opinion reading is depleted only by senility or death – events which are not in the model.

To allow that some indirect consequence of reading might be what depletes reading, ETHNO next asked for the abbreviation of the depleting event.

**Identify event that DOES deplete 'R read' (For none, enter Act.) Enter the abbreviation:** act

ETHNO allows for the possibility that none of the recorded events acts as a depleter and tells how to escape from specifying a depleting event, and that was the option I chose.

Even if no recorded event depletes reading, ETHNO allows that you may want to change the structure at this point and incorporate a new event that does deplete reading.

**Add a depleting event (y or n)?** N

I declined the offer. Thereupon ETHNO accepted the idea that reading is a non-depletable event.

The program started over and ran through all of the prior events in the series (just to make sure this solution did not create problems elsewhere). Then ETHNO proceeded to the next event, and the next interruption occurred.

**R funded externally**

**Problem! Conditions for this event are not fulfilled.**

This is the same kind of problem as before with the same kind of solution, so I simply list the ETHNO questions and my answers without further commentary.

**Is 'R received doctorate'** *not* **required for:**
  **Joi 'R joined faculty'**
  **Fin 'R funded externally'**
  **Enter abbreviation of non-dependent event.** Skipped.
**Can 'R funded externally' happen without depleting 'R received doctorate' (y or n)?** Y
**'R received doctorate' is depleted by 'R joined faculty' (y or n)?** N
**Identify event that DOES deplete 'R received doctorate' (For none, enter Act.)**
**Enter the abbreviation:** act
**Add a depleting event (y or n)?** N

The next event caused no problems.

**R joined faculty**

The event after that was a repetition of 'R read', and it caused another interruption.

**R read**

**Problem! This event undepleted since last occurrence.**
**Can this event be repeated without depletion (y or n)?** Y

ETHNO assumes by default that events are not repeated unless used up by consequences, but in this case we have specified that reading is not used up by any research events. ETHNO's suggested solution was that reading might be repeated whether it is depleted or not; and that was ETHNO's only offered solution in this case. I accepted the ETHNO suggestion, and the program continued with the analysis.

No additional problems were encountered with ACT events prior to 1966, the arbitrary stopping point for this illustration.

**R published database study**
**R contributed funding**

# 10

# The Upside and Downside of Hypertext Tools: the KANT Example

*Elizabeth (Betsy) S. Cordingley*

While on the Alvey/DHSS Large Demonstrator Project team at the University of Surrey, I was asked in 1985 to prepare a statement of user requirements for a qualitative data analysis tool and to 'be ambitious about it'. The prospect of having parts developed in time for us to use on the project put time constraints on how much 'research' could be done to broaden my own ideas. Even discussions with the dozen co-workers, colleagues and other analysts I had time to consult revealed a rich collection of approaches, personal styles and desired support for the analytic process (Cordingley, 1985). Two software tools were written in time for them to be trialed in the project, QUAT and KANT.

The 'annotation workbench', one of six 'workbenches' which were to have made up the projected Qualitative-data Analysis Tool (QAT), was selected for development. A user specification was prepared for the implementation team, and an initial version of the cut-down QAT was produced. It was promising but could not be made to run fast enough to use for the Claimant Information Systems (CIS) team's analysis it was designed to support – the analysis of the transcripts of interviews (some as long as two hours) with 50 potential users of an advice system demonstrator (Dawson and Buckland, 1986). Meanwhile the CIS team analysts and colleagues working on other demonstrator systems within the project had been experimenting with outliners and ideas processors such as ACTA, MORE, FACTFINDER and GUIDE. It was decided to use aspects of these to develop a tool, KANT (see below), to support the knowledge analysis of all teams working on the demonstrator project.

The metaphor of an outline, which was relatively well understood and therefore we hoped easily developed, was used in a number of these packages. The outline, which could hide details in various ways, plus some of the hypertext concepts, which supported the annotation facilities of QAT, were the basis for a second attempt to provide software support for analysis. This tool, Knowledge ANalysts Tool (KANT) (Storrs and Burton, 1989; Portman et al., 1989: 63–75), and a companion graphical tool, the Knowledge Base Builder (KBB) (Portman et al., 1989: 58–63), were used to analyse the knowledge for, and to construct most knowledge-bases of, the three systems the project demonstrated in March 1989. Toward the end of the project, facilities of KANT version 2 (KANT2) and KBB were combined into one package, KANT3, which was also demonstrated in its own right at the end of the project, although it was still under development. It is KANT2 that is described here, however, not only because its behaviour is better understood than that of KANT3, but also because it allows me to concentrate on the qualitative analysis facilities of the tools and only mention in passing the knowledge-base building support provided primarily by the KBB.

QAT and KANT2 reflect the two worlds which have an interest in computer-based qualitative analysis: the world of social sciences peopled by ethnographers, anthropologists and other social researchers; and the world of computer systems development, peopled with requirements and systems analysts, software and knowledge engineers, knowledge-base developers, logicians, user-interface and user-interaction designers, and others from the developer community. The populations of these worlds are no longer mutually exclusive. Their mingling has benefited both communities. It has highlighted both the common need for tools to support qualitative analysis and the contrast in how these needs are approached.

In general, social scientists performing qualitative analysis are looking for insights which can then be systematically checked against evidence. They value flexible tools which can be used in a variety of ways – tools which can accommodate individual differences in analytical style *and* the changing needs of analysis as it progresses. They want tools which support analysis, but leave the analyst firmly in charge.

Developers of computer systems lean more toward wanting tools to support standard styles of analysis and development such as those of Structured Systems Analysis and Design Methodology (SSADM), Jackson Systems Development (JSD) (for example, Sutcliffe, 1988; Page-Jones 1980). They typically want a tool to prevent analysts from including structures or elements which violate the constraints of the development method. Once the programming stage is reached, they want structured editors to prevent avoidable programming errors. There is pressure from this community to automate analysis where possible, 'since people make so many mistakes', and constrain it where automation is not yet possible.

KANT2 is a bit of both. On the one hand, the analyst is free to associate any meaning s/he wishes with relationships represented by *links* (described below). KANT2 also leaves the analyst entirely free to define how parts of their outlines 'automatically' relate to one another through the outline structure (in contrast with the relationships indicated by links). The analyst might decide to create an outline where a subheading, for example, names something which 'is a part of' whatever the heading was. The part–whole relationship would then be automatically implied just by creating the outline with headings and subheadings, but KANT2 has no way of being sure that appropriate headings and subheadings are used. It has no way of checking that whatever is named in the subheading is a part of whatever is named in the heading. There is no automatic check on these implied relationships. The analyst is free to use headings and subheadings which have a different relationship between them – for instance, first this then that – within an outline, even if this makes a nonsense of the analysis. There may be no problem with multi-relationship, heterogeneous, outlines where the text of the headings and subheadings contain indicators of what their relationship is, as the human brain can switch backwards and forwards between parts of heterogeneous outlines without difficulty. Problems would, however, arise if heterogeneous outlines were created and used with a tool whose automatic facilities expected homogeneous ones.

KANT2 (described below) does not automate analysis but has automatic facilities. It will automatically display the other end of a link the analyst wants to inspect, saving the analyst the overhead of keeping a separate record of where links lead. If the appropriate outline is not open to view at the time, KANT2 identifies the outline, opens it and displays the text that is the destination of the link. In addition, parts of a KANT2 outline could be defined as containing material with specific meaning; in our case it was rules which had to conform to the syntax of the 'Toolkit' language (Portman et al., 1989: 52–6) developed in the project. It was then possible for programmers to provide additional automatic facilities which exploited the rule field of nodes. In our case a parser was provided to check the syntax of the text in such fields.

So KANT2 allows flexibility and can permit the imposition of constraints on certain specially defined fields; there are both manual and automated features; it is a tool which bridges the two communities of users who have an interest in computer-supported qualitative analysis. Its machine-supported linking facilities and single coherent interface to its knowledge-base, the hallmarks of hypertext (Conklin, 1987: 18), make it a suitable example for discussing the upside and downside of hypertext tools to support such analysis. A brief description of KANT2 will aid understanding and the best 'way in' is through its metaphors.

## KANT2 and its metaphors

KANT2 utilizes four main metaphors – menus, windows, outlines and networks – each of which has subsidiary metaphors associated with it.

### Menus and windows
The KANT2 interface uses the metaphor of windows which will be familiar to anyone who has used an Apple Macintosh, Sun, Symbolics or other computer using a windowing system. Each KANT2 window has a title and a collection of 'drop-down' menus across the top and a scroll bar down its left side.

Each window contains either a KANT2 structure (see below) or a KANT2 source (see below). Several windows can be open at the same time, and if there are links (see below) between nodes (see below) in different windows, the user can take a hypertext-like journey through the environment from window to window by following links. If the journey includes a source or a structure which is not displayed in a window already, KANT2 creates a window and displays the appropriate material when the user selects the command SHOW LINK.

### Outlines
*Structures and nodes*   The next strongest metaphor incorporated in the KANT2 design is that of the outline. The analyst may create an outline such as the one for Work Status below:[1] it consists of a hierarchy of headings and subheadings (such as 'Employed' and 'Formally employed', respectively). A subheading can be broken down further, in which case the subheading ('Formally employed') acts as a heading for its subheadings ('Has regular employment with an employer', 'Has irregular/casual employment', and 'Is registered Self-Employed'). Hierarchies of an arbitrary number of levels can thus be created.

Work Status
   Employed
      Formally employed
         Has regular employment with an employer

> Has irregular/casual employment
> Is registered Self-Employed
> Informal employed
> 　Legal odd jobbing
> 　Black-economy work
> 　Both formally and informally employed (moonlighting)
> Not employed
> 　Unemployed and looking for work
> 　With domestic responsibilities, not looking for work
> 　Retired and not working
> 　Not doing paid work, and not looking for work
> 　Unemployable (e.g. babies)

Anyone who has used MORE, ACTA or the outlining facilities of WORD4 will be familiar with this sort of outline.

Subheadings are called *children* of the heading. The heading is called the *parent* of its subheadings. Subheadings of the same heading are called *siblings* of one another.

In KANT2 terminology, outlines which the analyst creates and can alter are called *KANT2 structures*. Each heading or subheading of such an outline is called a *node* in the structure, reminiscent of the terminology of networks, the third metaphor used in KANT2.

As with outlines that are partly fleshed out into documents, there may be more to each node than just the heading which serves as the title for the node. The title is held in the first (the *title field*) of the three parts of the KANT2 node. The other two parts, or fields, of a node are a *text field* (which may have something in it or be empty) in which the analyst can put any kind of text, and a *rule field* (which also may have something in it or may be empty).[2] Material in the text field is not given any special status by KANT2, but that in the rule field is and so must conform to the syntax expected of rules by the rule interpreter/compiler being used. The contents of the title field, which is used to name the rule associated with the node (where it exists) as well as naming the node, cannot be more than 132 characters long (including spaces), but no other particular constraints are imposed on it.

*Sources*　Material being analysed is held in files which are referred to as *KANT2 sources*. Because it is important that they be kept inviolate, it is not possible for the analyst to alter their content from within KANT2.[3] Each paragraph and heading/subheading of a KANT2 source is regarded as a node, but these nodes do not have the three distinct parts as nodes in structures do. Nor are sources regarded as having an outline structure. They are just regarded as 'documents' consisting of a collection of unnamed units of text. It is possible to page through the source, a screenful at a time, scroll through, or jump to a position in the document by moving an indicator on the scroll bar of the window in which the text is displayed.

## Links and networks

One of the main ways KANT2 differs from other outliners is that it provides facilities for explicitly linking nodes. A link, representing a relationship, can be created between any node in a structure and any other node within the KANT2 environment.

Links, like arcs in directed graphs, have direction – that is, they are regarded as going from one node (the originator) to another node (the destination) – and exactly two ends (no more, no less). A node may have zero, one, or more links coming into it. It may have zero, one, or more links going out from it. Two nodes may be linked by more than one link between them if they have more than one kind of relationship which the analyst thinks is worth emphasizing.

*Links within structures*  Links can be made between nodes in the same structure. For example, if every paragraph were considered to be a subsection and hence a node in its own right, then every paragraph in which the word 'node' is mentioned in this chapter might have a link going from it to the paragraph in which the word 'node' was first introduced.[4] Such a link might be labelled 'meaning of "node" given in'. Setting up links in this way would allow a user of the structure to check the meaning of the word 'node' by following such a link no matter where the user started inspecting the structure. Similarly, links labelled '"node" appears in' could be made from the first occurrence of the word 'node' to every paragraph in which the word 'node' was used, that is, links in the opposite direction from those above. This would enable a KANT2 user who was inspecting the initial characterization of the word 'node' to find all the other places where the word 'node' is used in the chapter.

*Links between structures*  Links can also be made between nodes of different structures. Thus if the analyst were setting up a separate glossary of terms used in the project, links might be made between every paragraph where the word 'node' was used in the chapter and the entry for 'node' in the glossary structure. This would mean that the characterization/definition of the term 'node' would not need to appear in the chapter itself but would be taken from the glossary. Creating links to a glossary is one way of increasing consistency across a team of analysts or across time when analysis is protracted.

*Links between structures and sources*  Links can also be made between nodes in structures and nodes in sources and vice versa. Sources–structure links are used, for example, where the analyst is creating analytical frameworks. Structure–source links on the other hand are used, for example, when the analyst is identifying where in the sources (for example, the interviews) examples of an analytical theme can be found.

The Work Status structure described above might have been devised from some theory of work. This could be made explicit by having the text of the theory and any relevant amplificatory material held as a KANT2 source and creating links from it to the Work Status structure, labelled perhaps 'suggests category'.

If the Work Status structure had emerged from the inspection of one or more key transcripts (an early step in the evolution of grounded theory), this could be made explicit in a similar way, that is, by creating links from those transcripts held as KANT2 sources to the Work Status structure.

When a structure such as the Work Status example is used as a framework for subsequent analysis of additional transcripts, its nodes are linked 'snippets' (selected portions of text) in the transcripts held as KANT2 sources. These links going from structure to source might be labelled 'an example is'. When a KANT2 user wants to inspect the analysis so far, the user can open the framework structure (for example, Work Status), select the node to explore (for example, Unemployable), show the links made from that node, and follow those labelled, say, 'an example is' to the relevant snippet. The snippet is still in the context of the particular interview of which it was a part. It has all of the co-text (the rest of the transcript) surrounding it to help the analyst assess its meaning/ significance. The analyst can follow other links onward from the snippet or return to the framework and follow other links in turn from the original node.

**Use of KANT2**

*Variety of uses*
In addition to the uses of KANT2 described in the previous section – creating a glossary to facilitate consistency, documenting analytical decisions such as what was used as the source of a framework for analysis, and using an analytical framework to study other material – KANT2 can also be used, for example:

–   as a project tool providing, for example, reminders of unfinished

work, highlighting areas of ambiguity, documenting progress, documenting the provenance[5] of each bit of analysis, and charting changes;
– as a way of expressing complex relationships between parts of different conceptual hierarchies.

Each structure can (and I would argue in most cases should) have nodes of a single type and single defining relationship relating parent nodes to their children. For example, in the Work Status structure, each subheading should be a work status which is '*is a kind of*' whatever work status its parent is. Thus the relationship established by the positioning of these headings in the outline is that 'Is registered Self-Employed' is a kind of formal employment. These constraints on the analyst are self-imposed and self-maintained. KANT2 does not require, nor can it check, that they are adhered to consistently.

Because KANT2 supports rather than performs analysis, the limits of its uses are, to a large extent, the limits of analysts' imaginations. Analysts can create any kind of structure that appears to be fruitful. They are free to create structures which are as constrained or as unconstrained as they wish.

*Manual and optional operation*
Since KANT2 does not automate any of these uses, the burden of consistency, completeness and the prompt updating of supplementary structures, such as those used for the management of a study, rests with the analysts who create, use and maintain them. The fact that they are optional and manual means, as with any manual optional system, there is considerable scope for inconsistencies to develop. These not only arise between analysts, but also within the work of a single analyst if the work is spread over a long enough period for the analyst to forget the details of previous analytical decisions.

*Automatic and forced operation*
Automatic and/or forced use during the Alvey/DHSS Demonstrator Project of some KANT2 facilities created certain problems which are worth noting. When logging of provenance was implemented, provenance details – the analyst's name, the purpose of the session, the data and the time – were automatically associated with every change the analyst made to the structure during the session. Analysts were required to indicate the purpose of the session when starting each session.

We could save our work without ending a session, and it often saved time for one analyst to take over from another without closing the tool down and starting it up again. Several analysts might each do some analysis once KANT2 was up and running and it was all recorded as having been done by the person who first logged in on the tool. In daily use, a great deal of not very useful provenance information was collected, including a note of every spelling correction and all the changes made to test rules written first one way and then another. As we discovered, in order for the provenance log to be of any use, a small set of relevant purposes needed to be identified and used consistently by all analysts. Analysts needed to discipline themselves to record (by closing down the tool and opening it up again) when there was a change of analyst and/or when the purpose of the session changed. We decided to abandon the use of the facility until we had given more thought to what exactly we wanted to record about the way, when and by whom structures were built up and changed.

## The upside of hypertext tools

There are three main strengths of hypertext tools like KANT2:

- multiple inspection trails can be set up for 'readers'[6] to follow;
- different parts of the corpus can be juxtaposed;
- 'readers' have navigational flexibility.

## Multiple inspection trails

Each way of moving through the material can provide an insight of its own. 'Authors' of environments (structures, sources and links between them) can, by judicious labelling of the links, set up inspection trails for subsequent 'readers' of the on-line material to follow. Providing a number of such trails is one way of conveying a variety of messages about the material effectively and efficiently.

The hypertext presentation increases efficiency and consistency by obviating the need for replication.[7] A node can be part of a number of different trails and will thereby seem to be replicated several times when in fact it is not. If a document, whether paper-based or electronic, were to provide its reader with the same insights, each hypertext journey would have to be represented as a separate discussion or argument. Revisited material would either be replicated each time it figured in the discourse or the reader would have to struggle with cross-references to find the material each time it was referred to.

Revisiting nodes rather than replicating them also reduces the likelihood of introducing errors during retyping or copying. It takes the burden of cross-references off the reader, while providing a variety of ways of using material. It provides a very efficient way for one analyst to convey to another, or document for oneself, themes and strategies which make up the rich texture of the analysis as it proceeds.

### *Juxtaposition*

Juxtaposition facilitates overview and verification by inspection. As analysis progresses, the analysts may want to see the overall content and structure of the material analysed so far, for which an overview facility is helpful. Alternatively the analyst may want to check that nothing has been lost or misrepresented in transforming the material from one form of expression to another. The latter is particularly an issue when material is being expressed in increasingly formal ways. Analysts often structure the original material and write it up in one document, then rewrite it more formally in another document, and want to check that the formal version has faithfully captured the appropriate features of the informal version. Comparing the two versions by looking at them together section by section is typically the first, and often the only, verification technique used in this situation. This kind of check, 'verification by inspection', is made much easier if the versions can be put side-by-side, that is, juxtaposed, and the two expressions of the same material seen simultaneously.

KANT2 enables juxtaposition in several ways. One is related to the internal structure of KANT2 nodes, that is, the existence of their three internal fields. Another depends on the multiple windows and links of the system. A third depends on hiding material.

*Juxtaposition of fields*   Using KANT2 it was possible to put an English-like rule in the text field of a node and express the same rule in the formal syntax of the language of the knowledge-base in the rule field (just below the text field in the Full display style). The material could be processed in one order for the English-like rules and in another order for the formal rules but, because the two versions were put in the same node of the KANT2 structure, they would appear next to one another in the display.[8] Three versions of the material could be inspected – its title, its informal expression and its more formal expression. KANT3 was to have allowed for more fields to be created in nodes and to allow the selective hiding of types of fields. These changes would have allowed a greater variety of forms of expression of the material held in a single structure to be juxtaposed to one another for inspection.

*Juxtaposition of nodes*    An alternative way to view versions of the
same material together would have been to create separate
structures with links between them. The node in the structure
containing the less formal version would be linked to the node
where the material was expressed in the formal syntax and vice
versa. One could inspect the transformation from a less formal to a
more formal expression by selecting a node in one structure with an
appropriately labelled link (for example, 'formalized as') and
displaying the node at the other end. This method could accommodate inspection of transformations involving a number of
different versions by linking together all the nodes which contain
versions of the same material. Because several windows can be open
on the screen at once – the number depending on the size of the
window and how much of the window one wants to see – it could be
possible to see all versions of the material at once. The links can be
set up (or activated in such an order) so that the user goes from
window to window around a circle with the last of the sequence next
to the first of the sequence. This would be a particularly interesting
arrangement for checking the translation of a short paragraph from
language to language and finally back into the language of the
original.

*Juxtaposition by hiding*    Another kind of juxtaposition involves
hiding material which, in an ordinary document, would always be
visible. The Brief display style of KANT2 hides everything except the
titles of nodes, a facility available in most outliners (the Full display
style shows the contents of the nodes as well). As with other
outliners, KANT2 allows the user to collapse structures so that lower
(the more detailed) levels of the structure are hidden. These two
ways of hiding material allow the user to get an overview of the
content and structure of the material.

*Navigational flexibility*
In hypertext-like systems such as KANT2, readers can select different
starting points and navigate the corpus in ways which reflect their
individual concerns and thought patterns. Thus they can seek their
own insights as well as having access to those of the author(s) of the
environment.
    Navigational flexibility also allows a number of different analysts
to use the same material comfortably, even though their cognitive
styles and analytical concerns differ. None is compelled to follow
trails set up by another.

**The downside of hypertext tools**

Some disadvantages of KANT2 are disadvantages of most currently available hypertext tools:

- non-linear features don't transfer to hard copy;
- hypertext material is not yet very transportable;
- complexity is encouraged;
- cognitive overheads are high owing to the extra degrees of freedom and the need to think about the nature of links when new related material is introduced;
- readers and authors can get disoriented, and have difficulty in finding particular material.

Other disadvantages are more specific to KANT2 and the use of tools for analysis:

- hybrid structures can be created;
- juxtaposition can inhibit analysis.

Several of these warrant further discussion.

*Non-linear features don't transfer to hard copy*
Journeys which are easy to follow on-line certainly cannot be easily captured in a hard copy document. The elegance of trails disappears when hypertext is printed. It is a lumbering tedious business, if it is possible at all, to follow the trails. The difficulty of presenting hypertext as hard copy is endemic to the concept. Conklin cites Ted Nelson, a father of hypertext, defining it as 'a combination of natural language text with the computer's capacity for interactive branching, or dynamic display . . . of a nonlinear text . . . which cannot be printed conveniently on a conventional page' (Conklin, 1987: 17).

KANT2 does allow the label and destination node of links to be printed out with each node, so trails can be followed. But this so spreads out the nodes on the printed page that it is counter-productive. Visual clues to structural information, for example sibling and parent–child relationships between nodes, can be lost entirely. Printouts were cumbersome to use and would not do for scrutinizing trails except for the most committed reader. Attempts to review analysis using hard copy were so frustrating and time consuming that in the end scrutiny was usually abandoned before the review was completed. Typically the links were ignored when they were printed out and, because their presence made it more difficult to appreciate other aspects of structures, they were rarely shown on printed versions.

It follows that if the hypertext tools of today were used for analysis, the analyst would have to rely on on-line scrutiny for validation, verification and negotiation of meanings in which links are crucial. This means that difficulties with reading from a VDU screen have to be overcome and the analyst must accept that the range of people who could be involved in the analysis process is reduced to those who can be connected on-line or can travel to the analyst. The constraint on who can be involved in scrutinizing analysis could be a major problem if the analysis leads to the development of a knowledge-base in which a number of parties have an interest. It works counter to democratization of computer developments by inhibiting the spread of their 'ownership', especially into the user community.

Even if hypertext trails were printed in some diagrammatic form showing the links and pointing somehow to text printed out in appropriate document modules, there would be difficulties. Readers bring prose reading strategies to the inspection of hard copy diagrams (Cordingley, 1987). Even when alternative sequences are explicitly indicated, the western strategies of reading left to right, and top to bottom are transferred to diagrams. It is very difficult to free readers from these habits. The tendency to read these 'natural orders' into diagrams is strong and largely unconscious. It is a real problem to those who want to represent in a diagram a collection of hypertext material where no sequencing between nodes is to be implied.

*Non-transportability*
Rahtz, Carr and Hall point out that:

> In many hypertext systems the assumption is usually that the magic system chosen is to be the final resting place of the data, and although tools are provided to import text and pictures, little effort is expended on tools to write out a generalized version of the knowledge suitable for other systems. Import and export facilities generally relate to the low-level elements of the document (words, numbers, bitmaps), and a general criticism can be made that hypertext shares with desktop publishing a view of documents as a continuous stream of words, which are broken up into pleasant-looking groups with no explicit decisions about what the groups represent. (1989: 2)

They have worked on Lace, a hypertext front end to documents which allows the structure of the material to be retained while having the advantages of treating it as hypertext.

> Lace aims to minimize the effort needed to take a document to a new medium; the intention is to protect the writer's investment, . . . a

document is seen here as an explicitly authored structure, rather than a simple 'dump' of facts at one level. (1989: 6)

Whatever tools are developed must consider both import and export, not only between computers but also between media.

## Complexity is encouraged

The extra degrees of freedom in hypertext encourage structural complexity. Multiple interconnected structures of different kinds are the norm. Even when a single structural form is used, as in KANT2 which is based upon outline hierarchies, the links the analyst can create within and between them increases the complexity by an order of magnitude.

## Multi-type structures allowed (hybrid)

KANT2 places few limits on its use. It automates little and it does not force conformation to a structured method or formal representation. Free-wheeling independent analysts would say that is a strength. Those who are looking for ways to help disparate individuals contribute to a single analysis process might contest that. The only standards (in the sense of ensuring similarity of representation) are achieved through individuals agreeing to and following the same conventions. If they forget or refuse, the tool will not know and will not enforce conformance.

In particular, the introduction of several defining relationships within a structure is not prohibited. Hybrid structures in which, say, some nodes are 'kinds of' whatever their parents are, other nodes are 'parts of' whatever their parents are, and yet others are 'caused by' or 'follow in time after' their parents, can be created. Typically this clouds analysis unless it is made explicit; unfortunately it usually is not.

## Juxtaposition may inhibit analysis

The ability to juxtapose material has a downside as well as the upside outlined above. The process of analysis involves the taking apart of material – identifying fundamental elements, breaking the material down into these elements – and (if synthesis is considered to be part of the analytic process) reforming it in more insightful ways. The new version may well be radically different from the original in form and representation, but faithful to its nature and content.

When the original is juxtaposed to the emerging new version, fresh and unfettered reformulation becomes more difficult. Visual separation seems necessary for analysts to reorganize material freely. Fundamental elements are usually identified as a result of considering similarities in a number of disparate portions of the material. If an analysis tool ties the analyst to a particular portion of the material – by juxtaposing the emerging representation with one portion of the material, as happened when a portion of the source was juxtaposed with a node whose fields were used for increasingly formal representations of it – the reformulation will almost inevitably be heavily influenced by the portion with which it is juxtaposed. The activity becomes transformation rather than analysis. As it happened, much of the work done using KANT2 was, correctly, transformation of material and so the tool was well suited to the task. However, many analysis tasks are not transformations. Hypertext-like tools should be selected and used with this distinction between radical analysis and incrementally formal reformulation in mind.

**Wish list**

There are a number of facilities on my hypertext wish list. It would be lovely, for example, to have multimedia annotation facilities, so, for example, sound could be annotated with pictures (and vice versa) and both could be annotated with text. It would be useful to be able to link diagrams to source text and to an automatically populated lexicon or set of templates designed by the analyst, all in a hypertext environment. The provision of graphical drawing and manipulation capabilities with analyst-definable constraints could be incorporated in a hypertext-like environment to great advantage.

Three requirements arising more directly from the KANT experience are: the provision of more operations on links; better ways of scrutinizing hypertext material off-line; and more ways of looking at structures.

*More operations on links*
It would be useful to be able to sort link labels and create a dictionary of relationships.

It would be useful to exploit the nature of relationships in analysis. For example, once a relationship such as 'lives in the same house as' was identified as being symmetrical, whenever a link was made and given that label a reverse link between the two nodes could also be made or perhaps proposed by the tool.

*Better ways of scrutinizing hypertext off-line*
KANT2 does have a provision for printing out the nature and destination of links, but there is no provision for printing out the

label and originator nodes of links coming into a node. Whatever way links are represented off-line, and a lot of work is needed to devise a satisfactory way of doing this, should allow a reader to see the node both as originating a set of links and as a destination for a set of links.

*More ways of looking at structures*
KANT2 does not allow level-by-level inspection, that is, the hiding of higher as well as lower levels. There are good theoretical reasons for not providing that facility, as the layers may have different meanings across the structure. For example, a third-level node in one part of a structure may be as detailed/refined/(or whatever) as a fifth-level node in another part, in which case level-by-level analysis would have no meaning. The fact that dependencies are not visible could be misleading. However, there are some analyses where levels do have meaning and an analyst would like to inspect structures a level at a time.

Brief and Full displays apply to the whole structure. It would be useful to have part of the structure with only headings showing, but others with the full node showing. This facility is available in some other (non-hypertext-like) outliners.

**Conclusions**

Hypertext tools may provide useful ways for analysts to structure, analyse and manage qualitative data. The upside is that it is an approach which frees the analyst from linearity; permits a number of items to be juxtaposed, facilitating critical scrutiny and/or the search for insight; provides facilities for analysts to set up multiple trails through material; and allows the material to be navigated in a number of different ways, suiting individual styles or analytical requirements.

The downside is that it can impose an additional cognitive burden on the analysts; it is easy for a reader or analyst to become disoriented and particular items of material to be 'lost'; it encourages complexity in analysis, including the creation of hybrid structures; hypertexts are not yet very transportable; it is difficult to scrutinize the hypertext features on hard copy versions; and juxtaposition, an advantage in some respects, may actually inhibit radical analysis.

There is no doubt that hypertext offers much that is promising, but its downside for analysts of qualitative data should not be overlooked.

## Notes

This chapter derives from work carried out on the Alvey/DHSS Large Demonstrator Project, which was supported by the UK Department of Trade and Industry through the Alvey Directorate and the Science and Engineering Research Council. The project collaborators were ICL, Logica, Imperial College London and the Universities of Lancaster, Liverpool and Surrey. I have derived great benefit from discussions with other members of the project and their assistance is gratefully acknowledged. However, the views expressed in this chapter are mine and may not represent those of the collaborators or be shared by all project members.

1. The way the structure is developed depends of course on the purpose for which it is devised. Typically where a concept is broken down, subheadings will be mutually exclusive, although it might make sense for the analysis to violate this constraint.

2. One of the enhancements of KANT3 was to allow for an arbitrary number of user-definable 'fields' in the nodes, rather than just the three (title, text and rule) permitted by KANT2. The rule field was a feature of KANT which allowed it to be a representation of the rules which, with the class definitions and class hierarchy, made up the knowledge-base. Facilities were provided in KANT2 to allow class definitions and rules to be created, altered and, in the case of rules, compiled directly from within a KANT structure.

3. Source text was 'KANTified' by a separate program, which identified its special features, such as headings of different styles and notes in the margin of legal statutes, and allowed a facsimile of even very complex publications to be available on-line. KANT3 had a *mode change* which would allow authorized analysts to alter source text. This would be used, for example, to correct errors in interview transcripts.

4. If links of this kind were made it would make sense to have a much deeper structure than the three levels of this chapter, perhaps giving every paragraph a title so it would be a node in its own right.

5. Provenance refers to details (by whom, when, in what analytical context) relating to the introduction and/or changing of the material handled by the system.

6. The terms 'reader' and 'author' are used to distinguish between those who are not altering the structures or making links (readers) and those who are (authors). Analysts are usually in the role of authors, but could be a reader in someone else's KANT environment of sources and structures.

7. This is not to suggest that a node cannot be copied and appear in more than one place in the corpus; just that it need not be.

8. If one is not intending to use the rule-checking capability of KANT, this really is no more than making special use of an outlining/word processing facility – with the title being like a heading of an outline and the two fields being like two paragraphs of text associated with the heading – not really hypertext.

# 11

# The Right Brain Strikes Back

*Michael Agar*

A few years ago I was contacted by an American arts foundation. They wanted to develop a system to assist art and architectural historians in their research. As a first step, they had commissioned a study where qualitative researchers had interviewed historians to learn something about the way they worked. The ETHNOGRAPH was used to come up with a final report. Somehow, said the foundation representative, it hadn't answered their question. Would I take a look at it and meet with them?

I read the report. The analysis was solid and competent, but it was of the 'cut the interview into topical segments and sort' variety. I use this approach all the time – as have countless qualitative researchers before me – and I describe it in *The Professional Stranger* (Agar, 1980b). But the segment-and-sort approach, the one for which the ETHNOGRAPH is an indispensable ally, missed the goals of the foundation's study.

The foundation wanted an utterance-by-utterance analysis to elucidate folk theories that represented how an individual researcher thought about his/her work as he/she did it. But when the qualitative researchers called up the ETHNOGRAPH, they committed themselves to multi-utterance cuts that cohered topically. The result was a report on shared topics of concern together with samples of how those topics were represented in an interview, rather than the more detailed theories of actions, states and results that were embedded, utterance by utterance, in those segments. The cuts were on the one hand too gross for such an analysis, and on the other hand too fine because chains of reasoning were interrupted at investigator-imposed topical shifts.

I don't mean to pick on the ETHNOGRAPH. On the contrary, later I shall describe a study where, if the ETHNOGRAPH had been available, I would have been the first in line. I do mean to say that a program like the ETHNOGRAPH represents a *part of* an ethnographic research process. When the part is taken for the whole, you get a pathological metonym that can lead you straight to the right answer to the wrong question.

The experience with the foundation, together with the growing number of computational conversations among colleagues, began to worry me. As more and more colleagues acquired computer know-how, I heard less about what ethnography was and how to think about it, and more about the newest hardware and software and what it could do, about memory capacity and hard disk access, about the latest laptop and illuminated screen. I worried that the means was beginning to replace the end, that the comfortable certainty of bytes and baud might replace the ambiguities of indeterminate pattern and emergent research.

I became even more worried about the trend as my paranoid political fantasies took hold. Though it is terribly superficial to try and summarize in a paragraph or two, recent American history, in my view, was driven by exhaustion after Watergate, Vietnam and Iran into an uncritical acceptance of some traditional American themes, like technology-driven productivity. Ethnography, in this worldview, has no value at all, except as an adjunct to marketing research or policy implementation. Ethnography, maybe, but only under control.

Extreme computer lust adapted one to this shift perfectly. Ethnographers weren't a threat to the uncritical *Zeitgeist*; they were just another kind of hacker, celebrating the same new technology that enhanced productivity in so many other domains. Social research didn't ferret out the current presuppositions and bring them to light as just one of a number of imaginable alternatives. Instead, social research busied itself with a new socially shared and culturally valued piece of technology that efficiently implemented pre-set problem definitions and categories of analysis.

I said that this was a paranoid fantasy, and I don't mean to say that the microcomputer doesn't have – and hasn't been demonstrated to have – powerful and positive consequences for what we do. On the contrary. But something kept gnawing away at my soul, telling me that this machine that was such a great help might take over a disproportionate share of the disciplinary show. The computer had shifted, in my worst-case scenario, from an aid in doing ethnography to a definition of what ethnography might do. It might mutate from an item in a context to the context itself. The arts foundation study was an example. Ethnography was the ETHNOGRAPH, and whatever analysis the ETHNOGRAPH enabled was ethnography.

At the same time, another movement, at least in American anthropology, started up and continues to flourish. This movement set up housekeeping with literary theory, began to talk about ethnography as genre, and visualized ethnographic reports as literature. I'm going to steal some of their insights shortly, but in its most extreme form the movement sets as devastating a set of limits as any hard-core ethnohacker could.

One no sooner lays out an ethnographic statement than one begins to deconstruct by showing the arbitrary webs of power, images of self and other, historical circumstances, and epistemological limits on which the statement rests. In the long run this movement will be seen as teaching us a great deal about the limits of what we do, but at the moment, in its strongest form, ethnography becomes a document that reflects mostly back on itself.

With these two worst-case models in mind – on the one hand, reducing massive amounts of texts to codes and sorting for eternity; on the other hand, asserting something on page one and spending the rest of the chapter telling the readers why they shouldn't believe it – I moved to Austria for my year as a visiting professor.

When writing this chapter I was working at the Linguistics Institute at the University of Vienna, trying to figure out how an ethnographer interested in language figures out something as complicated as Austria. I arrived in Vienna, flipped open the lid on my laptop, and stared at the screen. I wrote a couple of letters to warm up and then realized I had no idea what I was going to do or how I was going to do it.

The computer, of course, wasn't at fault. Our ideas about ethnography are currently chaotic, and the edges around our units of study have disappeared in the postmodern fog. These aren't problems that a computer can solve, and I found myself, for the first time in several years, snapping the laptop lid shut, because the machine looked more like a hindrance than a help. I didn't need more computational power; I didn't need software better suited to the problem; I needed a sense of what the problem was and how to begin to think about it.

Vienna handed me the perfect example of the computational dilemma, a research problem whose solution lay in an emergent way of seeing built on the dialectic of intense detail and global view that is such a critical part of the formative stages of a qualitative study. The computer, with its ability to handle massive amounts of material according to some system of categories, was simply irrelevant. Vienna (and the Surrey conference) were the combined opportunities to reflect on the question, what was going on that the computer couldn't handle? And the question led me to think back to my own history with the machine.

As an undergraduate in the 1960s I took advantage of the radical new idea that a student should be allowed to take a course outside his major subject on a pass/fail basis. I signed up for an introduction to computer programming. I'm not sure why, really, except that I grew up in the four-wheeled California valley subculture described in the film *American Graffiti* and I was tired of the existential novel and wanted to get my hands on the closest academic equivalent to a '55 Chevy. We were introduced to the new language that was going to be the international standard for all time, ALGOL, something most of you have probably never heard of.

I enjoyed the course. I would have received an A if I hadn't taken it pass/fail, but in the punitive tradition of university life you weren't allowed to switch back for a grade. The previous year I'd worked in India with an anthropology professor, Alan Beals, who had collected massive amounts of genealogies for a study of comparative fertility. For the next couple of years we worked together to code the genealogies and write ALGOL programs to analyze fertility by caste, lineage and family. It was, by today's standards, babytalk, but at the time I felt like we were on the way to a Nobel Prize.

I still remember how luxurious it felt to go to the computer center at 3 in the morning, a box of cards tucked under my arm, and run my programs. I had befriended the night-shift operator, so he gave me free rein and taught me about the machine. I remember how clear and precise everything was, without ambiguity, how my time in the computer center was a psychic vacation compared with the chaos outside in the years between 1966 and 1968.

Later in life I read the anthropologist/psychiatrist George Devereaux's book, *From Anxiety to Method in the Behavioral Sciences* (1967). His argument, as the title indicates, is that social research traditions carry a push to certainty and clarity, a push that causes anxiety until it is successfully resolved. The danger, he argues, is that the ambiguity is resolved too quickly, or even perhaps at all. I felt that push working on the genealogies, and the computer was an ideal and effective remedy. I felt it again in Vienna, but the epistemological crisis and the massive nature of the research problem forced me to push back. No rush to clarity and method, and, therefore, no machine.

The story now shifts to the late 1970s, when Radio Shack and Apple started to mass-market a microcomputer. I bought a TRS80 Model I. I can't even remember now what capacity it had – 48K in the keyboard and tape cassettes come to mind. I typed in three interviews I was doing on life histories and inserted simple codes after each statement about a social other that indicated things like affect and power versus solidarity, then wrote a simple BASIC program to go through the tape and pull out statements with certain code combinations. I sent an article to *Computers in the Humanities*

(1983), and I think it counts as one of the earliest published pieces on the use of microcomputers in ethnographic research.

The thing that bothered me at the time – I mentioned this in the article – was the reaction of colleagues. I was excited about the potential of the machine in handling a core ethnographic task. But colleagues – qualitative or quantitative – would walk by my open office door, hear a strange sound, and peek in. There, on the narrow silvery paper that slid out of those early printers, appeared statements that informant X had made about significant others, sorted by authority and effect. I can't tell you how impressed they were. I kept saying, 'Well, yes, but you see, it's the same thing I've always done.'

Of course it wasn't exactly the same thing. I saw, as they did, the potential for rapidly handling large amounts of qualitative data. But I kept having nightmares about two studies – a lousy computer analysis and a beautiful analysis done by hand – where the community of researchers would immediately gather around the printout and celebrate its form rather than its content. The computer was a rhetorical device to be feared. The problem has, in my experience, become more rather than less acute with discipline-wide computer sophistication. So, when I hit the research wall in Vienna, I decided that the computer would not provide the rhetoric of my research. I'd invent the rhetoric first, then fit the computer in, if and when it fitted in at all.

Now, one more scene shift to the early 1980s. I used a TRS80 Model III in a study of independent truckers from transcripts to finished book (1986). By then, more powerful machines and programs were available, but since I'd started things on the old Model I, and since Tandy had me by the operating system, I stayed with their product. I transcribed interviews and took notes on events, literature and documents. Then I used the Tandy database program to index a record to each content segment, and wrote a simple BASIC program that tacked back and forth between database and texts. It was a crude kind of ETHNOGRAPH, but the program wasn't around yet.

Nothing fancy or complicated, but my guesstimate is that full integration of the microcomputer into the ethnography saved me a quarter of the time I would have spent without it. Most important, something I haven't seen discussed in the qualitative literature, was the quasi-hypothesis test that the system enabled. One classic criticism of qualitative research is that the outsider can't evaluate the comparative weight of supporting versus non-supporting material, that Popperian falsification is impossible to attain.

The database system allowed me, at any given point in time, to call up all the records that represented texts that weren't accounted for in the analysis. At the end of the book, I told the reader what kind of material wasn't accounted for, what it was about, and I gave a rough idea of just how much text the leftovers represented. The microcomputer, in short, didn't just help handle the material and shape it into a book; it also let me, in a rough way, fulfill the qualitative Popperian dream by repeatedly trying to prove myself wrong.

But this study of independent truckers was unique. I came to it with more background knowledge that I'd ever had before. I'd dispatched trucks for a year, have a cousin who is an independent trucker, and generally found myself associating with the guys I'd gone to high school with. I also had a rough theoretical frame blending dependence and independence as cultural notions with the impact of deregulation of the US trucking industry. And finally, the segment-and-sort approach was suited to my analysis, since the primary question centered on shared categories of experience among a group. In Vienna, I had neither the cultural background, nor the theoretical framework, nor the shared category goal.

With this happy 20-year history with the machine, how could I possibly complain? I don't want to complain, just remind that, in spite of the potential of the machine to assist in *part of* any ethnographic study, it is not particularly useful in what I think of as the heart of ethnography, namely, the building through experience of a *way of seeing* a research problem, and in Vienna I had no idea how to start.

Related to my parodies of ethnohacking and destructive deconstruction, and the caution born of computational experience, I also had some problems figuring out what to study. The world that we so arrogantly set out to understand has ripped the edges of our old categories. Somewhere in Austria there's probably still a villager who doesn't have a TV, doesn't have one kid in college and another at home listening to Madonna, doesn't consciously participate in the world economy and discuss international politics, but I can't find them.

Traditional ethnography presupposes boundaries, social and cognitive edges, within which a small group can be picked out, lived with and eventually, one hopes, understood. This image of what our data are is increasingly difficult to support. In the so-called postmodern condition, everyone has something in common with any other person, but not everything in common with anyone. (Actually, Clyde Kluckhohn said something like that in 1949 in a book called *A Mirror for Man*.) The edges are gone.

When I voiced this delicate problem to colleagues in Vienna – 'How do I study Austria?' – their answers were telling. Gypsies or street people were popular suggestions, helpful efforts to push me in the direction of something like a tribe or band. But, even if such groups could be bounded like we used to, that's not what I wanted to do. I wanted to learn something about Austria. As an ethnographer. With or without a computer or a narrative structure. So what was I going to do?

Answering this question has preoccupied me for five months. I'd like to sketch the shape that the solutions are taking. The kind of patterns that ethnographers construct are multi-level things and, unlike the old linguistic model of phonology, morphology and syntax (itself problematic), it's not clear what the levels are or what they should be called. For now I'll simplify and fall back on the simple two-level discussion that usually gets jargonized by 'micro/ macro'. Given my current interests in discourse analysis on the one hand and political economy on the other, I had a rough idea of what the bottom and the top would be.

As usual in my career, I wound up studying something that the world handed me instead of something I had picked out beforehand. That something was a political scandal. Since the late 1970s, Austria has been embroiled in a series of scandals that have shaken the foundations of the postwar Second Republic. The Waldheim affair and the recent Lainz hospital deaths are the two that most of the world knows about. A recent cover of *Der Spiegel* called Austria 'the scandal republic'.

When I arrived in early February 1989, conversations and media were full of a new scandal, something called the '*Lucona* affair'. *Lucona* is the name of a ship that sank in the Indian Ocean in early 1977. Udo Proksch, social lion, wit and entrepreneur, owned the freight that was aboard and filed his insurance claim. Right from the beginning, weights and costs on the shipping invoices didn't accord with current market values, so the insurance company refused to pay.

The story continues over the years, through several Austrian civil courts and, since 1983, through the criminal justice system as well. A book about the case – a Truman Capote style 'true crime' story – appeared as recently as 1988. Suspicion grew that Udo Proksch had intentionally blown up the ship to collect insurance on worthless freight. It looked more and more like Proksch's highly placed friends in the ruling socialist regime had intervened to delay criminal investigations of the case. In 1988 Proksch fled the country, and in the Fall the Austrian parliament voted to conduct a hearing, a remarkable hearing, since it was the first in the history of the Second Republic where media coverage would be allowed. There is a great deal more to tell you about the *Lucona* scandal, but I don't want to do that here. Instead, I just want to say that the *Lucona* scandal caught my attention – how could it not? Since I was teaching two seminars at the Institute, and since transcripts of the hearing were published by the Austrian newsweekly *Profil*, I decided that my students and I would use them as data.

We approached the transcripts from the point of view of argumentation theory (van Eemeren et al., 1987). Once again, this isn't the time to spell it all out, but argumentation theory is grounded in the work of Toulmin and Habermas and sets out the relationships between Data and Conclusions, or between Grounds/ Goals and Actions, the Justifications that support those links, the Norms that support those justifications, and the possible Exceptions to the relationships those links define. The theory is intended to generate models of how people argue, or sometimes of how people *should* argue, and it leads naturally to attempts to map the theory onto actual texts.

In the literature, the mapping is always problematic, if not a full disaster. Most of the literature is based on constructed examples rather than argumentation transcripts. My students and I took the theory and laid it over the texts of the hearings. We did find some cases where the mapping was fairly straightforward, and we did observe that there was obviously a relationship between text and theory, but we had – as expected – problems filling in the gap between the two. I asked the students to work on the gap; most of them never came back. But together with the ones that did, some interesting relationships surfaced. Let me offer you an example of the material, translated casually for comprehension.

Rieder, socialist member of parliament, representative of the party responsible for the scandal, is interrogating Guggenbichler, a private detective, a fascinating figure out of *film noir*. Guggenbichler was hired by the insurance company after they were told by the courts to pay up. He found enough evidence of insurance fraud to file criminal charges against Udo Proksch.

Guggenbichler had taped and photographed a conversation between Proksch and a socialist minister. Rieder wants to label that action '*bespitzeln*'. The word has negative connotations, like 'spying' or 'snitching' in English. Guggenbichler fights the label by comparing Rieder's definition of *Bespitzelung* with what the socialist government did to him, and then he shifts the labels for his actions to 'beschatten' (shadow) and 'ermitteln' (investigate), terms that neutrally describe the actions of a detective.

*Rieder*: Dann werde ich anders fragen. Nach dem Bericht der Wochenpresse ging es um ein Zusammentreffen des damaligen Außenministers Gratz mit Udo Proksch, also um diese beiden Personen. Ist Ihnen mitgeteilt worden, um jetzt den Begriff der Bespitzelung zu definieren, daß sich Personen bemühen, den Wortlaut ihrer Gespräche, den Inhalt ihre Informationen wahrzunehmen?

(Then I'll ask it another way. According to the Weekly Press's report it deals with a meeting between then foreign minister Gratz with Udo Proksch, with these two people. Were you informed – now the concept of 'spying' is defined – that individuals were trying to record the details of their conversation, the contents?)

*Guggenbichler*: Also irgendwie komme ich mit Ihrer Sprechweise nicht klar. Ich verstehe Sie noch immer nicht. Was wollen Sie von mir wissen?

(Somehow I'm not getting what you're trying to say. I still don't understand. What do you want to know from me?)

*Rieder*: Sie haben gesagt, Sie können mit dem Begriff 'Bespitzelung' nichts anfangen. Meine Einschätzung des Begriffes Bespitzelung ist, daß hinter dem Rücken der Betreffenden ohne ihr Wissen Bemühungen im Gange sind, den Inhalt von Gesprächen wahrzunehmen, aufzuzeichnen.

(You said you couldn't get anywhere with the concept of 'spying'. My evaluation of the concept of 'spying' is that efforts are made, behind the backs and without the knowledge of those concerned, to hear, to record the contents of their conversation.)

*Guggenbichler*: Aha. Sie meinen so ähnlich, wie wenn man zum Beispiel auf illegalem Weg das Datenschutzgesetz verletzt und Akten behändigt, um einer politischen Partei irgendwie Hilfestellung zu erleisten. Das meinen Sie?

(Ah, you mean similar for example to when one helps out a political party by handing over files illegally against confidentiality laws? Is that what you mean?)

*Rieder*: Das muß nicht illegal sein, sondern unter Bespitzelung verstehe ich, daß hinter dem Rücken der Betreffenden ohne ihr Wissen von persönlichen Gesprächen Wahrnehmung erlangt werden kann.

(It doesn't have to be illegal. Instead, by 'spying' I understand that one can hear personal conversations behind the backs of those concerned without their knowledge.)

*Guggenbichler*: Jetzt habe ich verstanden, jetzt kann ich antworten. Es ist so, wenn ich einen Ermittlungsauftrag habe, wegen sechsfachem Mord und Betrug in Höhe von 300 Millionen Schilling zu ermitteln, dann führe ich keine Bespitzelungen durch, sondern ermittle und beschatte Personen, die im engen Umfeld und Zusammenhang mit dem

Betreffenden stehen. Und so leid es mir tut, darunter is auch der Herr Gratz gefallen, wenn Sie das wissen wollten.
(Now I understand, now I can answer. It's like this. When I have a contract to investigate sixfold murder and fraud in the amount of 300 million Schillings, then I don't 'spy'. Instead, I investigate and shadow persons who associate and have something to do with the concerned. And sorry as I am, Herr Gratz was among them, if that's what you wanted to know.)

This is an argument, but it has more to do with how to label an action rather than with a justification of the grounds or goals of that action. Depending on what you call it, a frame of quite different grounds and goals and justifications travels along in the background knowledge that hearing participants and media consumers share. If it's *'bespitzeln'*, the grounds are sleazy and the goals unfair to the target; if it's *'beschatten'* and *'ermitteln'*, it's the duty of the professional private investigator; the grounds and goals are not only acceptable, they are the responsibility of the detective vis à vis his client, in this case an insurance company that is a central institution of Austrian society.

The example is only one of many, but the point is that the argumentation theorists actually defined a type of *schema* or *frame*, a general relationship among different kinds of know-how and know-that. There are times when a particular frame models the process in terms of which an exchange takes place, when the frame accounts for the data like a theory should, but these are the exceptions. The argumentation theorists don't have a theory of argumentation; they have a theory of a *frame type* that has several potential relationships to an argument, or to other types of text as well.

Hammering together a modified theory of argumentation in light of the *Lucona* transcripts of course involves more than this one example illustrates. My point at the moment is just that this critical micro-level work requires looking at a few detailed passages, over and over again, doing the dialectic dance between an idea about how text is organized and a couple of examples, figuring out what I was looking at, how to look at it, and why. The computer had no role to play in this, except in the trivial sense of word processing.

Now I want to consider the second problem, the macro level. I could stop with argumentation theory and texts, but I wanted to look at *Lucona* and figure out how to say something about Austria as well. I needed a way to think about the *Lucona* hearing, not only in terms of its internal structure, but also in terms of the larger picture it fits into.

Once again, I started by trying to use the machine. I thought about collecting and entering newspaper and magazine articles and notes from conversations. And once again, this sort of slash and burn empiricism seemed to miss the point. Instead, I just read, listened, and tried out my own opinions, not for any particular detail, but rather for a global sense of what the *Lucona* affair said about the postwar Second Republic.

Then one day I wandered into Kolisch's bookstore, famous in Vienna because it's set up so you can browse without knowing which book you want. There on the lower shelf sat a new book, edited by two German sociologists, called *Anatomy of the Political Scandal* (Ebbighausen and Neckel, 1989). It had articles on scandals as necessary parts of liberal democracy, scandal as theater, scandal structure, even a contribution on scandals in ancient Greece.

The book helped pull together a macro view of *Lucona*. Here's the general idea that's taking shape, an ideal also rooted in Turner's (1957) discussion of the social drama. Scandal is a drama that the social order stages to tell itself a story about itself, to use Geertz's (1976) formulation. The conflict that the scandal dramatizes is the same kind of conflict that makes for good theater. I began to see that *Lucona* – the first public legislative hearing in Austrian postwar history – was a drama about a centuries-old political culture lumbering in the direction of liberal democracy.

The character I referred to earlier, Guggenbichler, is the private detective who started the criminal proceedings against Udo Proksch back in July 1983. The field of 'scandalology' – really, that's what they call it – suggests that certain key roles will be found in any scandal. I decided to pull out some statements by Guggenbichler and arrange them thematically to see how he characterized himself, what kind of a role he played.

He represents himself as a classic type, the shadowy outsider who stands on the edges and sees more clearly than the insiders the webs of hypocrisy in which they live. In contrast to the insiders, he is a figure of integrity, even if – as he freely admits – he uses some questionable means to achieve his results. But more generally, and more importantly, Guggenbichler and other figures like him in the hearing represent forces of outspoken individuality that call for open government. To appreciate what a departure this is, you need more background in Austrian history than I have time to provide.

Maybe I can best sum it up with another story. Just last week I had dinner with a group that included an Austrian novelist. We were talking about what a good paper the *Neue Züricher Zeitung* is and how horrible the Viennese papers are. 'Why doesn't Austria have a NZZ?' I asked. 'Because', said the writer, 'what happened in 1848 upset the Kaiser.' We all laughed, but the other Austrians nodded and said 'That's right' and 'Really'. *Lucona* is so dramatic because it represents the conflict between a closed government style with roots in the old hand of imperial authority and the newer trend to a style of open individuality.

Austrian politics is going through a sea change right now – new parties on the left and right, increasing voter discontent, personalization of candidates and use of television – the story, as I said, is more than I can do justice to here. But the point is that the theory of scandal as a theater in which key contradictions are given dramatic representation is just the one I needed. It ties in with symbolic anthropological notions, links the *Lucona* event to political economy, and provides a broader context into which the micro analysis of argumentation can be placed. This second critical research task, tinkering with the macro frame, didn't have much to do with the computer, either.

To conclude I'd like to tell you how I might have used the machine earlier, except that a piece of hardware has been neglected in the microcomputing world. Recently, a computer social science colleague called me. He was writing an article and asking several people for a telephone interview. In my computational dream world, what would I want that I didn't have now? My answer didn't convince him that I was certifiable, so I'd like to try it here. Actually, as I hallucinated a response, I wondered why I hadn't talked about these aspects of my ethnographic style before.

I could have used the computer earlier in Vienna, if I'd had a screen that I could sit inside of. Let me explain, first at the macro level. A couple of times during the early stages of an ethnography I'll find an empty classroom, usually in the evening when the building is deserted, a classroom with blackboards on several walls. I start writing things on the boards, erasing and writing again, not data, but rather thoughts, patterns. I'll often stand in the middle of the room and turn slowly around, looking at the boards, then go to another board and write something else. One colleague still accuses me of 'research deviance', but I think its similar to something that we all do.

What's important is the large space that I can visualize all at once. There is a famous quote attributed to Lévi-Strauss that if he had a card table big enough, he could figure out all of France. If I could sit in the middle of a room-sized screen, I would be telling you about how I had used the computer in the early stages of my research instead of why I didn't. The large, simultaneously accessible visual space is critical for me in snapping the macro frame for an ethnography into focus.

The large screen would also have played a role in the micro analysis. In that phase, I need to lay out a couple of stretches of transcript on a table so I can look at it all at once. Then I need to mark different parts in different ways to find the pattern that holds the text together and ties it to whatever external frame I'm developing. The software problem here would be simple to solve. You'd need to be able to quickly insert different colored marks of different kinds at different points so you could see the multiple connections across the text all at once, sort of a multi-thread DNA laid on the text so you could look at the patterns that each thread revealed and then the patterns among the patterns. But once again you'd need a much bigger screen, because simultaneous visual access to material is what makes the ideas happen.

Computational trends in qualitative research carry a logic that runs like this: Isolate those aspects of ethnographic research that lend themselves to computer assistance and develop software to implement them. So far, so good. But then comes the potentially destructive step – conduct an ethnography to maximize fit between the process and the available software. This second step is supported by everything from individual researcher anxiety about systematic results to broader historical pressures for efficient technology.

The problem is that use of software presupposes a way of seeing the problem and the situation, the pinnacle of the top-down framework that guides one into gathering of material, development of research categories, and perceptions of relationships among them. That critical way of seeing, in my experience at least, comes out of numerous cycles through a little bit of data, massive amounts of thinking about that data, and slippery things like intuition and serendipity. An electronic ally doesn't have much of a role to play.

In some ways, this is a simple echo of the old chant, 'Know the problem before you look for software.' But I mean something more than just that, because 'knowing the problem' is exactly where ethnography shines in comparison with other social research frameworks. Figuring out the problem is part of the research process, often requiring most of the time and energy of a researcher, always involving more creativity than laying marks on text and moving them around.

Creation of macro and micro frameworks has more to do with synthesis and pattern-perception than with analysis and data processing. Computer applications in qualitative research have mostly been of the segment-and-sort variety. At this they are without equal, and that task will remain a core part of ethnographic work. But some of ethnography, especially in the critical, framework-setting stages, emphasizes the interrelated detail in a small number of cases rather than the common properties across a large number. For that, you need a little bit of data and a lot of right brain.

# Resources

This section provides a listing of programs with brief details of their features and hardware requirements. Where appropriate, information is also provided about pricing and distribution. By no means *all* the available programs are listed here.

We believe the information contained in this section to be up to date and accurate. Specification and prices can, of course, change without notice. Prospective purchasers are advised to ensure that a particular program will meet their needs before buying it. The editors regret that they cannot normally answer queries about specific programs.

Dr Renata Tesch provides advice and consultancy on the use of computers in qualitative research. She also distributes a number of the programs listed below. She can be contacted at:

> Qualitative Research Management
> 73425 Hilltop Road
> Desert Hot Springs
> CA 92240, USA
> Tel: (619) 329-7026

**Program:** ETHNO™        **Version:** 2

**Developer:** David R. Heise, Indiana University.

**Description:** Program for studying concepts and their logical connections, and for discovering systems of rules that govern action, ETHNO offers computer-assisted construction and testing of action grammars to interpret texts, behaviour transcripts, narratives, historical episodes, etc.

**Required hardware:** PC compatible, 512K RAM, DOS 2.1 or higher. Colour monitor desirable but not required. Program prints to Hewlett-Packard or Epson printers or to ASCII files.

**Price:**

| | |
|---|---|
| Single pack | $35 |
| Lab pack (5 programs, 1 documentation) | $70 |
| Site licence, 2-year colleges | $350 |
| Site licence, other institutions | $525 |

Add $5 for Alaska, Hawaii, Canada; $20 for other countries.

**Distributed by:** National Collegiate Software of Duke University Press, 6697 College Station, Durham, NC 27708, USA. Tel: (919) 684-6837 or (919) 737-2468 (sole distributor)

**Program:** ETHNOGRAPH™    **Version:** 3.0 (version 4.0 is under development)

**Developer:** John V. Seidel, PhD, Qualis Research Associates.

**Description:** The ETHNOGRAPH allows the qualitative/ethnographic researcher to identify and retrieve text from documents. The basic unit is the segment. Each segment can be identified by up to 12 'codewords'. Segments can be nested and overlapped seven levels deep. Search results are sensitive to nests and overlaps. Searches can be done on the basis of a single codeword or multiple codewords. Entire data files can be identified by face sheet variables. Existing coding schemes can be selectively or globally modified.

**Required hardware:** Runs on all IBM PCs and compatibles. Hard disk recommended; essential for version 4.0.

**Price:**

|  | USA | Shipping Canada | Other |
|---|---|---|---|
| 1 copy | $150 | $5 | $10 | $20 |
| 3–10 copies | $100/copy | $3 | $5 | $15 |
| 10+ copies | $75/copy | $2 | $5 | $15 |

Classroom Use Discounts and Site Licences available. Additional information available from distributor.

**Distributed by:** Qualitative Research Management (address above).
Qualis Research Associates, PO Box 2240, Corvallis, OR 97339, USA.

## Program: HyperQual™            Version: 2.1 (version 3.0 pending)

**Developer:** Raymond V. Padilla, Arizona State University.

**Description:** HyperQual provides an integrated environment for data entry, memory and illustrations. The program is designed to assist in the analysis of text data from interviews, observations and documents. HyperQual is a HyperCard application (stack) that requires a Macintosh.

**Required hardware:** Macintosh plus or higher (SE, SE/30, MacII); 1 MB RAM; word processor, hard disk; HyperCard version 1.2 or higher.

**Price:**
In USA:        $125.00    plus $5.00 shipping and handling
Outside USA:   $125.00    plus $10.00 shipping and handling

**Distributed by:** Renata Tesch, Qualitative Research Management (address above).
Dr Raymond V. Padilla, 3327 N. Dakota, Chandler, AZ, 85224, USA.

## Program: HyperResearch™            Version: 1.0

**Developer:** Sharlene Hesse-Biber, Paul DuPuis, Scott Kinder, Boston College.

**Description:** HyperResearch is a HyperCard-based application that allows for qualitative and quantitative analysis of textual, audio and video materials. Coding of text, audio and video are supported. An expert system provides a semi-formal mechanism for theory-building. A statistical option allows for the simple analysis of coded data. Reporting allows for the displaying or printing of text and the replay of coded segments of audio or video.

**Required hardware:** Apple Macintosh with System 6.0 (or later) and HyperCard version 1.2 (or higher).

**Price:** $175

**Distributed by:** Researchware Inc., 20 Soren Street, Randolph, MA 02368-1945, USA. Tel: (617) 961-3909.

**Program:** Hypersoft™      **Version:** Hypersoft Beta-1 (pre-release)

**Developer:** Ian Dey, University of Edinburgh.

**Description:** Hypersoft offers facilities for filing, copying, indexing, searching and extracting textual data. The package includes procedures for summarizing, annotating, categorizing, mapping, coding and quantifying data.

**Required hardware:** Apple Macintosh with System 6.0 (or later), and HyperCard version 1.2 (or higher).

**Price:** £50.

**Distributed by:** Ian Dey, 45 Colinton Road, Edinburgh, EH10 5EN, UK.

**Program:** MECA™ (Map Extraction Comparison and Analysis)

**Developer:** Kathleen Carley, Carnegie Mellon University.

**Description:** Suite of 15 programs for textual analysis.

**Required hardware:** IBM PC/XT/AT, PS2 or IBM compatible with hard disk, 640K or more RAM; MacII, Mac-IIci, Mac-SE with hard disk, 1 MB or more RAM; SUN, 1 MB RAM.

**Price:** $200.00 (includes all 15 routines).

**Distributed by:** Professor Kathleen Carley, Department of Social and Decision Science, Carnegie Mellon University, Pittsburgh, PA 15213-3890, USA.

**Program:** NUDIST™ (Non-numerical Unstructured Data Indexing Searching and Theorising)      **Version:** 2.1

**Developer:** T.J. Richards and M.G. Richards, La Trobe University.

**Description:** Supports qualitative analysis of on-line and off-line unstructured data. Uses flagging and text search to construct a possibly large and highly structured hierarchical indexing database into the documents to be analysed. Retrievals use a complete set of Boolean operators on the indexing categories, as well as a set of non-Boolean operators which encourage the generation and exploration of new ideas. Importantly, all retrievals are added back to the indexing system as additional indexing categories, and are available as the basis of further and more abstracted retrievals. To support emerging theory, indexing categories are independent objects which may be modified, titled, have text comments added, and be shifted to other locations in the indexing structure. Nudist for Macintosh file compatible with mainframe version of NUDIST 2.1.

**Required hardware:** Mainframe version: supports multi-user multi-database projects; minis or mainframes that have any version of Common LISP. Macintosh version: any Macintosh with a minimum of 2 MB free main memory; 2 MB+ Macs on Appleshare network. Hard disk needed. PC 386 version to be announced late in 1991.

**Price:**
Mainframe version: AUS $1500 (approx. US $1125 or £700)
Macintosh version: single user AUS $250; network AUS $1000; site AUS $3000

**Distributed by:** NUDIST Project, ACRI, La Trobe University, Bundoora, VIC 3083, Australia. Tel: (613) 479-2857. Fax: (613) 470-4915.

**Program:** QUALOG™

**Developer:** Ernest Sibert and Anne Shelly, Syracuse University.

**Description:** QUALOG is a group of computer programs developed to facilitate the mechanical tasks of analysing qualitative data.

**Required hardware:** Mainframe systems only: DEC VAX/VMS or IBM/CMS/VM.

**Price:** $700.00 site licence.

**Distributed by:** Ernest Sibert and Anne Shelly, Syracuse University, 4-116 CST, School of Computer and Information Science, Syracuse, NY 13244-4100, USA.

**Program:** QUALPRO™                                            **Version:** 3.3

**Developer:** Bernard Blackman, Florida State University.

**Description:** Provides all the basic functions needed by a researcher who does qualitative analysis. Text segments can be identified flexibly, codes attached and segments retrieved.

**Required hardware:** IBM PC/XT/AT or 100% compatible with DOS 2.0 or higher; at least 128K RAM.

**Price:**
In USA:         $125.00
Outside USA:   $160.00

**Distributed by:** Qualitative Research Management (address above).

**Program:** TAP™ (Text Analysis Package)                      **Version:** 1.0

**Developer:** Kriss A. Drass, Southern Methodist University.

**Description:** TAP is a set of procedures for analysing any type of text data. With TAP you can: add codes to a text file; search for patterns among the codes; retrieve lines of text associated with codes or code patterns; compute frequency tables for codes.

**Required hardware:** IBM PC (or clone) with 640K RAM and 2 floppy disk drives; MS-DOS 2.1 or higher.

**Price:**
In usa: $75.00
Outside usa: $75.00
These prices apply only to copies purchased directly from Kriss Drass.

**Distributed by:** Qualitative Research Management (address above).
Kriss A. Drass, Department of Sociology, Southern Methodist University, Dallas, Texas, 75275, usa.

**Program:** Textbase Alpha™

**Developer:** Bo Sommerlund and Ole Steen Kristensen.

**Description:** Permits the coding of data which have an internal structure, as well as narrative texts of any kind. Searching and assembling of coded segments is supported along with frequency counts, and data matrix output.

**Required hardware:** ibm/xt and fully compatible computers; 640k ram and dos 2.00 or higher.

**Price:**
In usa: $150.00
Outside usa: $160.00

**Distributed by:** Qualitative Research Management (address above).

# Bibliography

Abell, Peter (1987) *The Syntax of Social Life: The Theory and Method of Comparative Narratives*. New York: Oxford University Press.

Abell, Peter (1988) 'The "structuration" of action: inference and comparative narratives', in Nigel G. Fielding (ed.), *Actions and Structure: Research Methods and Social Theory*. Beverly Hills, CA: Sage.

Accu-tech Software Services, *Accu-Type Keyboard Tutor Version 4.0* UK (MS-DOS) (computer program). Rushden.

Agar, Michael (1980a) 'Getting better quality stuff: methodological competition in an interdisciplinary niche', *Urban Life*, 9 (1): 34–50.

Agar, Michael (1980b) *The Professional Stranger: An Informal Introduction to Ethnography*. New York: Academic Press.

Agar, Michael (1983) 'Microcomputers as field tools', *Computers in the Humanities*, 17: 19–26.

Agar, Michael (1986) *Independents Declared: The Dilemmas of Independent Trucking*. Washington, DC: Smithsonian Institution Press.

Agar, Michael (1990) 'Text and fieldwork', *Journal of Contemporary Ethnography*, 19 (1): 73–88.

Akeroyd, A.V. (1984) 'Ethics in relation to informants, the profession and governments', in R.F. Ellen (ed.), *Ethnographic Research: A Guide to General Conduct*. London: Academic Press. pp. 133–54.

Akeroyd, A.V. (1988) 'Ethnography, personal data and computers: the implications of data protection legislation for qualitative social research', in R.G. Burgess (ed.), *Conducting Qualitative Research*. Greenwich, CT: JAI Press. pp. 179–219.

Altheide, David L. (1987) 'Ethnographic content analysis', *Qualitative Sociology*, 10 (1), Spring: 65–77.

Anderson, R.E. and Brent, E. (1989) 'Computing in sociology: promise and practice', *Social Science Computer Review*, 7 (4): 487–502.

Appell, G.N. (1978) *Ethical Dilemmas in Anthropological Inquiry*. Waltham, Mass: Crossroads Press.

Baecker, R.M. and Buxton, W.A.S. (1987) 'Cognition and human information processing', in R.M. Baecker and W.A.S. Buxton (eds), *Readings in Human–Computer Interaction: a Multidisciplinary Approach*. California: Morgan Kaufman. pp. 207–18.

Bailey, Kenneth D. (1978) *Methods of Social Research*. New York: Free Press.

Barnes, J.A. (1979) *Who Should Know What? Social Science, Privacy and Ethics*. Harmondsworth: Penguin Books.

Barnes, J.A. (1984) 'Ethical and political compromises in social research', *Wisconsin Sociologist*, 21 (4): 100–10.

Barzun, Jacques and Graff, Henry F. (1977) *The Modern Researcher*. New York: Harcourt Brace Jovanovich.

Bazillion, R.J. (1984) 'The effect of access and privacy legislation in the conduct of scholarly research in Canada', *Social Science Information Studies*, 4 (1): 5–14.

Becker, H.S. (1985) 'Software for sociologists: finding facts and mastering data' (software review), *Contemporary Sociology*, 4 July: 450–1.

Becker, H.S., Gordon, A.C. and LeBailly, R.K. (1984) 'Fieldwork with the computer: criteria for assessing systems', *Qualitative Sociology*, 7 (1–2): 16–33.

Bell, C. and Newby, H. (1977) *Doing Sociological Research*. New York: Free Press.

Berelson, B. (1952) *Content Analysis in Communications Research*. New York: Free Press.

Bergin, T.J. Jr (1989) 'Ethical issues in federal computing: an overview and a research agenda', in G. Garson and S. Nagel (eds), *Advances in Social Sciences and Computers, v.I.* Greenwich, CT: JAI Press. pp. 277–98.

Bigelow, R.P. (1986) 'Computers and privacy – an American perspective', *Information Age*, 8 (3): 134–40.

Bing, J. (1980) 'Personal data systems – a comparative perspective on a basic concept in privacy legislation', in J. Bing and K.S. Selmer (eds), *A Decade of Computers and Law*. Oslo: Universitetsforlaget. pp. 72–91.

Bing, J. (1985) 'Personal data: the international legal regime', in J.J.P. Kenny (ed.), *Data Privacy and Security: The State of the Art Report*. Oxford: Pergamon Infotech. pp. 3–12.

Bing, J. (1986) 'Beyond 1984: the law and information technology in tomorrow's society. Data protection and social policy', *Information Age*, 8 (2): 85–94.

Blank, G. (1989) 'Introduction: new technology and the nature of sociological work', in G. Blank et al. (eds), *New Technology in Sociology: Practical Applications in Research and Work*. New Brunswick, NJ: Transaction Publishers. pp. 1–14.

Blank, G., McCartney, J.L. and Brent, E. (eds) (1989) *New Technology in Sociology: Practical Applications in Research and Work*. New Brunswick, NJ: Transaction Publishers.

Blumer, Herbert (1969) *Symbolic Interactionism*. Englewood Cliffs, NJ: Prentice Hall.

Bogdan, Robert and Taylor, Steven J. (1975) *Introduction to Qualitative Research Methods: A Phenomenological Approach to the Social Sciences*. New York: John Wiley.

Bond, G.C. (1990) 'Fieldnotes: research in past occurrences', in R. Sanjek (ed.), *Fieldnotes: the Makings of Anthropology*. Ithaca and London: Cornell University Press. pp. 273–89.

Boonzaier, E., Skalnik, P., Thornton, R., West, M. and Gordon, R. (1985) 'Review discussion' [of V. Crapanzano's *Waiting: The Whites of South Africa*, New York, 1985], *Social Dynamics*, 11 (2): 65–71.

Boruch, R.F. and Cecil, J.S. (eds) (1983) *Solutions to Ethical and Legal Problems in Research*. New York: Academic Press.

Brajuha, M. and Hallowell, L. (1986) 'Legal intrusion and the politics of fieldwork: the impact of the Brajuha case', *Urban Life*, 14 (4): 454–78.

Brent, Edward (1984) 'Qualitative computing: approaches and issues', *Qualitative Sociology*, 7 (1/2): 34–60.

Brent, E. (1986) 'Knowledge based systems: a qualitative formalism', *Qualitative Sociology*, 9 (3): 256–79.

Bulmer, M. (ed.) (1979) *Censuses, Surveys and Privacy*. London: Macmillan.

Burgess, R.G. (1984) *In the Field: An Introduction to Field Research*. London: Allen & Unwin.

Burgess, R.G. (ed.) (1988) *Conducting Qualitative Research* [Studies in Qualitative Methodology v.1]. Greenwich, CT: JAI Press.

Burgess, R.G. and Bulmer, M. (1981) 'Research methodology teaching: trends and developments', *Sociology*, 15 (4): 477–89.

Burkert, H. (1986) 'International data protection', *Computer Law and Practice*, 2 (5): 155–60.

Burt, Ronald S. (1990) STRUCTURE Network Analysis System, Version 4.1, New York: Research Program in Structural Analysis, Center for the Social Sciences, Columbia University.

Busa, R. (1980) 'The annals of humanities computing: the Index Thomisticus', *Computers and the Humanities*, 14 (2) Oct.: 83–90.

Cain, Maureen and Finch, Janet (1981) 'Towards a rehabilitation of data', in P. Abrams et al. (eds), *Practice and Progress: British Sociology 1950–1980*. London: Allen & Unwin. pp. 105–19.

Card, Stuart K., Moran, Thomas P. and Newell, Allen (1983) *The Psychology of Human–Computer Interaction*. London: Lawrence Erlbaum.

Cartwright, Dorwin P. (1953) 'Analysis of qualitative material', in L. Festinger and D. Katz, *Research in the Behavioral Sciences*. New York: Holt, Rinehart & Winston.

Cavendish, R. (1982) *Women on the Line*. London: Routledge.

Chambers, E. (1980) 'Fieldwork and the law: new contexts for ethical decision making', *Social Problems*, 27 (3): 330–41.

Choueka, Yaacov (1980) 'Computerized full-text retrieval systems and research in the humanities: The Responsa Project', *Computers and the Humanities*, 14: 153–69.

Clarke, David D. (1983) *Language and Action: A Structural Model of Behaviour*. Oxford: Pergamon Press.

CoE (1981) *Convention for the Protection of Individuals with Regard to Automatic Processing of Personal Data*. Strasbourg: Council of Europe.

Computer Knowledge (1985) *Tutor.Com Version 4.2: Tutorials about PC Computing* (computer program), Los Angeles, CA.

Conklin, Jeff (1987) 'Hypertext: an introduction and survey', *IEEE Computer*, 209: 17–41.

Conrad, P. and Reinharz, S. (1984) 'Computers and qualitative data: editors' introductory essay', *Qualitative Sociology*, 7 (1/2): 3–15.

Cordingley, Betsy (1985) 'User requirements for a qualitative-data analysis tool', Alvey/DHSS Demonstrator Project Report (ALVIN 390), Social and Computing Sciences Group, University of Surrey, Guildford.

Cordingley, Elizabeth S. (1987) 'Knowledge acquisition for the advice system', *Proceedings of the First European Workshop on Knowledge Acquisition for Knowledge-Based Systems*. Reading: University of Reading.

Corsaro, W.A. and Heise, D.R. (1990) 'Event structure models from ethnographic data', in C. Clogg (ed.), *Sociological Methodology: 1990*. San Francisco, CA: Jossey Bass.

Davies, John (1988) 'Automated tools for qualitative research in the social sciences'. Unpublished thesis, Department of Computer Science, University of Edinburgh.

Davis, William S. (1989) *Computing Fundamentals: Concepts*. Reading, MA: Addison-Wesley.

Dawson, Patrick and Buckland, Sarah (1986) 'The potential user study: interim report', Alvey/DHSS Large Demonstrator Project Publication AD31.

Devault, M. (1990) 'Feminist interviewing and analysis', *Social Problems*, 37 (1): 96–116.

Deveraux, George (1967) *From Anxiety to Method in the Behavioral Sciences*. The Hague: Mouton.

Dey, Ian (1988) Unpublished documentation on the 'Hypersoft' computer system (under development). *Department of Social Policy and Social Work, University of Edinburgh.*

Diaper, D. (1987) 'Designing systems for people: beyond user-centred design', *Proceedings of the Share European Association (SEAS) Anniversary Meeting*, pp. 283–302.

Donnan, Hastings (1988) *Marriage among Muslims: preference and choice in northern Pakistan.* London: E.J. Brill.

Douglas, J. (1976) *Investigative Social Research.* London: Sage.

Drass, Kriss A. (1980) 'The analysis of qualitative data', *Urban Life*, 9 (3): 332–53.

Drass, Kriss A. (1989) 'Text analysis and text-analysis software: a comparison of assumptions', in Grant Blank, James L. McCartney and Edward Brent (eds), *New Technology in Sociology: Practical Applications in Research and Work.* New Brunswick: NJ: Transaction Publishers.

Ebbighausen, Rolf and Neckel, Sighard (1989) *Anatomie des politischen Skandals.* Frankfurt: Suhrkamp.

Emeroth, B. (1988) 'The invisibility of qualitative sociology in Sweden', *Qualitative Sociology*, 11 (1–2): 113–22.

Ericsson, K.A. and Simon, H.A. (1985) *Protocol Analysis: Verbal Reports as Data.* London: MIT Press.

*Ethnos* (1982) 'The shaping of national anthropologies' [special issue], *Ethnos*, 47 (1–2): 6–186.

Etzkowitz, H. (1989) 'The electronic focussed interview: Email as a dialogic interviewing medium', in E. Stefferud, O.-J. Jacobsen and P. Schicker (eds), *Message Handling Systems and Distributed Applications.* Amsterdam: Elsevier Science Publishers BV (North Holland). pp. 525–37.

Fiderio, Janet (1988) 'A grand vision', *Byte*, 13 (10): 237–44.

Fielding, N. (1982) 'Observational research on the National Front', in M. Bulmer (ed.), *Social Research Ethics.* London: Macmillan. pp. 80–104.

Fielding, Nigel and Fielding, Jane (1986) *Linking Data.* Beverly Hills, CA: Sage.

Fienberg, S.E., Martin, M.F. and Straf, M.L. (eds) (1985) *Sharing Research Data.* Washington, DC: National Academy Press.

Finch, Janet (1986) *Research and Policy: the Uses of Qualitative Methods in Social and Educational Research.* London: Falmer Press.

Finlay, M. (1987) *Powermatics: a Discursive Critique of New Communications Technology.* London and New York: Routledge & Kegan Paul.

Fischer, M.D. (1986a) 'Expert systems and anthropological analysis', *Bulletin of Information on Computing in Anthropology*, 4.

Fischer, M.D. (1986b) 'Computer representations of ethnological knowledge', *Bulletin of Information on Computing in Anthropology*, 6.

Fischer, M.D. (1991) 'Marriage and power: tradition and transition in an urban Punjabi community', in Hastings Donnan and Pnina Werbner (eds), *Economy and Culture in Pakistan: Migrants and Cities in a Muslim Society.* London: Macmillan. pp. 97–123.

Fischer, M.D. (forthcoming) 'Computer representation of anthropological data: a perspective', in Michael Fischer and Gurcharan Khanna (eds), *Computing Solutions to Anthropological Problems.*

Flaherty, D.H. (1986) 'Governmental surveillance and bureaucratic accountability: data protection agencies in Western societies', *Science, Technology and Human Values*, 11 (1): 7–18.

204   *Using computers in qualitative research*

Freedman, W. (1987) *The Right of Privacy in the Computer Age.* Westport, CT: Quorum Books, Greenwood Press.

Freidman, Elizabeth A. (1984) 'Field research and word processor files: a technical note', *Qualitative Sociology,* 7 (1/2): 90–7.

Gallaher, A. Jr (1964) 'Plainsville: the twice studied town', in A.J. Vidich, J. Bensman and M.R. Stein (eds), *Reflections on Community Studies.* New York: Wiley. pp. 285–303.

Garson, G.D. (1989a) 'Microcomputers and social sciences research', in G. Garson and S. Nagel (eds), *Advances in Social Sciences and Computers v.1.* Greenwich, CT: JAI Press. pp. 3–10.

Garson, G.D. (1989b) 'News and notes', *Social Science Computer Review,* 7 (1): 81–101.

Garson, G.D. (1989c) 'News and notes', *Social Science Computer Review,* 7 (4): 535–58.

Garson, G.D. and Nagel, S.S. (eds) (1989) *Advances in Social Sciences and Computers, v.1.* Greenwich, CT: JAI Press.

Geertz, Clifford (1973) *The Interpretation of Cultures.* New York: Basic Books.

Geertz, Clifford (1976) 'From the native's point of view: on the nature of anthropological understanding', in K. Basso and H. Selby (eds), *Meaning in Anthropology.* Albuquerque: University of New Mexico Press.

Gerson, E. (1984) 'Qualitative research and the computer', *Qualitative Sociology,* 7 (1/2): 61–74.

Gerson E. (1986) 'Where do we go from here?', *Qualitative Sociology,* 9 (2): 209–11.

Gerson, E. (1987) 'Computing in qualitative sociology: do we sincerely want to be programmers?', *Qualitative Sociology,* 10 (4): 407–9.

Gerson, E. (1989) 'Scientific evaluation criteria and the rationalization of research'. Paper for National Science Foundation, San Francisco: Tremont Research Institute.

Glaser, Barney G. and Strauss, Anselm L. (1967) *The Discovery of Grounded Theory: Strategies for Qualitative Research.* Chicago: Aldine.

Gold, S.J. (1989) 'Ethical issues in visual fieldwork', in G. Blank et al., *New Technology in Sociology: Practical Applications in Research and Work.* New Brunswick, NJ: Transaction Publishers. pp. 99–109.

Golzen, G. (1989) 'Giving the boss Qwerty power', *Sunday Times,* 18 June.

Goodson, Ivor (1985) 'History, context and qualitative method in the study of curriculum', in Robert G. Burgess (ed.), *Strategies of Educational Research: Qualitative Methods.* Philadelphia PA: Falmer Press. pp. 121–52.

Gray, S. (1989) 'Electronic data bases and privacy: policy for the 1990s', *Science, Technology, and Human Values,* 14 (3): 242–57.

Greenleaf, G.W. and Clarke, R.A. (1984) 'Database retrieval technology and subject access principles', *Australian Computer Journal,* 16 (1): 27–32.

Greenwell, M. (1988) *Knowledge Engineering for Expert Systems.* Chichester: Ellis Horwood.

Gubrium, Jaber (1988) *Analyzing Field Reality.* Beverly Hills. CA: Sage.

Halfpenny, Peter (1979) 'The analysis of qualitative data', *Sociological Review,* 27 (4): 799–825.

Halfpenny, P. (1981) 'Teaching ethnographic data analysis', *Sociology,* 15 (4): 564–9.

Hammersley, Martyn and Atkinson, Paul (1983) *Ethnography: Principles in Practice.* New York: Tavistock.

Hedrick, T.E. (1985) 'Justifications for and obstacles to data sharing', in S. Fienberg, M. Martin and M. Straf (eds), *Sharing Research Data*. Washington DC: National Academy Press. pp. 123–47.

Heise, D.R. (1974) 'Prologue', *Sociological Methodology 1975*. San Francisco: Jossey-Bass.

Heise, D.R. (1979) *Understanding Events: Affect and the Construction of Social Action*. New York: Cambridge University Press.

Heise, D.R. (1988) 'Computer analysis of cultural structures', *Social Science Computer Review*, 6 (1), Spring: 183–96.

Heise, D.R. (1989) 'Modeling event structures', *Journal of Mathematical Sociology*, 14: 139–69.

Heise, D.R. (1990) 'Careers, career trajectories and the self', in J. Rodin, C. Schooler and K. Schaie (eds), *Self-Directedness: Causes and Effects throughout the Life Course*. New York: Lawrence Erlbaum.

Heise, David R. and Lewis, Elsa M. (1988) *Introduction to* ETHNO*, Version 2*. Raleigh, NC: National Collegiate Software Clearinghouse.

Highland, H.J. (1990) 'Demise of passwords', Pt. II, *Computers and Security*, 9 (3): 196–200; 'Demise of passwords', Pt. III, *Computers and Security*, 9 (4): 286–90.

Hiller, H. (1979) 'Universality of science and the question of national sociologies', *American Sociologist*, 14 (3): 124–35.

Hinze, K.E. (1987) 'Computing in sociology: bringing back balance', *Social Science Microcomputer Review*, 5 (4): 439–51.

Hockey, S. (1980) *A Guide to Computer Applications in the Humanities*. London: Duckworth.

Hofferbert, R.I. (1977) 'Social science archives and confidentiality', in R.I. Hofferbert and J.S. Clubb (eds), *Social Science Data Archives: Applications and Potential*. Beverly Hills, CA: Sage. pp. 93–114.

Holsti, O.R. (1969) *Content Analysis for the Social Sciences and Humanities*. Reading, MA: Addison-Wesley.

*HyperCard User's Guide* (1987). Cupertino, CA: Apple Computer Inc.

IBM Corp. and Microsoft Inc. (1987) DOS 3.30 *User's Guide*. IBM.

*Inside Macintosh, Promotional Edition* (1985). Cupertino, CA: Apple Computer Inc.

*International Sociology* (1989) [Section on] 'Universalism and indigenisation', *International Sociology*, 3 (2): 155–99.

Jacob, Evelyn (1987) 'Qualitative research traditions: a review', *Review of Educational Research*, 57 (1), Spring: 1–50.

Jones, Gareth R. (1983) 'Life history methodology', in G. Morgan (ed.), *Beyond Method*. Beverly Hills, CA: Sage.

Jones, John (1986) 'MacCadd, an enabling software method support tool', *Proceedings of the Conference of the British Computer Society Human–Computer Interaction Specialist Group*, pp. 132–54.

Kant, L. and Brown, M. (1983) *Jobs for the Girls? An Analysis of the Role of Education in Vocational Choice and Careers Opportunities for Girls*, Schools Council Pamphlet 22, London: Schools Council.

Kelly, J.F. (1984) 'An iterative design methodology for user-friendly natural language office information applications', *Association for Computing Machinery Transactions on Office Information Systems*, 2 (1): 26–41.

Kirk, R.C. (1981) 'Microcomputers and anthropological research', *Sociological Methods and Research*, 9 (4): 473–92.

## 206  Using computers in qualitative research

Kidder, L. and Judd, C. (1986) *Research Methods in Social Relations*, 5th edn. New York: CBS College Publishing.

Kling, Rob and Iacono, Suzanne (1988) 'The mobilization of support for computerization: the role of computerization movements', *Social Problems*, 35 (3): 226–43.

Klopp, C. (1990) 'Microcomputer security systems attempt to lock up desktops', *Computers and Security*, 9 (2): 139–41.

Kluckhohn, Clyde (1949) *A Mirror for Man: The Relation of Anthropology to Modern Life.* New York: Whittlesey House.

Krippendorf, Klaus (1980) *Content Analysis: An Introduction to its Methodology.* Beverly Hills, CA: Sage.

Langefors, B. (1987) 'Distinction between data and information/knowledge', *Information Age*, 9 (2): 89–91.

Latour, Bruno (1987) *Science in Action: How to Follow Scientists and Engineers through Society.* Cambridge, MA: Harvard University Press.

Laudon, K.C. (1986) *Dossier Society: Value Choices in the Design of National Information Systems.* New York: Columbia University Press.

Lieberson, Stanley (1985) *Making It Count: The Improvement of Social Research and Theory.* Berkeley: University of California Press.

Lincoln, Y.S. and Guba, E.G. (1984) *Naturalistic Inquiry.* Beverly Hills, CA: Sage.

Lofland, J. and Lofland, L. (1984) *Analysing Social Settings: A Guide to Qualitative Observation and Analysis.* Belmont: Wadsworth.

Longley, D. and Shain, M. (1987) *Data and Computer Security: Dictionary of Standards, Concepts and Terms.* London: Macmillan.

Lyman, P. (1984) 'Reading, writing and word processing: towards a phenomenology of the computer age', *Qualitative Sociology*, 7 (1/2): 75–89.

Lyman, P. (1989) 'Sociological literature in an age of computerized texts', in G. Blank et al. (eds), *New Technology in Sociology: Practical Applications in Research and Work.* New Brunswick, NJ: Transaction Publishers. pp. 17–32.

McCullagh, C. Behan (1984) *Justifying Historical Descriptions.* New York: Cambridge University Press.

Macfarlane, A. (1990) 'The Cambridge Experimental Videodisc Project', *Anthropology Today*, 6 (1): 9–12.

Mack, Robert L., Lewis, Clayton H. and Carroll, John N. (1983) 'Learning to use word processors: problems and prospects', *Association for Computing Machinery Transactions on Office Information Systems*, 1 (3): 254–71.

McLean, J. (1990) 'The specification and modelling of computer security', *Computer*, 23 (1): 9–16.

Maibaum, T.S.E. (1986) 'A logic for the formal requirements specification of real-time/embedded systems'. Alvey FOREST Deliverable Report 3. Chelmsford: GEC Research Laboratories.

Martin, C.D. and Martin, D.H. (1989) 'Professional codes of conduct and computer ethics education', *Social Science Computer Review*, 8 (1): 96–108.

Martin, P. and Turner, B. (1986) 'Grounded theory and organisational research', *Journal of Applied Behaviour*, 22 (2): 141–57.

Marx, G.T. and Reichman, N. (1984) 'Routinizing the discovery of secrets: computers as informants', *American Behavioral Scientist*, 27 (4): 423–52.

Menkus, B. (1990) 'Understanding data communication security vulnerabilities', *Computers and Security*, 9 (3): 209–13.

Merton, R. (1967) *On Theoretical Sociology.* Toronto: Collier-Macmillan.

Miles, M.B. (1979) 'Qualitative data as an attractive nuisance', *Administrative Science Quarterly*, 24: 590–601.

Miles, Matthew B. and Huberman, A. Michael (1984) *Qualitative Data Analysis: A Sourcebook of New Methods.* Beverly Hills, CA: Sage.

Mills, C. Wright (1959) *The Sociological Imagination.* New York: Oxford University Press.

Mitchell, J. (1983) 'Case and situation analysis', *Sociological Review,* 31 (2): 187–211.

Mochman, E. and Müller, P.J. (eds) (1979) *Data Protection and Social Science Research: Perspectives from Ten Countries.* Frankfurt, New York: Campus Verlag.

Morton, A.G. (1980) 'The annals of computing: the Greek Testament', *Computers and the Humanities,* 14 (2): 197–200.

Moyser, G. (1988) 'Non-standardized interviewing in elite research', in R. Burgess, (ed.), *Conducting Qualitative Research.* Greenwich, CT: JAI Press. pp. 109–36.

Murphy, B.M. (1986) *The International Politics of New Information Technology.* London: Croom Helm.

Murphy, M.D. and Johannsen, A. (1990) 'Ethical obligations and federal regulations in ethnographic research and anthropological education', *Human Organization,* 49 (2): 127–34.

Murphy, R.F. (1972) *The Dialectics of Social Life.* London: Allen & Unwin.

Norman, D.A. (1987) 'Some observations on mental models', in R.M. Baecker and W.A.S. Buxton (eds), *Readings in Human–Computer Interaction: a Multi-disciplinary Approach.* California: Morgan Kaufman. pp. 241–4.

Norris, Margaret (1981) 'Problems in the analysis of soft data', *Sociology,* 15: 337–51.

OECD (1980) *Guidelines for the Protection of Privacy and Transborder Flows of Personal Data.* Paris: Organization for Economic Cooperation and Development.

Øyen, O. and Olaussen, T.G. (1985) 'Social science and the data protection issue in Norway: a case of accommodation to conflicting goals'. Unpublished paper prepared for the European Consortium for Political Research, Workshop on Confidentiality, Privacy and Data Protection, Barcelona, 25–30 March 1985.

O'Neil, D.H. (1990) 'Roots III' [Review], *Social Science Computer Review,* 8 (2): 288–94.

Paczuska, A. (1986) 'Thinking woman's way', *The Guardian,* 6 March.

Page-Jones, Meilir (1980) *The Practical Guide to Structured Systems Design.* New York: Yourdon Press.

Payne, G., Lyon, E.S. and Anderson, R. (1989) 'Undergraduate sociology: research methods in the public sector curriculum', *Sociology,* 23 (2): 261–73.

Peterson, J. (1984) 'Promises, compromises, and commitments', *American Behavioral Scientist,* 27 (4): 453–80.

Pfaffenberger, B. (1988) *Microcomputer Applications in Qualitative Research.* Beverly Hills, CA: Sage.

Podolefsky, A. and McCarty, C. (1983) 'Topical sorting: a technique for computer assisted qualitative data analysis', *American Anthropologist,* 85 (4): 886–90.

Portman, C., Currie, A., Burton, C., Gilbert, N., Forder, J. and Storrs, G. (eds) (1989), *Alvey DHSS Demonstrator 1984–89: Final Report.* Manchester: ICL Ltd. (Knowledge Based Systems).

Potter, W.D. and Trueblood R.P. (1988) 'Traditional, semantic and hyper-semantic approaches to data modeling', *Computer,* 21 (6): 53–63.

Potts, C., Finkelstein, A., Aslett, M. and Booth, J. (1986) '"Structured common sense": a requirements elicitation and formalization method for model action logic'. Alvey Initiative FOREST Report R2. London: Imperial College of Science and Technology.

Pritchard, J. (1980) 'Electronic filing and retrieval: developments in full-text systems', *Information Media and Technology*, 23 (2): 63–6.

Raffe, D., Bundell, I. and Bibby, J. (1989) 'Ethics and tactics: issues arising from an educational survey', in R.G. Burgess (ed.), *The Ethics of Educational Research*. Lewes: Falmer Press. pp. 13–30.

Ragin, C.C. and Becker, H.S. (1989) 'How the microcomputer is changing our analytic habits', in G. Blank et al. (eds), *New Technology in Sociology: Practical Applications in Research and Work*. New Brunswick, NJ: Transaction Publishers.

Rahtz, Sebastian, Carr, Les and Hall, Wendy (1989) 'Creating multimedia documents: hypertext-processing'. Paper P9 in the delegates' collection of papers presented at Hypertext II, University of York, June 1989.

Reynolds, P.D. (1982) *Ethics and Social Science Research*. Englewood Cliffs, NJ: Prentice-Hall.

Richards, L. (1990) *Nobody's Home: Dreams and Realities in a New Suburb*. Melbourne: Oxford University Press.

Richards, Lyn (forthcoming) 'Software for soft data: computing qualitative research', in Jeanne Daly, Ian McDonald and Evan Willis (eds), *The Social Sciences and Health Care Research*. Melbourne: Victorian Health Association.

Richards, Lyn and Richards, Tom (1987) 'Qualitative data analysis: can computers do it?' *Australian and New Zealand Journal of Sociology*, 23: 23–35.

Richards, Lyn and Richards, Tom (1989) 'The impact of computer techniques for qualitative analysis', *Technical Report*, no. 6/89, Dept. of Computer Science, La Trobe University.

Richards, Tom and Richards, Lyn (1990) *NUDIST 2.0: User's Manual*. Melbourne: Replee.

Richards, Tom and Richards, Lyn (1991) 'Computing in qualitative analysis: a healthy development?', *Qualitative Health Research*, 1 (2).

Richards, Tom and Richards, Lyn (forthcoming) 'The NUDIST qualitative data analysis system', *Qualitative Sociology*.

Ripp, A. (1987) 'Whose picture is it anyway?', *American Photographer*, June: 74–9.

Robinson, W.S. (1951) 'The logical structure of analytic induction', *American Sociological Review*, 16: 812–18.

Rogers, E.M. (1987) 'Progress, problems and prospects for network research: investigating relationships in the age of electronic communication technologies', *Social Networks*, 9: 285–310.

Rohde, R. and Haskett, J. (1990) 'Disaster recovery planning for academic computing centres', *Communications of the ACM*, 33 (6): 652–7.

Satyanaryanan, M. (1990) 'Scalable, secure and highly available distributed file access', *Computer*, 23 (5): 9–19, 20–21.

Scheper-Hughes, N. (1981) 'Cui Bonum – for whose good?: a dialogue with Sir Raymond Firth', *Human Organization*, 40 (4): 371–2.

Schneiderman, B. (1983) 'Direct manipulation: a step beyond programming languages', *Institute of Electrical and Electronics Engineering Computer*, August: 57–67.

Seidel, J.V. (1988) *The Ethnograph Version 3.0* (computer program). Littleton, CO: Qualis Research Associates.

Seidel, J.V. (1990) 'Epistemological musings', *Cut and Paste*, 2 (1): 5–6.

Seidel, J.V. and Clark, J.A. (1984) 'The Ethnograph: A computer program for the analysis of qualitative data', *Qualitative Sociology*, 7 (1/2): 110–25.

Seidel, J.V., Kjolseth, R. and Seymour, E. (1988) *The Ethnograph: A User's Guide*. Littleton, CO: Qualis Research Associates.

Selvin, H.C. (1965) 'Training for social research', in J. Gould (ed.), *Penguin Survey of the Social Sciences*. London: Penguin.

Shakel, B. (1986) 'Ergonomics in design for usability'. *Proceedings of the Second Conference of the British Computer Society Human–Computer Interaction Specialist Group*. pp. 44–64.

Shapiro, Ezra (1984) 'Text databases', *Byte*, October: 147–50.

Sharrock, W. and Anderson, B. (1986) *The Ethnomethodologists*. New York: Tavistock Publications.

Shelly, Anne and Sibert, Ernest, (1986) 'Using logic programming to facilitate qualitative data analysis', *Qualitative Sociology*, 9 (2): 145–61.

Sherani, S.R. (1988) 'Ritual and symbol in Pakistani politics'. Canterbury: University of Kent.

Shetler, T. (1990) 'Birth of the BLOB', *Byte*, 15 (2): 221–2, 224, 226.

Shipman, F.M., III, Chaney, R.J. and Gorry, G.A. (1989) 'Distributed hypertext for collaborative research: the Virtual Notebook System', *SIGCHI Bulletin*, special issue, November: 129–35.

Shipman, M. (1979) 'The effectiveness of graduate education in sociology: employment in local authority research'. Paper presented at the SSRC Warwick Methodology Conference, December.

Sieghart, P. (1982) 'The data protection debate', in P. Sieghart (ed.), *Microchips with Everything*. London: Comedia Publishing Group.

Silverman, J. (1985) *Qualitative Methodology and Sociology*. Aldershot: Gower.

Simitis, S.D. (1981) 'Data protection and research: a case study of control', *American Journal of Comparative Law*, 29 (4): 583–605.

Smith, M. (1989a) 'Computer security – threats, vulnerabilities and counter-measures', *Information Age*, 11 (4): 205–10.

Smith, M. (1989b) *Commonsense Computer Security: Your Practical Guide to Preventing Accidental Error and Deliberate Electronic Data Loss*. London: McGraw-Hill (UK).

Smith-Lovin, Lynn and Heise, D.R. (eds) (1988) *Analyzing Social Interaction: Advances in Affect Control Theory*. New York: Gordon and Breach.

Southward, C.D. IV (1989) 'Individual privacy and governmental efficiency: technology's effect on the government's ability to gather, store and distribute information', *Computer/Law Journal*, IX (3): 359–74.

Spradley, James P. (1979) *The Ethnographic Interview*. New York: Holt, Rinehart & Winston.

Sproull, Lee S. and Sproull, Robert F. (1982) 'Managing and analyzing behavioral records: explorations in non-numeric data analysis', *Human Organization*, 41: 283–90.

Stone, Phillip J., Dexter, C., Smith, Marshall, S. and Ogilvie, Daniel M. (1966) *The General Inquirer: A Computer Approach to Content Analysis*. Cambridge, MA: MIT Press.

Storrs, Graham E. and Burton, Chris P. (1989) 'The Alvey DHSS Large Demonstrator Project Knowledge Analysis Tool: KANT2'. Alvey/DHSS Large Demonstrator Project Publication AD 114.

Strauss, Anselm L. (1987) *Qualitative Analysis for Social Scientists*. New York: Cambridge University Press.

210    *Using computers in qualitative research*

Stubbs, Michael (1983) *Discourse Analysis: The Sociolinguistic Analysis of Natural Language.* Chicago: University of Chicago Press.

Suchman, L.A. (1983) 'Office procedure as practical action: models of work and system design', *Association for Computing Machinery Transactions on Office Information Systems*, 1 (4): 320–8.

Sutcliffe, Alistair (1988) *Jackson Systems Development.* London: Prentice Hall.

TDCR (1986) 'Sweden: hidden profiles de-identified', *Transnational Data and Communications Report*, IX (3): 24.

TDCR (1989a) 'Protection of personal data used for employment purposes', *Transnational Data and Communications Report*, XII (3): 26–8.

TDCR (1989b) 'Special Report' [of the 11th Annual Data Commissioners Conference], *Transnational Data and Communications Report*, XII (9): 5–7.

TDCR (1989c) 'UN Guidelines concerning computerized personal data files', *Transnational Data and Communications Report*, XII (9): 35–6.

TDCR (1990a) 'Status of data protection/privacy legislation – February 1990', *Transnational Data and Communications Report*, XIII (2): 25.

TDCR (1990b) 'UN Privacy Guidelines delayed', *Transnational Data and Communications Report*, XIII (4): 4.

TDCR (1990c) 'Special Report: telecom privacy policy elements', *Transnational Data and Communications Report*, XIII (3): 9–19.

Teitelbaum, L.E. (1983) 'Spurious, tractable, and intractable legal problems: a positivist approach to law and social science research', in R. Boruch and J. Cecil (eds), *Solutions to Ethical and Legal Problems in Research.* New York: Academic Press. pp. 11–48.

ten Have, Paul (1990) 'Text analysis programs and routines: the challenge of computer analysis'. Paper given to the International Sociological Association XIIth World Congress of Sociology, Madrid.

Tesch, Renata (1988) 'Computer software and qualitative analysis: A reassessment', in G. Blank, L. McCartney and E. Brent (eds), *New Technology in Sociology.* New Brunswick, NJ: Transaction Books. pp. 141–54.

Tesch, Renata (1989) 'The correspondence between different kinds of qualitative analysis and different kinds of software'. Paper presented at the Symposium on Qualitative Knowledge and Computing, University of Surrey, 11–12 July.

Tesch, Renata (1990) *Qualitative Research: Analysis Types and Software Tools.* London and Philadelphia: Falmer Press.

Thom, J.A. and Thorne, P.G. (1983) 'Privacy legislation and the right of access', *Australian Computer Journal*, 15 (4): 145–50.

Trend, M.G. (1980) 'Applied social research and the government: notes on the limits of confidentiality', *Social Problems*, 27 (3): 342–9.

Tuma, Nancy B., Hannan, Michael J. and Groeneveld, L.P. (1979) 'Dynamic analysis of event histories', *American Journal of Sociology*, 84: 820–54.

Turner, Barry (1981) 'Some practical aspects of qualitative data analysis: one way of organising the cognitive processes associated with the generation of grounded theory', *Quality and Quantity*, 15: 225–47.

Turner, Victor W. (1957) *Schism and Continuity in an African Society.* Manchester: Manchester University Press.

Tyler, S.A. (1969) 'Introduction', in S.A. Tyler (ed.), *Cognitive Anthropology.* New York: Holt, Rinehart & Winston.

van Dijk, Teun A. (ed.) (1985) *Handbook of Discourse Analysis Vol. 4.* London: Academic Press.

van Eemeren, Frans H., Grootendorst, Rob and Kruiger, Tjark (1987) *Handbook of Argumentation Theory*. Dordrecht: Foris Publications.

Vidich, A.J. and Bensman, J. (1964) 'The Springdale case: academic bureaucrats and sensitive townspeople', in A.J. Vidich, J. Bensman and M.R. Stein (eds), *Reflections on Community Studies*. New York: Wiley. pp. 313–49.

Wacks, R. (1989) *Personal Information and the Law: Privacy and the Law*. Oxford: Clarendon Press.

Wakeford, J. (1968) *The Strategy of Social Inquiry: A New Programme in Methods and Measurement for the Student of Sociology*. London: Macmillan.

Wakeford, J. (1981) 'From methods to practice: a critical note on the teaching of research practice to undergraduates', *Sociology*, 15 (4): 505–12.

Walden, I. (1988) 'Data protection responding to trends in technology', *Transnational Data and Communications Report*, XI (1): 12–13.

Walsh, J.P. and Gordon, A.C.C. (1989) 'Intellectual property and new technology: some possible futures in sociology', in G. Blank et al. (eds), *New Technology in Sociology: Practical Applications in Research and Work*. New Brunswick, NJ: Transaction. pp. 33–43.

Weinberg, Daniela (1974) 'Computers as a research tool', *Human Organization*, 33: 291–302.

Werner, Oswald and Schoepfle, G. Mark (1987) *Systematic Fieldwork, Vol. 2*. Beverly Hills, CA: Sage.

Winer, L.R. and Carrière, M. (1990) 'The use of a relational database in qualitative research on educational computing', *Computers and Education*, 15 (1–3): 213–20.

Winograd, E. (1987) 'Separate bias: A microcomputer program to assist in the textual analysis of qualitative data', *Western Journal of Speech Communication*, 51 (1): 52–67.

Wiseman, Jacqueline (1970) *Stations of the Lost*. London: Routledge.

Wiseman, J.P. and Aron, M.S. (1972) *Field Projects in Sociology*. Land: Transworld Student Library Books.

Wood, C.C. (1990) 'Principles of secure information systems design', *Computers and Security*, 9 (1): 13–24.

Woolgar, Steve (ed.) (1988) *Knowledge and Reflexivity: New Frontiers in the Sociology of Knowledge*. Beverly Hills, CA: Sage.

Znaniecki, R. (1934) *The Method of Sociology*. New York: Farrer & Rinehart.

# Index

## 214    *Using computers in qualitative research*